STUDIES IN NEW ENGLAND TRANSCENDENTALISM

BY

HAROLD CLARKE GODDARD

Assistant Professor of English Literature
Northwestern University

HILLARY HOUSE PUBLISHERS, Ltd.
New York
1960

First Published in 1908
by Columbia University Press

Reprinted 1960
by
Hillary House Publ. Ltd.

Printed in the U.S.A.

NOBLE OFFSET PRINTERS, INC.
NEW YORK 3, N. Y.

PREFACE

Since the scope and purpose of this study are stated at some length in the introductory chapter, it will here be sufficient, perhaps, to call attention to the fact that, as its title indicates, the essay makes no pretence of being a history of New England transcendentalism. Such a history would necessarily be a far more ambitious undertaking than the present work, which is restricted to a consideration of a few definitely selected questions. The discussion of these points, moreover, is even further narrowed by being carried on with reference, in the main, to the so-called leaders of the movement. The reasons for these limitations are given in the introduction, where, also, the emphasis placed on Dr. Channing and the comparative neglect of Thoreau—features of the treatment which at first sight may cause surprise—are fully explained. Perhaps the only other comment that is needed is the observation that the term " Platonism," especially in the concluding chapter, is used in a very elastic and untechnical sense, and where a man is spoken of as a Platonist it is not necessarily implied that he embraced in detail the philosophy of Plato.

This essay was submitted in partial fulfillment of the requirements for the degree of Doctor of Philosophy in Columbia University, and the author takes this opportunity of expressing to the faculty of the English Department at Columbia his gratitude for their valuable assistance—to Professor Brander Matthews, Professor G. R. Carpenter, Professor A. H. Thorndike, and, above all, to Professor W. P. Trent, at whose suggestion the study was undertaken and under whose supervision it was written. To Professor Trent's generous help and to his wide knowledge of American literature, any merits which the book may have are, in no inconsiderable measure, due ; the author alone is responsible for its shortcomings.

The writer wishes, furthermore, to thank Mr. Frank B. Sanborn, whose intimate knowledge of transcendentalism

proved of great assistance.   To Dr. Stuart P. Sherman, who
read the work in manuscript and made many pertinent suggestions, he is also deeply indebted.   He appreciates highly the
unfailing courtesies of the authorities of the Columbia University, Harvard University, and Worcester Public Libraries;
and he would acknowledge, finally, the kindness of Messrs.
Houghton, Mifflin and Co. in permitting citations from works
of which they hold the copyrights.

H. C. G.

NORTHWESTERN UNIVERSITY,
June, 1907.

CONTENTS

NOTE

The following biographies are referred to in the footnotes merely by the names of the authors:

Cabot = J. E. Cabot, Memoir of Ralph Waldo Emerson.

Chadwick = J. W. Chadwick, Theodore Parker, Preacher and Reformer.[1]

Chadwick = J. W. Chadwick, William Ellery Channing, Minister of Religion.[1]

Channing = William Henry Channing, The Life of William Ellery Channing.

Cheney = Mrs. E. D. Cheney, Life, Letters, and Journals of Louisa May Alcott.

Cooke = G. W. Cooke, Ralph Waldo Emerson, his Life, Writings, and Philosophy.

Frothingham = O. B. Frothingham, Theodore Parker, a Biography.

Garnett = R. Garnett, Life of Ralph Waldo Emerson.

Higginson = T. W. Higginson, Margaret Fuller Ossoli.

Holmes = O. W. Holmes, Ralph Waldo Emerson.

Sanborn = F. B. Sanborn (and W. T. Harris), A. Bronson Alcott; His Life and Philosophy.

Weiss = J. Weiss, Life and Correspondence of Theodore Parker.

Memoirs = Memoirs of Margaret Fuller Ossoli, by Emerson, et al.[1]   E. W. Emerson's *Emerson in Concord;* and *The Genius and Character of Emerson* (Ed. F. B. Sanborn) are referred to merely by their titles.   Emerson's *Works* are referred to in the Riverside Edition.

[1] Fuller designation is given where there can be any doubt as to the book referred to.

"TRANSCENDENTALISM"—AN INTRODUCTORY CHAPTER

What was the nature of the transcendental movement in New England? The critics can hardly be said to have reached a final answer to this question. There has been a good deal of innocent merriment. There has been a still larger amount of foolish scoffing and silly laughter—harmless, however, in the main. There have been knowing and indulgent smiles, telling, even better than condescending words, how deeply the pity of certain persons has been stirred at the sad vagaries of the transcendentalists. On the other hand there have been eulogies and esoteric utterances; or, where words have failed, there has been a bowing of heads in silent veneration. Between these two extremes, however, have appeared, fortunately, many saner and more critical estimates. But entire agreement, even here, has not by any means emerged; and there seem to be some reasons for believing that the word *transcendental* is itself responsible for much of the confusion.

The word *transcendental*, as applied to this movement, has been used in at least two distinct senses—one popular, the other more or less technically philosophical. The latter usage is to be traced of course to Kant and the *Critique of Pure Reason*. For a full understanding of the philosophical side of New England transcendentalism it is necessary to know somewhat of this technical meaning of *transcendental*;[1] to have sojourned for a time in the kingdoms of the *Transcendental Aesthetic,* the *Transcendental Analytic,* and the *Transcendental Dialectic;* to have at least a bowing acquaintance with such

[1] "I call all knowledge *transcendental* which is occupied not so much with objects, as with our *a priori* concepts of objects. A system of such concepts might be called Transcendental Philosophy. . . . Transcendental Philosophy . . . is a system of all principles of pure reason. . . . Transcendental philosophy is the wisdom of pure speculative reason." Introduction to the *Critique of Pure Reason* (pp. 9, 11, 12, translation of F. Max Müller, Macmillan, 1896).

2 1

formidable inhabitants of these realms as the *A Priori Synthetic Cognition* and the *Transcendental Ego of Apperception;* to recognize, for instance, what Schelling means by a *System of Transcendental Idealism;* and to understand somewhat of the nature of the German and other transcendental seeds that Coleridge[1] sowed and tried to bring to flower in English soil. But fortunately for our present study, we may escape many of these difficulties that seemingly confront us; nor shall we have to excuse ourselves by saying that these matters belong to the professional metaphysicians, reasonable, perhaps, as such a plea might be; for the fact is that the question, What was the philosophy of the New England transcendentalists? is about the least mooted point in the whole discussion, and, if this alone were the question to be answered, such an essay as the present one would hardly be in order.

Transcendental, in its philosophical sense, was used in connection with this New England movement in a broad and often very elastic way; yet, after all, it had a quite definite and unmistakable meaning, nor can that meaning be said to have undergone any development or change. Emerson, at the beginning of his lecture, *The Transcendentalist,* tells us plainly what that usage was:

" It is well known to most of my audience, that the Idealism of the present day acquired the name Transcendental, from the use of that term by Immanuel Kant of Königsberg, who replied to the sceptical philosophy of Locke, which insisted that there was nothing in the intellect which was not previously in the experience of the senses, by showing that there was a very important class of ideas, or imperative forms, which did not come by experience, but through which experience was acquired; that these were intuitions of the mind itself; and he denominated them *Transcendental* forms. The extraordinary profoundness and precision of that man's thinking have given vogue to his nomenclature, in Europe and America, to that extent, that whatever belongs to the class of intuitive thought is popularly called at the present day *Transcendental.*"

[1] See, e. g., " On the difference in kind of Reason and the Understanding," *Aids to Reflection* (Complete Works, N. Y., 1858, vol. i, 241).

Theodore Parker's lecture *Transcendentalism* is an extended amplification of the same definition, and shows, with especial clearness, how the term was then employed.

Kant had taught that time and space are not external realities[1] or even concepts derived from external experience,[2] but *ways* in which the mind " constitutes " its world of sense. In terms of the familiar illustration, they are the mental spectacles through which we look. Again, cause and effect, he says, and all the other " categories " are forms or methods in accord with which the mental content is arranged. The ideas of God, furthermore, of freedom, and of immortality, are inevitable intuitions of the practical nature of man; and these intuitions, since man *is* essentially a practical and moral being, have therefore not a merely sentimental but a real validity. Now from these and other Kantian conceptions a broad generalization was made[3] (as the passage from Emerson just quoted renders clear), and the word *transcendental* came to be applied—by the New England transcendentalists and others —to whatever in man's mental and spiritual nature is conceived of as " above " experience and independent of it. Whatever transcends (sensational) experience is transcendental. Innate, original, universal, *a priori*, intuitive—these are words all of which convey a part of the thought swept under the larger meaning of the term. To the transcendentalists the name John Locke stood for the denial of innate ideas. " Sen-

[1] *Critique of Pure Reason*, 22 and 28 (tr. Müller).

[2] *Ibid.*, 18 and 24.

[3] A passage from the Introduction to the *Critique* (11) will show how much more restricted and technical Kant's use of the term was: " The most important consideration in the arrangement of such a science [the science of which Transcendental Philosophy is an idea] is that no concepts should be admitted which contain anything empirical, and that the *a priori* knowledge shall be perfectly pure. Therefore, although the highest principles of morality and their fundamental concepts are *a priori* knowledge, they do not belong to transcendental philosophy, because the concepts of pleasure and pain, desire, inclination, free-will, etc., which are all of empirical origin, must here be presupposed. Transcendental philosophy is the wisdom of pure speculative reason. Everything practical, so far as it contains motives, has reference to sentiments, and these belong to empirical sources of knowledge."

sationalism " was the prevalent description of the doctrine of his Essay. Transcendentalism and sensationalism!—these were the poles of the philosophy of mind, and among the elect of the new movement to call a man a sensationalist was a polite way of informing him that he was an intellectual and spiritual dullard.[1]

Transcendentalism was, then, first and foremost, a doctrine concerning the mind, its ways of acting and methods of getting knowledge. Upon this doctrine the New England transcendental philosophy as a whole was built. What the nature of that philosophy was, as has been said, is a matter of general agreement, and in setting down, briefly, its most important elements one is certain only to be repeating what has been often and well said before. Of course on minor points there is still plenty of room for controversy. One may discuss endlessly, for instance, how far Emerson's God was a personal being. It may be pointed out wherein in one respect Theodore Parker contradicts Bronson Alcott, or how in another Emerson differs from Margaret Fuller; and indeed in this connection it should not be forgotten that these transcendentalists were variously adapted, by both nature and training, for pure metaphysical thinking. But after everything has been said, there remains no possible doubt that in its large outlines they all held an identical philosophy. This philosophy teaches the unity of the world in God and the immanence of God in the world. Because of this indwelling of divinity, every part of the world, however small, is a microcosm, comprehending within itself, like Tennyson's flower in the crannied wall, all the laws and meaning of existence. The soul of each individual is identical with the soul of the world, and contains, latently, all which 'it contains. The normal life of man is a life of continuous expansion, the making actual of the potential elements of his being. This may occur in two ways: either directly, in states which vary from the ordinary perception of truth to moments of mystical rapture in which there is a conscious influx of the divine into the human; or indirectly, through the instrumentality of nature. Nature is the em-

[1] See Emerson's words quoted below, p. 71.

bodiment of spirit in the world of sense—it is a great picture to be appreciated; a great book to be read; a great task to be performed. Through the beauty, truth, and goodness incarnate in the natural world, the individual soul comes in contact with and appropriates to itself the spirit and being of God. From these beliefs as a center radiate all those others, which, however differently emphasized and variously blended, are constantly met with among the transcendentalists, as, for example, the doctrine of self-reliance and individualism, the identity of moral and physical laws, the essential unity of all religions, complete tolerance, the negative nature of evil, absolute optimism, a disregard for all "external" authority and for tradition, even, indeed, some conceptions not wholly typical of New England transcendentalism, like Alcott's doctrine of creation by "lapse." But always, beneath the rest, is the fundamental belief in the identity of the individual soul with God, and—at the same time the source and the corollary of this belief—an unshakable faith in the divine authority of the intuitions of the soul. Insight, instinct, impulse, intuition—the trust of the transcendentalists in these was complete, and whenever they employ these words they must be understood not in the ordinary but in a highly technical sense. Through a failure to observe this point, and on the supposition that the word "instinct"—in the phrase "Trust your instincts"—has its usual meaning, scores of persons have completely misunderstood and grossly misrepresented the teaching of Emerson and his associates.[1] Intuition—that is the method of the transcendental philosophy; no truth worth the knowing is susceptible of logical demonstration.[2] Herein is seen the predominance, in the Kantian influence on this movement, of the *Critique of Practical* over the *Critique of Pure Reason.*[3]

[1] See for further comment on this point, p. 142.

[2] "Foolish people ask you, when you have spoken what they do not wish to hear, 'How do you know it is truth, and not an error of your own?' We know truth when we see it, from opinion, as we know when we are awake that we are awake." Emerson, *Works,* ii, 262.

[3] It is worthy of note that that part of the *Critique of Pure Reason* which teaches the impossibility of the mind's knowing external things as they really are and the futility of metaphysical speculation finds no

No one seems to know just how or just when the term *transcendentalists* was first applied to Emerson and his circle; but there is evidence that those on whom it was bestowed were not overwhelmed with gratitude at the gift.[1] What was the reason for the resentment? Surely these men were far enough from being ashamed of a kinship with Kant and Kant's "idealist" successors. That there was a degree of such resentment, however, seems certain, and so we are compelled to suspect that the term—if indeed it were not maliciously applied in the beginning—very early took on somewhat of that popular significance which has clung to it ever since. With this second meaning, completely to be distinguished from the philosophical one we have been considering, *transcendental* has been used as practically synonymous with "transcending common-sense," airy, flighty, "ideal" in the uncomplimentary sense of that word. It may be objected at once that this second use is merely a colloquial, satirical perversion of the term.[2] Whatever it may be, this is the meaning that has been most widely attached to it; it is the meaning that the word conveys to the majority of readers today. The critic of transcendentalism will reckon ill who leaves it out.

There are other reasons besides its wide prevalence that entitle this popular use of the word to consideration. In the first place it embodies the most frequent and serious charge that has been brought against the New England transcen-

reflection in the New England use of *transcendental*. It troubled these men as little as it did Kant's "idealist" successors in Germany. As an example of the way in which the *Critique of Practical Reason* appealed especially to the transcendentalists, see the words of Theodore Parker, quoted below, p. 89.

[1] See *Dial,* ii, 382.

[2] The transcendentalists themselves used the term in both senses. For example, compare Theodore Parker's words from his Journal (1840), "I intend, in the coming year, to let out all the force of Transcendentalism that is in me" (Weiss, i, 155), and this extract from another of his sentences: "You remember the stuff which Margaret Fuller used to twaddle forth on that theme [the absence of art in America], and what transcendental nonsense got delivered from gawky girls and long-haired young men" (Weiss, ii, 377; the whole passage is given below, p. 165). And Emerson makes a similar distinction, see p. 166 sq.

dentalists: that they were "lost in the clouds," out of touch with real, practical life, and out of joint with common-sense. In the second place a mere glance is sufficient to show that the actual history of the times does much to explain and something to sanction the popular application of the word. During the same years when Emerson was writing and lecturing, when Theodore Parker was preaching, and Margaret Fuller was editing the *Dial,* currents of religious and social unrest, some of them of the wildest types, were pulsing through New England. "Dissent" and "reform"—these were the watchwords of the hour; and every "cause," from the maddest and the most insignificant to such mighty questions as those of temperance and anti-slavery, was given its hearing. Listen to Emerson's description of the members of the Chardon Street Convention who gathered in Boston in November, 1840: "Madmen, madwomen, men with beards, Dunkers, Muggletonians, Come-outers, Groaners, Agrarians, Seventh-day Baptists, Quakers, Abolitionists, Calvinists, Unitarians, and Philosophers."[1] Surely these were wild and "transcendental" times!

Now all the radical tendencies of that day may be considered, perhaps, as parts of a single movement, and even the extremes, as we look back, may seem to blend quite imperceptibly together. But the point is that if we glibly call the whole transcendentalism, we shall certainly be meaning something very different from what we mean when we speak of the transcendentalism of Emerson or Parker. No one can dictate how the term shall finally be used, but we shall inevitably fall into great confusion if we employ it in several senses, or if he who criticizes means one thing while he who reads may understand another. The significance often given to Brook Farm in discussions of this movement is an illustration of just this confusion. That Brook Farm was very typical of the times doubtless no one will deny; but transcendental in the more narrowly philosophical sense of the term it certainly was not

---

[1] *Works,* x, 351. See also the opening paragraphs of Lowell's essay on Thoreau; and Cooke, 92.

—as indeed its latest historian clearly recognizes.[1] It was an attempt at collectivism, contrasting very markedly with the extreme individualism of a more strictly interpreted transcendentalism.   Said Emerson, when George Ripley invited him to take part in the enterprise: " At the name of a society all my repulsions play, all my quills rise and sharpen."   And it is worthy of remark that not one of the four whom common consent seems to have selected as the leading transcendentalists, Alcott, Emerson, Parker, and Margaret Fuller, had any active share in the enterprise, and that most of them, while sympathizing with the spirit of its founders, expressed themselves as disagreeing with the theories underlying it.[2]   Indeed Mr. Lindsay Swift has put it in a way which cannot be improved on when he says that Emerson " never refers to Brook Farm without conveying to the finest sense the assurance that someone is laughing behind the shrubbery."

This is but one illustration of the confusion caused by the word *transcendental*.   When we speak of the Elizabethan Age, of the Restoration Drama, of the Victorian Poets, we use terms purely or mainly temporal in their significance.   But when we speak of the Transcendental Movement, we go further, we indulge in criticism in the very name; and this is likely to prove dangerous, for we are tempted, if not compelled, to assume at the beginning what really should be the outcome of our discussion—a definition of transcendentalism.   Well may we take warning from the more famous parallel case of *romantic* and the *Romantic Movement!*

We wish, therefore, instead of starting with a definition of transcendentalism, to impose on ourselves a limitation of another sort, to confine our study almost exclusively to those

[1] " Brook Farm was a Transcendental movement without doubt, but only, after all, in that it was a speculation of pure idealists, and that its inspiration came from the sources here so imperfectly outlined." Lindsay Swift, *Brook Farm*, 11. The same view is taken by Frothingham in his life of Ripley, 119.

[2] See Emerson's *Works*, iii, 251; x, 331; xii, 44 and 99; Holmes, 165 and 191; Frothingham, *George Ripley*, 307. Weiss, i, 108. *Memoirs*, ii, 73. Chadwick, *William Ellery Channing*, 322. Sanborn, 382; notice that this last is not in Alcott's own words.

whom, as we have just said, common consent has selected as the leaders of this movement. In other words we would restrict not the meaning of the term but the field to be examined; and if, for instance, Brook Farm is almost completely excluded from our pages, it will not be because of any abstract difference between individualism and collectivism, but because of the concrete fact that Alcott, Emerson, Parker, and Margaret Fuller had little hand in the experiment. Let it be clearly understood, then, that in the following studies transcendentalism is being treated in this restricted sense, and the discussion will center accordingly around the four chief names already mentioned.[1]

Within the realm, thus limited, of transcendental criticism, there are, we think, two questions in particular that must be looked on as distinctly " open."

As has been said, there is little dispute as to what the New England transcendental philosophy was; but as to just whence it came, just what its various sources truly were, no answer really definite has been given. Concerning certain general points in the inquiry, there can, to be sure, exist no serious doubt or difference of opinion. But among proposed solutions of the problem there is still, in even important respects, wide divergence, and the final word in the matter has not by any means been spoken. The object of the second chapter of these studies is to examine the evidence on this point, *as far as the leading transcendentalists are concerned.*

[1] The passing of time has made the name of Henry David Thoreau of greater significance than that of any of the other transcendentalists except Emerson, and it may seem strange, therefore, that his name should not be included among those singled out for special treatment. But the fact that Thoreau was much younger than the four others we have mentioned, and that the transcendental movement was already beyond its formative stage at a time when he was still hardly more than a boy, make him at once of far less importance than the others in connection with any investigation of the sources of the movement; while to those parts of our discussion on which the date of his birth has a less vital bearing, the relation of Thoreau is so unmistakably clear that it has been found possible to summarize the facts in a brief paragraph of the concluding chapter.

For the reasons for the attention given to William Ellery Channing, see p. 27 sq.

The second of the open questions is this: How far justified, *as applied to the leaders of this movement,* is the popular definition of transcendental, " transcending common-sense "? This seems in many ways the very crux of transcendental criticism. Surely in the past it has been the chief bone of critical contention. The third and fourth chapters of the present essay are devoted to a consideration of this question. In the former, especially, some of the grounds of the popular criticism are examined. In the latter, the main point at issue is directly treated.

For the purpose of throwing light on these discussions and of affording a slight historical setting, the first chapter is given to a short summary of the streams of tendency, American and foreign, leading toward the transcendental movement, and to an enumeration—in the briefest form—of some of the most important events of the transcendental period itself. It is designed especially to make clear the relation between Unitarianism and transcendentalism. As a complete study of these early currents of influence would amount to little less than a history of the entire political, philosophical, and religious thought of the eighteenth and early nineteenth centuries, it will be sufficiently apparent that what is offered here is merely the most fragmentary summary. Obviously this inquiry is ultimately bound up with the question of the sources of transcendentalism; indeed the two are in a way identical. But a distinction has been preserved—just wherein, the parts of the essay devoted to these subjects should make clear—between forces only indirectly and those directly influencing the transcendental group. Several statements made in the course of Chapter I depend for their proof, it is true, upon the facts of Chapter II. Anticipated conclusions of this sort will be indicated in the footnotes.

A glance at the chief books bearing on New England transcendentalism will be sufficient to show in what sense the two main questions proposed for discussion are still " open."

The most important general work is O. B. Frothingham's *Transcendentalism in New England, a History,* a work of permanent value, founded on sympathetic insight, and showing wide personal knowledge of the men and conditions treated. Even its unsupported statements have much of the weight of original authority. Its method, however, is largely expository and biographical, and while the book contains not a little that concerns the two questions we have singled out, its author cannot be said to have treated either of them except incidentally, much less to have gathered the evidence together. Indeed, in his opening paragraph, he distinctly disclaims any attempt to study in detail the sources of the movement.

There are various accounts of Brook Farm, the best being Mr. Lindsay Swift's excellent little history. But since we have chosen to restrict our study to men who were only remotely connected with this enterprise, these books can have little bearing on the points of our discussion.

For the rest, the most important works are the biographies of the transcendentalists, and it is to these, it is needless to say, that the writer is principally indebted for his facts. They differ much in the attention they give to the two specific inquiries we have raised. Mr. Higginson's admirable life of Margaret Fuller, for instance, seems to have been written with very especial reference to our second question; while in the case of Emerson of course both of the problems have been pretty fully considered. But for the most part the points are treated incidentally, the pertinent facts being scattered through many pages; and even though these matters had been handled exhaustively in every case, it is quite conceivable that the individual results might take on an entirely new meaning when considered collectively. The chapters on transcendentalism in these various biographies, while full of suggestive points of view (and to these the writer is deeply indebted, more deeply doubtless than he is himself aware), are in their very nature too brief for any massing of the evidence. The same may be said of the almost endless number of essays and magazine articles that have treated various phases of the subject.

These observations are made in order to justify the present study; and if it supplies material for answers to the two main questions that have been proposed, it is hoped that it will serve a useful purpose, whether or not the reader feels that the data warrant the induction of the brief concluding chapter. If, however, that conclusion does seem to follow from the facts, unity is then given to the two parts of the discussion, and its scope is considerably widened. The chapters may, in that case, be regarded from a slightly different point of view. Some critics have looked upon transcendentalism as simply a New England importation from abroad; others have found in it a strictly indigenous product. In its extreme form either of these opinions is easy to refute, but the thought underlying them supplies an interesting and highly suggestive way of treating the whole matter. Under this aspect and in the light of the conclusion, the essay falls into three main parts, and a fourth part summing up the other three, somewhat as follows:

I. A brief study of blended American and European influences leading toward New England transcendentalism. (Chapter I.)

II. A study of the immediate European contribution to transcendentalism.

   (*a*) As shown in the reading and studies of these men. (Chapter II.)

   (*b*) As shown in the finished transcendental product. (Chapter III.)[1]

III. A study of the immediate American contribution to transcendentalism. (Chapter IV.)

IV. Summary of I, II, and III, and general conclusion. (Chapter V.)

[1] Chapter III incidentally shows some aspects of the immediate American contribution.

CHAPTER I

Unitarianism and Transcendentalism

The eighteenth century, we have often heard, was an age
of prose and reason. The phrase is certainly a useful one,
useful and illuminating; but we must be on our guard against
too simple a formula for a period of extraordinary complexity.
The eighteenth century was an age of transition; it gathered
up and criticized the life of Europe since the Renaissance; it
made ready, too, for the Europe that was to come. It was,
in a peculiar sense, a meeting ground of the future and the
past, a time, as Leslie Stephen has well put it, of compromise
and truce. Such an age, manifestly, must refuse to be
crowded into a pigeon-hole or to be embodied in a phrase. It
was, for instance, not merely an era of prose and reason, but,
as has often been pointed out, an era of the rebirth of emotion.
Even in its earliest decades signs were not absent of a re-
kindling enthusiasm; and more and more, as its years went
by, imagination and poetry, spirituality and the sense of mystery, reawakened from torpor into a new life. The age of
rationalism and the age of the return of feeling—while even
this description is far from exhausting the nature of the time,
the contrast which these two aspects of the century present,
becomes, for the purposes of our study, highly significant.

For a long time the intellectual[1] and emotional currents of
the eighteenth century flowed on with little or no blending of
their streams, and neither of them, alone, it is clear, was adequate to bring the nineteenth century. The intellectual tendency was not adequate: the spirit of reason and criticism
accomplished no transient nor despicable results, yet the logical
end of the century's most radical, and it may be said, most
progressive thought, was, as it took the genius of a Hume to

[1] Those "intellectual" currents especially are meant which time has
shown were really potential with great results.

13

perceive, the abyss of skepticism; rationalism concluded, not unfittingly, its salutary reign—by digging its own grave. Here then, plainly, we have no sufficient explanation of the early nineteenth century with its intensity of life and action, its rich fruition of fresh ideals and faiths. Nor on the other hand is the new age to be fully accounted for by the emotional tendency of the preceding one: it, alone, could bring only a blind extravagance, a mawkish sentimentality, or a piety which, however beautiful, fixed its face resolutely on the past; the Richardsons, the Whitefields, and the Ossians were in no final sense the forerunners of the coming era.

Skepticism and sentimentalism—these, then, were the two gulfs that seemed to await the intellectual and emotional currents of the eighteenth century. But the age was destined to another end; for once let these isolated streams of influence come together, once let this feeling and progressive thought unite, and instantly—whether positive or negative—a power was abroad in the land, a Rousseau, a Lessing, or a Tom Paine. Reason had germinated in the congenial soil of common-sense, but the seed could be saved from skeptical decay and death only as it forced its way up into the atmosphere of feeling. And this union of thought and feeling was, indeed, exactly what was taking place on all sides at the beginning of the revolutionary[1] era. Everywhere ideas were catching fire; everywhere theories were being infused with the red blood of life. Pale abstractions, touched with passion, took on, in a moment, a strange vitality; weak sentiment, fastening upon thought, assumed a sudden power. Out of this ferment of emotions and ideas, profound changes at the very heart of European life could scarcely fail to come. Far enough from revolutionary in temper was the author of the *Essay on the Human Understanding,* or the little English printer whose novels made the whole of Europe weep; yet—we might almost say—Locke plus Richardson gives us Rousseau.

It is customary to regard the new era as a revolt from the

---

[1] This term, throughout the discussion, it need hardly be said, is used with reference to the whole period of change at the end of the century, with no limited application to the French Revolution.

old. And so it was. But it was also its positive culmination.
Indeed, as the scene shifts, it sometimes seems wellnigh impossible to tell whether the figures that we now behold have
come to inter the dead bones of the passing age, or whether in
these figures we see those very bones themselves, risen, re-
clothed in a new flesh and blood. If Wordsworth came to
bury Pope's couplets, he came too to raise his pantheism from
the dead.[1]

Again and again it is possible to point out thoughts of the
late eighteenth or of the nineteenth century which—as mere
thoughts—seem hardly distinguishable from those of a hundred or a hundred and fifty years before; but the spirit in
which they are held and the implications they involve differ
often as widely as the poles. It is a far cry from the social
contract of Hobbes, or even of Locke, to the social contract of
Rousseau; from the pantheism of Spinoza to the pantheism
of Schelling, or from that of the *Essay on Man* to that of
Adonais; from Pope's " Whatever is, is right " to Browning's
" God's in his heaven—All's right with the world! " But the
analogies are not merely fanciful. And so, during the great
epoch of change of which we speak, we have a curiously ironic
spectacle: we behold men repudiating the age that is passing,
yet, not infrequently, accepting its thought and transforming
its cold intellectual propositions into their own revolutionary
watchwords. The touch of feeling on eighteenth century
thinking wrought a result scarcely less astonishing than the
famous contact of Ithuriel's spear. Indeed, we might apply
Milton's figure, in at least one case, in further detail. The
orthodox would have been far from unwilling to compare
early English deism with a toad, and the seeming half-hearted-
ness of its apostles, in the age of prose and reason, made it
appear, in many ways, as completely insignificant. But when
at the touch of feeling English deism flared up in the figure
of Thomas Paine, the orthodox surely must have admitted
that the old enemy had assumed, if not a more diabolical, at
least a far more dangerous and appalling form. The reason

[1] Or, more strictly, the pantheism of Shaftesbury, Bolingbroke, and
others—the men from whom Pope got his own.

to which early eighteenth century thinkers appealed was a dim abstraction; the Reason to whom the French Revolutionists built altars was a living goddess.

Now this transformation of old ideas by new emotion, of which we have just given an example, let loose upon the planet sometimes constructive, sometimes destructive, forces. Indeed nothing could prove more clearly the point on which we are insisting, could show more conclusively that the world had reached one of the great turning points of its history, than the character of the French Revolution itself, a movement at once so conspicuously an end and a beginning.

> "Heaven smiles, and faiths and empires gleam
> Like wrecks of a dissolving dream,"

wrote Shelley, and he condensed a wonderful amount into those two short lines. Smiles and wrecks—these were the characteristic products of the age, blasted institutions and blossoming ideals; and it is partly because they were its characteristic products that this age assumes, frequently, an aspect of such wild confusion. What can be more startling, for instance, than the fact that, at the very time when the historical way of regarding things was grounding itself firmly in the minds of men, a movement should occur whose very essence was the denial of history?—what more startling than at just the moment when the world was learning that society and civilization are the products of an evolution, to have the thesis propounded that both may be brought, outright, into perfect being? Yet in this very paradox, this very contradiction, we perceive the contending forces of the age. Vitalized by passion, two mighty conceptions—and to recognize what those conceptions were we need only pronounce the names Rousseau and Burke —had come to the grapple, and each was to be vanquished, each victorious. Each was to be vanquished: the French Revolution was the funeral pyre alike of reason and the old regime. Each was to be victorious: the French Revolution was a terrible vindication of authority, experience, and the past, demonstrating, in the face of its own principles, the immense significance of historical continuity and evolution; but it was not less a staggering blow to all blind worship of custom and tradition, to all unreasoning acceptance of the sacredness of creeds and institutions. And so, when the smoke of the Revolution began to clear away, to those who had eyes to see, both reason and the established order stood discredited. Never again with hope of general countenance could "reason" put forth such arrogant pretensions, never again could the established order, simply because it was the established order, claim such authority. The world was convinced that there was something rotten at the heart of the existing state; but the world began to look for some other means of removing that rottenness than the deification of reason, to search for some other avenue than that of the pure intellect through which to approach the deepest problems of life. A new standard of truth was demanded; and seeking to discover such a standard, men began more and more to favor the belief that other faculties beside the understanding, that the imaginative, the practical, and moral sides of man's nature play a part in his apprehension of the truth. To the wonderful accuracy with which they embody this fundamental shifting of the view-point of the world, not less than to their own intrinsic merit, must be attributed the immense significance and influence of the two Critiques of Immanuel Kant,[1] and of the two parts of Goethe's *Faust;* while, on the other hand, the failure of a philosophy like that of Hegel to retain vitality and power must be attributed, in no small measure, to its vain attempt to re-enthrone the dialectic method. Varied as have been the faiths and ideals of the nineteenth century, it is not a little remarkable to note how the attempt to find some more satisfactory basis of truth to replace the rejected standard of pure reason imparts a certain unity of purpose to views of life which, in other respects, differ oftentimes widely enough. To take only a few examples where many might be chosen, and to confine these few to England: Coleridge's exaltation of "Reason" over the understanding, Wordsworth's nature-worship, the mysticism of Shelley, Carlyle's gospel of work, the art-philosophy of Ruskin, the "culture" of Arnold, Tenny-

[1] Kant's two Critiques (1781 and 1788), to be sure, both antedate the fall of the Bastile.

son's trust in " faith " and " wisdom " rather than in " knowledge," Browning's appeal from the intellect to the heart, even
the agnosticism of Spencer, the utilitarianism of Mill, and the
Catholicism of Newman—each of these reveals some aspect
of this search for a deeper way of seeking after truth, each,
in one manner or another, aims a blow at the ascendency of
reason.

This much has been said of European tendencies in the
eighteenth century, and of some of their results, because it
is only in their light—or indeed as a part of them—that the
story of American religious development can be understood.
The history of American thought is, in its largest outlines,
identical with that of Europe, though generally, save in politics,
America lagged several decades, sometimes nearer a whole
century, behind.   Just as the various movements of the revolutionary age in Europe were both culminations of the eighteenth
century and revolts against it, so New England transcendentalism—whatever else it may have been—was both a culmination of that typically eighteenth century movement, early American Unitarianism, and at the same time a revolt against it.
Transcendentalism, furthermore, was just such a union of
thought and feeling as those we have been describing.   And
just as there emerged in Europe with the passing of the age
of reason the longing for a new and deeper standard of truth,
so transcendentalism was, in part, a search for some such pro-
founder and more comprehensive way of grasping the nature
of man and of the world.
    New England took no plunge, as England did, from the
moral heights of Puritanism into the abyss of Restoration
licentiousness.   But there was a descent, which, if more
gradual, was not on that account less real.   Extreme Puritanism
held within itself the germ of its own disintegration.   As a
mere matter of psychology, the intensity of Massachusetts
Puritanism of the first generation could not be indefinitely
continued, and some decline from earlier religious fervor was
even more inevitable in a pioneer community where material
development and protection from the Indians were crying neces-

sities. Already, by the second generation, the falling off in piety was conspicuous, and at the time when Increase Mather was instrumental in calling the "Reforming Synod" of 1679 there was sad evidence, he believed, of "decay of godliness in the land; of the increase of pride; neglect of worship; sabbath breaking; lack of family government; censurings, intemperance, falsehood, and love of the world."[1] Though the widespread belief in witchcraft and the frequent occurrence of witchcraft delusions throughout the seventeenth century may make one hesitate to say so, it seems difficult not to regard Salem Witchcraft, from some points of view at least, as the *reductio ad absurdum* of the extreme religious spirit. It showed, apparently, that the old Puritanism had passed its prime, and it surely hastened the advent of more rational and common-sense ideas; while, to make the reaction stronger, all through the eighteenth century, especially in the neighborhood of Boston, the commercial and political questions of the day were sufficient to render impossible any exclusive absorption of the community's attention in things religious.

But the causes of these changes in the spiritual atmosphere were not wholly indigenous. English rationalistic and free-thinking tendencies penetrated to the colonies—and not always so slowly as might be imagined—and they had, particularly in the accessible region about Boston, their immediate effect. "Heresies" began to creep into the religious world. Reflecting the contemporary English interest in questions of morality, Arminianism[2] appeared in Massachusetts, giving an unorthodox importance to matters of conduct, and attacking, though insidiously, the Calvinistic doctrine of election. The early Arminians in America, though they still believed that man was saved by the sovereign grace and mercy of God, held nevertheless that man could aid the operation of that grace by putting himself in a proper attitude for its reception, by attending, as it were, to what were called the "means" of

[1] Quoted from Williston Walker, *A History of the Congregational Churches in the United States,* 187.

[2] See *Ibid.,* 85 et seq., and 252; also, Cooke, *Unitarianism in America,* 37.

grace; and gradually more and more efficiency was attributed to these "means." Arianism, too, appeared, subtly undermining the doctrine of the Trinity.

Nothing could show more clearly the religious condition of New England during the first half of the eighteenth century than the career of Jonathan Edwards and the story of the Great Awakening. The apprehensions of Edwards were aroused by two causes, and the Great Awakening was designed to remedy two evils—the spiritual deadness and the doctrinal heresies of the time. It need hardly be added that to Edwards these were aspects of one thing. The great wave of enthusiasm that swept over the colony was the protest against the decline of piety, the treatise on *The Freedom of the Will* the most famous part of the protest against the doctrinal Arminianism of the day. But what could better prove that New England, too, was living in the same eighteenth century with Europe, and that she was even less ready than England for any high manifestation of feeling, than the rapidity with which the emotional wave subsided and the completeness with which the old apathy returned? While the religious views of Jonathan Edwards were too spiritually lofty and too intellectually original and profound to be properly termed retrogressive in any age, and while in him and in his remarkable wife we find many anticipations of transcendentalism itself, it cannot be denied that, historically, his influence proved on the whole reactionary. Put Edwards beside any one of his Boston Arminian opponents. Can there be a moment's hesitation as to which was the greater man, the greater genius? But on the other hand, can there be any more question as to which was in closer touch with the dominant spirit of the time? The Great Awakening is the American analog of the Methodist movement[1]—emotionally prophetic, theologically, in the main, reactionary.

The New England revival did not close the opening gulf in the religious world. It widened it rather. The efforts of Edwards had increased and consolidated the enemies he sought

---

[1] The part that Whitefield played in the American movement is well known. For the influence of the Great Awakening on Wesley, see Allen, *Jonathan Edwards*, 133.

to slay; and the adherents of the opposing views continued in constantly diverging paths. The New Calvinists,[1] as the followers of Edwards were called, went on to develop an American theology, uninfluenced essentially by European thought, and the large product of doctrinal discussion that resulted is the orthodox contribution to the age of reason. The liberal school, on the other hand, confirmed by the excesses of the Great Awakening in their dislike of enthusiasm, and constantly closer in touch with various forms of English thinking, grew more and more liberal, until, as the differences between their own and the New Calvinist views became wider and wider, the term Unitarian was finally applied to them.[2]

It must not be forgotten that this movement had little direct connection with the English Unitarianism of Priestley and that it exhibited practically none of his materialistic and Socinian tendencies. This is only one reason why the term Unitarian is in some ways unfortunate, in some ways apt to prove misleading. It must be made to cover—if names are to correspond with realities—the whole early movement for freedom of thought and release from tradition within the New England religious world, and of that movement, discussions of the Trinity and of the nature of Christ were manifestly but single aspects.[3] Unitarianism was something more than a passing agitation over a few theological doctrines. It was the product within this New England religious world of the combined rational and questioning tendencies of the age. It was contributed to not merely directly, from within, by writers or thought-currents of a religious sort; but it was contributed to also indirectly, from without, by whatever struck at tradition. Skeptical opinions that were in the air, the turmoil that accom-

[1] The distinction between the Old Calvinists and the followers of Edwards may be practically neglected for the purposes of this essay.

[2] The term was not employed until very late. See Walker, *A History of the Cong. Churches in the U. S.*, 338.

[3] Indeed the doctrines of total depravity and eternal punishment seem, in some ways, to have been even more conspicuously the center of the controversy.

panied the Revolutionary War,[1] speculations from France that preceded 1789 and echoes that followed it[2]—these things had various effects in various spheres of New England life, but within the religious sphere they tended, for the time, to strengthen the Unitarian position. Early American Unitarianism was eminently typical of the *critical* century in which it appeared. It seems, in many ways, much more a negative than a positive movement, or—if the term negative be objectionable—much more preparatory than final. Its essence consists more than in anything else in this: that it was a reaction from Calvinism. Its most immediate positive product was, perhaps, the atmosphere of tolerance it created.

If we have characterized the movement correctly, its continuity, then, cannot be insisted on too strongly. In 1785 King's Chapel became Unitarian by the revision of its liturgy[3]—the first open denial of the doctrine of the Trinity by a New England church organization. This year is accordingly frequently chosen to mark the beginning of the movement. But the singling out of any one initial date is useless and confusing. The King's Chapel event was but one incident in a long development, and its real significance is that of an unmistakable sign that toward the end of the century the struggle between

[1] See, "Life in Boston in the Revolutionary Period," by Horace E. Scudder, being Chapter iv of Volume iii of *The Memorial History of Boston.*

[2] William Ellery Channing's account of conditions at Harvard at the time he entered college (1794) gives an idea of the feeling of unrest that pervaded the country. "College was never in a worse state than when I entered it. Society was passing through a most critical stage. The French Revolution had diseased the imagination and unsettled the understanding of men everywhere. The old foundations of social order, loyalty, tradition, habit, reverence for antiquity, were everywhere shaken, if not subverted. The authority of the past was gone. The old forms were outgrown, and new ones had not taken their place. The tone of books and conversation was presumptuous and daring. The tendency of all classes was to skepticism." (Channing, 30. See also Miss Peabody, *Reminiscences*, 253.)

[3] Both the pastor, Rev. James Freeman, and the people were of advanced views, but Rev. William Hazlitt (father of the essayist), who was then in America, was especially influential in bringing about the change.

the liberals and the orthodox was approaching a critical stage. In this sense only it was a beginning.

In 1801, because their new pastor (Rev. James Kendall) exhibited, they thought, too advanced views, half the members of the original Pilgrim Church at Plymouth withdrew, founding a new organization that kept to the old faith. In 1805 Harvard College, which from the first had been a stronghold of the more radical thought, passed into the complete control of the Unitarians by the appointment of Rev. Henry Ware as Hollis Professor of Divinity[1]—an event which soon caused the establishment of Andover Theological Seminary by the opposition. Another influence toward liberalism was the *Monthly Anthology*.[2] This publication was begun (but soon abandoned) by a young graduate of Harvard. It was then assumed and continued through ten volumes by Emerson's father, the Rev. William Emerson, and the friends whom he gathered round him. This group was known as The Anthology Club,[3] and their organ, though dedicated to the service of literature and general culture, discussed theology to some extent. In 1815 the whole controversy reached a climax, for then began—and continued for a quarter of a century—the open division of the Congregational churches[4] into the Unitarian and the Trinitarian, a division accelerated, and on the orthodox side embittered, by the decision of the Massachusetts Supreme Court in the famous Dedham Case.[5]

When we remember the varied tides of emotion that during these years were sweeping over Europe, the condition of New England life in the earlier decades of the nineteenth century seems, at first sight at least, somewhat inexplicable. It is clear that there had come no general invasion of European enthusiasm. Beginning about 1790—and lasting for two gen-

[1] Cooke, *Unitarianism in America*, 94.

[2] *Ibid.*, 95.

[3] Other members were Samuel Cooper Thacher, Joseph Stevens Buckminster, Joseph Tuckerman, and John S. J. Gardiner. *Ibid.*, 96.

[4] *Ibid.*, 117.

[5] For discussions of this decision, see Ellis, *A Half-Century of the Unitarian Controversy*, 415; Walker, *A History of the Cong. Churches in the U. S.*, 342.

erations—a new series of revivals took place in the Trinitarian churches, and it is impossible to believe that these had no connection with the wider emotional currents of the day, though such a relationship it might be somewhat difficult to establish. It is obvious, too, that of the controversial sort there was no lack in the religious world of most intense and bitter feeling. But, after all, it seems plain that the spirit of the earlier eighteenth century, with all its lethargy and lack of fire, had lasted over, widely, in New England. Much of the community was still emotionally starved, and the young people especially must have looked about them in vain for that which could offer any lasting satisfaction to their deeper feelings.

The prevalent philosophy was the common-sense philosophy of Locke; the prevalent literature was still that of the uninspiring "classical" school. The educational world, conspicuously, within which the feelings of the young would naturally be fed, was infected with apathy. There is no reason to doubt that the descriptions given, for instance, by George Ticknor and James Freeman Clarke,[1] of conditions prevailing at Harvard, are just and characteristic. Of Professor John Farrar, who lectured in philosophy and the sciences, Clarke says, " He was a true teacher, but almost the only one in the whole corps of the professors." And then, as an example, is given an account of the Greek teacher, who never displayed any enthusiasm or the slightest appreciation of the poetry of the Iliad. The result was that the students began seeking emotional satisfaction outside the curriculum.[2]

It should be remarked too that, during much of the period we are discussing, the young New Englander who turned to politics did not find the prospect bright. New England, the stronghold of Federalism, was, during the ascendency of the Democratic party, to a considerable degree politically isolated.

[1] J. F. Clarke, *Autobiography*, 36–39. *Life, Letters, and Journals of George Ticknor,* i, chapter xviii.

[2] "They did not read Thucydides and Xenophon, but Macaulay and Carlyle. . . . Our real professors of rhetoric were Charles Lamb and Coleridge, Walter Scott and Wordsworth."—a statement which shows that the condition of emotional indifference still survived at the time when the writings of Macaulay and Carlyle were becoming known.

In the words of Professor Trent, " it was a period of American history in which politics offered no great allurements to young men trained as the best New Englanders were. Although Daniel Webster had already become the idol of his countrymen, it was plain that the democratic rule of Jackson offered more opportunities to the tricky politician than to the trained states-man,"[1]—a condition of things highly favorable, it will be realized, to the advent of transcendentalism.

But this lack of enthusiasm, so widespread, was hardly any-where more noticeable than in the Unitarian world. The Unitarians were, indeed, in a peculiarly untenable position. Their eighteenth century spirit had survived its usefulness—yet they clung to it tenaciously. The eighteenth century was an age of transition—and they were seeking to make its views and temper permanent. The eighteenth century was an age of compromise—and they would render its position final. The eighteenth century was an age of preparation—and they re-mained unwilling to advance. They had no philosophy to give their views consistency, and indeed no philosophy can be conceived that could have performed, even superficially, a task so hopelessly gigantic. With the orthodox and their " super-stitions " on the one side and the kindly abyss that Hume with his logic had prepared for the reception of all rationalism on the other, the Unitarians were, most veritably, between the devil and the deep sea. And their enemies perceived their dilemma better, probably, than they did themselves. They were charged with lack of boldness in defending their posi-tion, even with cowardice and duplicity. Emerson's phrase " the pale negations of Boston Unitarianism " had, beyond doubt, justification, while Theodore Parker summed up their spiritual coldness in words that, at the same time, reveal how among the Unitarian preachers the eighteenth century interest in morality had still survived: " I felt early that the ' liberal ' ministers did not do justice to simple religious feeling; to me their preaching seemed to relate too much to outward things, not enough to the inward pious life; their prayers felt cold; but certainly they preached the importance and religious

[1] *A History of American Literature*, 303.

value of morality as no sect, I think, had done before. . . .
The defect of the Unitarians was a profound one. . . . It is
a dismal fault in a religious party, this lack of Piety, and dis-
mally have the Unitarians answered it; yet let their great
merits and services be not forgot."[1]   It is indeed important
that the merits of the Unitarians—in spite of the fact that
their present position was a prosaic and in some respects a
ridiculous one—should be remembered, for many and high
those merits surely were.   The typical Unitarian of the time,[2]
as far as there was any such, was a man of tolerance, of intellect, of cultured tastes, of unexceptionable private morality
and notable civic virtue, as well as of many other admirable
qualities, but not—let it be repeated—either metaphysical or
emotionally spiritual in his temperament.   Philosophy and
enthusiasm he did not have; yet philosophy and enthusiasm
were exactly the things of which his religion stood most
lamentably in need.

Now the time was bound to come when the intense fervor
and the new ideals of Europe should make their way to New
England.   And at that hour there were bound to be young
people there ready to welcome and receive them.   In so far
as the new spirit was to enter the religious world—and it must
not be forgotten that New England was still pre-eminently a
religious community—it was natural, if like conditions were
to produce the same or similar effects, that it should appeal
most strongly to the Unitarians.   Why?   Precisely because
the Unitarians, having taken their course in the (rational)
spirit of the eighteenth century, were ready for that of the
nineteenth, ready for it in a way in which the orthodox were
not and could not be.   If the Unitarians had carried over into
the nineteenth the temper of the eighteenth century, it may
almost be said—if the statement is not taken too literally—
that the orthodox had carried over into the nineteenth the
temper of the seventeenth century.   Significant changes might

[1] Weiss, ii, 481 *et seq.*

[2] See Garnett, *Life of Ralph Waldo Emerson,* 84; Frothingham, *George
Ripley,* 42; Frothingham, *Theodore Parker,* 151; Channing, *Works,* iii,
147; Trent, *A History of American Literature,* 298.

first be expected then within the ranks of the " liberals," and signs were not completely lacking that changes were at work.

A man who early showed symptoms of appreciating the religious needs of the time, and who, had not early death cut short a career of exceptional promise, would inevitably have played an even more important part than he did in the development we are discussing, was the Rev. Joseph Stevens Buckminster (1784–1812). He was a preacher of great scholarship and eloquence, and of considerable literary power. The letters between the father, Rev. Joseph Buckminster (1751–1812), the stern old Calvinist, and his Unitarian son, throw much light on the times.[1] In his sermons the latter opposed the doctrinal in favor of the spiritual and practical, and in Biblical scholarship, with the critical material and tools gained in Europe, accomplished so much that he was appointed the first lecturer in Biblical criticism at Harvard, and George Ticknor wrote of him, " It has, in our opinion, hardly been permitted to any other man to render so considerable a service as this to Christianity in the western world."[2]

But there was another man who, more than anyone else in the religious world, showed himself open to the influence of the *Zeitgeist,* and who, largely because of this, became a power in the land whose effect is not likely to be overrated. This man, it need scarcely be added, was William Ellery Channing (1780–1842). Channing is usually spoken of as the great Unitarian, and his famous sermon on " Unitarian Christianity,"[3] preached at the ordination of Jared Sparks at Baltimore in 1819, is generally looked on as being in a sense the formulation of the denomination's creed. But if Channing was a Unitarian, he was one of an entirely new type ; and with him—if we are to give him that name—the continuity of Unitarian development seems almost broken. Indeed the more one studies his character and beliefs in relation to his time, the more one must feel that he was scarcely a Unitarian at all, but rather

[1] See Trent, *A History of American Literature,* 293. Mrs. E. B. Lee, *Memoirs of the Buckminsters,* 141.

[2] Cooke, *Unitarianism in America,* 390. See also *Christian Examiner,* xlvii, 186 ; Channing, 124 ; *Memoirs of the Buckminsters.*

[3] *Works,* iii, 59.

the first of the transcendentalists. He had precisely what the Unitarians of the day had not—enthusiasm, a deeply spiritual character, and a liking for philosophy. His true position is seen in his own declaration that Unitarianism is "only the vestibule"[1] of truth. This claim, to be sure, must not be pressed too far.[2] In his theology and philosophy Channing appears not infrequently about half way between the Unitarian and the transcendental position. In such a sermon as his *Likeness to God*[3] he is almost completely transcendental; but when he discourses on miracles[4] or the future state[5] he seems very far from Emerson and Parker.[6] The point is, however, that he shows a development in the transcendental direction, and that all those distinctive doctrines which gave his preaching uniqueness and significance in his own day and which give him historical importance now, flowed from the transcendental elements in his belief. An example will make this clear. The Calvinists believed that human nature is totally depraved; the Unitarians denied this, their denial carrying with it the positive implication that human nature is essentially good; the transcendentalists believed that human nature is divine. What could show more clearly where Channing really stood than the fact that his "one sublime idea" was no other than this of the divinity of human nature? And further than this his temper and general spirit were singularly like those of the transcendentalists. He was, to

[1] Miss Peabody, *Reminiscences,* 56.

[2] The whole question after all is mainly a matter of definition, the definition of Unitarianism. The contention merely is that to call both Channing and the typical Unitarian of the time Unitarians is quite like making no distinction between the orthodox and the liberals of a hundred years before. There was at this time, as then, a very real distinction, and new names or at least new qualifying adjectives are demanded.

[3] *Works,* iii, 227.

Ibid., 107.

Ibid., iv, 228.

[6] For Channing's criticism of the transcendentalists, see (from a letter to Dr. Martineau) Conway, *Emerson at Home and Abroad,* 187; and for his differences with Parker, Miss Peabody, *Reminiscences,* 427. See also *Ibid.,* 364.

be sure, much more conservative, but his conservatism[1] was the inevitable outcome, among other things, of the earlier date of his birth. That his influence on the transcendentalists was so powerful and their sympathy for him so great—Emerson called him "our Bishop"[2]—is the surest proof of the transcendentalism of his own nature. These are some of the reasons for giving Channing a fairly full treatment in the present study, even to the exclusion of men who, at a cursory glance, may seem more intimately connected with the movement under consideration. To omit Channing in discussing transcendentalism would be to omit a large part of the first act of the play.

A few sentences of his own will perhaps best make clear the general truth of these contentions and show how fully he saw the hour's need and felt the wider spirit of the time. He wrote in 1820:

"I have before told you how much I think Unitarianism has suffered from union with a heart-withering philosophy. I will now add, that it has suffered also from a too exclusive application of its advocates to biblical criticism and theological controversy, in other words, from a too partial culture of the mind. I fear that we must look to other schools for the thoughts which thrill us, which touch the most inward springs, and disclose to us the depths of our own souls."[3]

And these words were spoken in 1824:

"Now, religion ought to be dispensed in accommodation to this spirit and character of our age. Men desire excitement, and religion must be communicated in a more exciting form. . . . Men will not now be trifled with. . . . They want a religion which will take a strong hold upon them. . . . Much as the age requires intellectual culture in a minister, it requires still more, that his acquisitions of truth should be instinct with life and feeling."[4]

But it was not merely a new religious spirit to which Chan-

---

[1] These points are more fully discussed in chapters II and IV.

[2] Miss Peabody, *Reminiscences*, 371.

[3] Channing, 276.

[4] *Works*, iii, 146.

ning was awake; he appreciated as well the significance of the
romantic note in the new fiction and poetry:

"The poetry of the age . . . has a deeper and more im-
pressive tone than comes to us from what has been called the
Augustan age of English literature. The regular, elaborate,
harmonious strains, which delighted a former generation, are
now accused, I say not how justly, of playing too much on
the surface of nature and of the heart. Men want and de-
mand a more thrilling note, a poetry which pierces beneath the
exterior of life to the depths of the soul, and which lays open
its mysterious workings, borrowing from the whole outward
creation fresh images and correspondences, with which to
illuminate the secrets of the world within us. So keen is this
appetite, that extravagances of imagination, and gross viola-
tions both of taste and moral sentiment, are forgiven, when
conjoined with what awakens strong emotion."[1]

Such words as these show plainly what was taking place
—especially the references to " other schools " that must be
looked to for " the thoughts which thrill us." That very
phrase, " the thoughts which thrill us," tells it all. At last
within the New England religious world was happening what
had long since been happening across the water: radical ideas
were being kindled with emotion. The theological and spiritual
revolution that long had threatened now had come. There
had been reasons for its delay. Revolutionary Europe had
indeed already wrought some confusion by battering harshly
on the outside of the conservative New England meeting-house;
but even revolutionary Europe could cause a vitally transforming change inside only as it was the author of some new and
larger ideal of truth, of some influence that could operate
from within, some *positive* influence that could touch and
move the very hearts of those that worshipped. The words
of Channing show that such influences were now at work.
German idealistic thought (especially that aspect of it which
asserted new validity for the moral and religious instincts of
man) and the new romantic literature[2]—these things could

[1] *Ibid.,* 146.

[2] Fuller proof of these statements is given later (especially in Chapter
II), but we may remark here that the original impetus toward German

operate from within, these things could appeal to the heart; and they supplied, moreover, exactly what the current Unitarianism needed most—philosophy and feeling.   Their effect —as obvious reasons led us to predict—was strongest upon certain emotionally starved young people of the time and most conspicuous within the Unitarian world.

One result of this influx of radical speculation and fresh feeling was an inevitable division in the Unitarian church between those who welcomed and assimilated the new thought and spirit, and those who opposed them as dangerous and revolutionary, between the transcendentalists, that is, and the conservative Unitarians.   In connection with this division it is important to notice, in passing, that the significant question is not one—for us at least—of approximation toward the truth, but one rather of adjustment to the spirit of the age; and just as there is no doubt that a hundred years before Charles Chauncy was nearer that spirit than was Jonathan Edwards, so there is no doubt that now Channing and Emerson were nearer it than—let us say—Professor Andrews Norton.

The history of this whole development may be represented roughly in some such way as this:

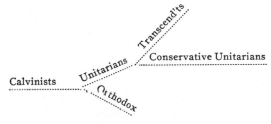

literature had come, about 1819, with the return to America from Göttingen of Edward Everett, George Bancroft, and George Ticknor. From this time on, knowledge of the German language and interest in the works of German writers increased, slowly at first, but, with the spread of the works of Coleridge and the appearance of Carlyle's, more and more rapidly. (See Appendix, in which the question of the early interest in German in New England is more fully considered.) This interest was enhanced and the obtaining of this knowledge facilitated by the coming to Harvard, about 1825, as instructor in German—he was made professor in 1830—of Charles T. Follen, a political exile. Other Germans who came to New England about the same time were Francis Lieber and Dr. Charles Beck, the latter being given in 1832 a place as University Professor of Latin at Harvard.

Of course such a diagram is far enough from explaining what transcendentalism—that complex product of most varied forces —really was. But it does, we think, fairly well represent its New England religious ancestry. It shows that the later division was not less real than the earlier; and it indicates in a way also that analogy with the development of European thought, on which we cannot, again, too strenuously insist. Just as the critical age succeeded the Puritan age in England, so "liberalism" came with the waning of the earlier New England spirit; and just as revolutionary Europe both repudiated the eighteenth century and at the same time accepted and transformed it, so the New England transcendentalists both repudiated and transformed with new life "the pale negations of Boston Unitarianism." They rejected its compromises; they rejected its cold spirit; but they accepted and carried further its rational method, so informing it with feeling, however, that it passed over into something quite unlike itself, the method of spiritual intuition. The diagram illustrates, too, why—though not impossible—it was hard for others[1] than Unitarians to become transcendentalists. Individuals might and did pass rapidly over from the orthodox to the transcendental view. But after all, however unconscious of it they might be, it was Unitarianism that had made that easy transit possible. The rational spirit is the logical predecessor of the transcendental spirit. The enthusiasm of the opening sentences of Emerson's *Nature* and their easy disregard for all tradition are so spontaneous and sincere that they seem purely original. And purely original, in a sense, they are. But behind them, in another sense, are all the doubts and questionings of the age of reason, and in them the feeling of an entire epoch of European life.

It must not be understood, when we speak of a division within the Unitarian church, that there was an open schism or even, in every case, a definite taking of sides on the new issues. No; like the "liberal" movement of the previous century

---

[1] Those who started as Calvinists, in most cases, seem to have passed through something corresponding to a Unitarian stage in their development.

this movement was a gradual development, and it is impossible
to put one's finger on any point and call it a beginning. Such
an event, however, as Emerson's withdrawal from the ministry
in 1832—owing mainly to a feeling that he could not con-
scientiously administer the communion—is comparable to the
King's Chapel occurrence of 1785, already mentioned, and
shows clearly the direction in which things were moving.

But it is especially in various publications and addresses of
the fourth decade of the century that the progress of the
" new " thought is most easily traced; and in confirmation
of what we have said of the gradual growth of the transcendental spirit it is significant to remark that a number of these
publications reached their readers through the columns of the
Christian Examiner, the official organ of the Unitarian church.
One of the most influential of them, probably, was an article
on Coleridge—and incidentally on German philosophy—by Rev.
Frederick Henry Hedge, which appeared in the *Examiner* for
March, 1833. Hedge, who had been a pupil of George Bancroft, knew the German language well, was a man of ripe and
sound scholarship, and would have played—had he lived nearer
to Boston, and had his nature been a little more aggressive
—a far more prominent part than he did in the movement.
As it is, he must be reckoned one of the earliest and most
influential of transcendentalists. There were other radical
articles in the *Examiner.* George Ripley, between 1830 and
1837, wrote ten such papers, " all either stating or foreshadow-
ing his later conclusions."[1] One of these, that on Martineau's
Rationale of Religious Inquiry (November, 1836), caused
somewhat of a sensation in conservative Unitarian circles. It
elicited a reprimand for Ripley from Professor Andrews Norton in the *Boston Advertiser.*

In 1836 Emerson published *Nature*—a little work which
comes nearer perhaps than anything else to being the philosophical " constitution " of transcendentalism. It was a call
on the author's part to the world around him to realize that
" the sun shines today also," and hence to cast aside conformity
and live lives in touch with nature—" nature " in the sense

[1] Frothingham, *Life of Ripley,* 94.

4

of the natural constitution of things. He followed this up
the next year with his Phi Beta Kappa oration, *The American
Scholar,* simply an application of the conceptions of *Nature*
to the world of literature and scholarship in the widest sense,
a plea for originality and individualism in the realm of letters.
Though in this address Emerson was careful not to let his philosophy obtrude itself, transcendental thought, nevertheless,
forms the real essence of the essay. In 1839 came the *Divinity
School Address,* another specific application of Emersonian
philosophy, this time to the world of theology and religion.
This utterance was widely considered the most radically dangerous declaration of the new school which had appeared up
to that time, and called forth an immediate answer in behalf
of the conservatives from Professor Andrews Norton. This,
under the title, *The Latest Form of Infidelity,* was a vigorous
attack on the intuitional philosophy,[1] and elicited, in its turn,
from George Ripley, a spirited rejoinder, *"The Latest Form
of Infidelity" Examined.* Theodore Parker's declaration of
war, his South Boston sermon on *The Transient and Permanent in Christianity,* was delivered in 1841. In connection
with these various publications and addresses, here is perhaps
the best place to note that the year 1838 was marked by the
appearance of the first two of a significant and influential series
of fourteen volumes, *Specimens of Foreign Standard Literature*
(reprinted in Edinburgh in 1857), of which Ripley was the
main editor. The opening volumes were called *Philosophical
Miscellanies,* and contained among other things, translations
from Cousin and Jouffroy. The same year saw the appearance of Emerson's collection of some of Carlyle's " Review "
articles, under the title of *Critical and Miscellaneous Essays.*
The American edition of *Sartor Resartus* had been issued two
years earlier.

But meanwhile, long before the latest of the events we have
just been chronicling, something approaching a transcendental
organization had been effected. It is characteristic of the
extreme individualism of the movement that it never attained
a really formal organization. The dissenters did not withdraw

[1] See also two articles in the *Princeton Review,* XI, 37, and XII, 31.

from Unitarianism and form a new church. It was natural however, that kindred spirits who, in the words of Emerson, " perhaps . . . only agreed in having fallen upon Coleridge and Wordsworth and Goethe, then on Carlyle, with pleasure and sympathy,"[1] should find one another out. This they had done many months before any regular transcendental gatherings seem to have been contemplated. It was not until 1836 that these were begun, when on September 19—after a still smaller preliminary conference—Ralph Waldo Emerson, Frederick Henry Hedge, Convers Francis, James Freeman Clarke, and Amos Bronson Alcott, met with George Ripley at the latter's house and formed the germ of an organization to aid an exchange of thought among those interested in the " new views " in philosophy, theology, and literature.[2] How far the later meetings were simply informal gatherings of sympathetic souls and how far there was a real distinction between members and non-members is a question concerning which there is little evidence. We may be perfectly certain, however, on *a priori* grounds, that they found it possible to dispense with all such mundane things as by-laws, minutes, and membership rolls. It was in connection with these meetings, probably, that the popular, satirical use of " transcendental " first arose. At any rate to the outside world those who attended them made up the Transcendental Club. To the initiated the group was known as the Symposium or the Hedge Club—the latter name being due to the fact that meetings of the Club were frequently called when Dr. Hedge, whose home was in Bangor, made a trip to Boston. From 1836 the Club continued to come together occasionally for a number of years—how occasionally or for how many years we do not know, for only the most meagre reports and records of the gatherings now exist.

Among those who were not at the first but who joined the group at later meetings, or were present now and then, were: Theodore Parker, Margaret Fuller, Orestes A. Brownson,

[1] *Works*, x, 323.

[2] The accounts in Frothingham's *Ripley* (54), Cabot's *Emerson* (244, Dr. Hedge's account), Cooke's *Emerson* (56, from Alcott's Journal), and Higginson's *Margaret Fuller Ossoli* (142), differ slightly as to those present at the early meetings.

Cyrus A. Bartol, Caleb Stetson, Elizabeth and Sophia Peabody, Thoreau, Hawthorne, Jones Very, Christopher P. Cranch, Charles T. Follen, and William Henry Channing. Dr. Channing and George Bancroft seem to have been present on one occasion. Of the men just mentioned to whom we shall not make further extended reference, there are two to whom, partly from their eccentricities, there attaches a peculiar interest—Jones Very and Orestes A. Brownson. We may pause here, then, long enough to remark that Very was a clergyman and poet of an extreme mystical tendency, whose capacity for soaring above terrestrial conditions of time and space gave rise to many amusing anecdotes of varying degrees of authenticity. Of Brownson and his erratic career we may note that, having passed through successive stages of Presbyterianism, Universalism, Socialism, and Unitarianism, and having coquetted with transcendentalism (and, it might be added, with politics), he completed the cycle of his intellectual and religious experiences by emerging in 1844 as a full-fledged Roman Catholic. He spent much of the rest of his long life in administering ferocious chastisement to Protestantism—and incidentally to transcendentalism—in the columns of *Brownson's Quarterly Review*. The militant element in his nature is hinted at in Dr. Hedge's remark *apropos* of the Transcendental Club: " Brownson met with us once or twice, but became unbearable, and was not afterward invited." Yet there is no doubt that Brownson was a man of exceptional ability.

For some time before anything definite came of the desire,[1] it was felt by the apostles of the new movement that they ought to have a literary organ, and in 1840, with the appearance of the first number of the *Dial*,[2] this long-projected tran-

[1] See e. g., Higginson, 141.

[2] The *Dial* has been reprinted by the Rowfant Club of Cleveland (see bibliography) ; for the authorship of the various articles and accompanying biographical data, see G. W. Cooke's *An Historical and Biographical Introduction to accompany the Dial* (see bibliography). Also see *Journal of Speculative Philosophy*, xix, 262.

The *Dial* was in some respects inspired by and modeled after the *New Monthly Magazine* of the Englishman, John A. Heraud, of whom Carlyle has given a portrait. The proposal of Orestes A. Brownson that the new enterprise be merged in his *Boston Quarterly Review* (1838–1842) was rejected.

scendental magazine became—to use a phrase which in different senses will satisfy all—a realized dream, with Margaret Fuller for editor and George Ripley as assistant editor. It never even approached financial success, and it was only through real devotion and sacrifice on the part of its editor and Miss Elizabeth Peabody that it was continued as long as it was. Miss Fuller resigned the editorship after two years and Emerson assumed it for a like period, after which the magazine was discontinued. Whatever defects the *Dial* may have had— and it obviously had many—a comparison of its pages with the dusty contemporary numbers of, let us say, the *North American Review,* is enough to convince one that the claim of its main contributors that they were dealing with subjects whose interest in a measure transcends time, is not entirely without foundation. The journal discussed questions of theology and philosophy; it contained—besides many other things—papers on art, music, and literature, especially German literature; translations from ancient " Oriental Scriptures "; original modern " scriptures " in the form of Alcott's *Orphic Sayings;* and finally, a good deal of verse. In this latter connection, one of the most interesting aspects of the *Dial* today is the opportunity and encouragement it afforded to the genius of Thoreau. Besides his and Emerson's, there were, among others, metrical contributions from Lowell, Ellery Channing, and Christopher P. Cranch—the latter one of the most picturesque figures of the period (an ex-minister who gave up preaching to study art abroad), poet, painter, musician, and ventriloquist. The *Dial,* it is needless to remark, did not satisfy the public. Hundreds of parodies, especially of the *Orphic Sayings,* were forthcoming, and " epithets, too, were showered about as freely as imitations; the Philadelphia ' Gazette,' for instance, calling the editors of the new journal ' zanies,' ' Bedlamites,' and ' considerably madder than the Mormons.' "[1] Nor did it even fulfil the hopes of the transcendentalists themselves. Alcott thought it tame and compromising: " It satisfies me not, nor Emerson. It measures not the meridian but the morning ray; the nations wait for the gnomon that shall mark the

[1] Quoted from Higginson, 159.

broad noon." On the other hand Theodore Parker's declaration that his own *Massachusetts Quarterly Review* (1848–1850) was to be the *Dial* "with a beard" indicates that he thought the earlier periodical had offended in quite an opposite direction. On the whole, however, whatever our judgment of its intrinsic merit may be—and the mere fact that it contains some of Emerson's best known poems and essays is enough to establish a degree of such merit—we shall not be likely to overrate its significance in the history of American literature or the importance of the part it played in our literary emancipation.

Much more remotely connected with the Transcendental Club than the *Dial* was the Brook Farm enterprise. George Ripley, to be sure, was the leader in the experiment, but "none of the original members [of the Club] accompanied Ripley to Brook Farm, and of the later members only Hawthorne and Dwight followed him." These last are the words of Mr. Lindsay Swift,[1] and a glance at the two chapters of his history of Brook Farm which are entitled "The Members" and "The Visitors" respectively is in itself sufficient to show that, whatever kinship of spirit there may have been among all these men, it is not fanciful to draw a line of distinction between the Brook Farmers and the transcendentalists in the stricter sense. Indeed, the relation between these two groups of men may be pretty well grasped by a mere comparison of the names treated in the two chapters of Mr. Swift's book just referred to. Singled out for particular mention among "The Members" are, after the Ripleys: Charles A. Dana, John S. Dwight, Hawthorne, John Orvis, John Allen, Minot Pratt, George P. Bradford, Warren Burton, Charles K. Newcomb; to whom should be added George William Curtis, James Burrill Curtis, and Father Hecker, discussed in the chapter, "The School and its Scholars." Among "The Visitors," on the other hand, we find: Margaret Fuller, William Henry Channing, Emerson, Alcott, Charles Lane, Brownson, Parker, Francis G. Shaw, Cranch, and Elizabeth Peabody (together with Albert Brisbane and Horace Greeley, treated in another

---

[1] *Brook Farm; Its Members, Scholars, and Visitors*, 9.

connection). These lists require no comment; yet a few words may be said of the history of Brook Farm.

George Ripley, its head, was a graduate of Harvard and a Unitarian minister. As we have already seen, the nature of his beliefs was too radical for the Unitarian audience that listened to him, a fact which, together with his wide studies of European writers, led him gradually to see his duty more and more along the line of social reform. He accordingly left the pulpit; and in 1841 he and his enthusiastic wife gathered around them a number of supporters, subscriptions were received at $500 a share for the "Brook Farm Institute of Agriculture and Education," and the enterprise was begun with ten signers of the "Articles of Association" and by the purchase of a farm at West Roxbury, nine miles from Boston. While Brook Farm must not be considered an attempt at socialism, it was nevertheless collectivistic and communistic in its tendency. The hope was to make it a self-supporting group of men and women, where all should share in the manual labor, the leisure, and the educational and cultural advantages, and life be lived under something approaching ideal conditions. There has been ample testimony from the members that the attempt was far from being entirely unsuccessful. The adoption in 1844, with some modifications, of the principles of Fourier, seems, however, to have put an end to some of the more Arcadian features of Brook Farm; and this, together with the fact that the efforts of inexperienced farmers on a rather poor farm yielded insufficient financial return, was enough to doom the experiment to ultimate failure. The disbanding of the members was immediately occasioned by the burning in 1847 of the new "phalanstery," erected at a cost of ten thousand dollars, and—by an appropriate "transcendental" irony, some will be inclined to comment—uninsured. We must not forget to remark that for a time the Brook Farmers had a literary organ, *The Harbinger*.

There were other attempts during the transcendental period at ideal living. Of Bronson Alcott's communal experiment, "Fruitlands," which with his family and two English friends he undertook on a farm in Harvard, Massachusetts, and which cold weather brought to a speedy and disastrous conclusion, we shall have occasion to say something later on. Of Thoreau's two years at Walden Pond (1845–1847) almost everyone has heard. There, with a small cabin for headquarters, he practised an extreme form of the " simple life," studying the phenomena of nature, communing with her spirit, and noting down his observations and reflections in voluminous diaries. Both these enterprises—Alcott's and Thoreau's—were in most respects strikingly different in intent from Brook Farm. Especially was the Walden Pond episode, in its individualism, the most completely transcendental of any of these experiments.

Mention should not be omitted of one other feature of the period—we mean the well-known " conversations." These seem on the whole to have been of the nature of informal lectures, the audience generally being small and the speaker willing to be interrupted by questions or comments. Sometimes the " talk" was more evenly distributed among those present, and the leader acted more as the chairman of a conference who had also the privilege of the floor. The conversations of Alcott and Miss Fuller have attained much notoriety and some fame. Alcott made use of the conversational method in his school teaching, but it was not till after the failure of his Temple School in 1839 that he ventured a trial of his theory in public. From that time, off and on, for a good many years he gave lectures of the conversational type. Miss Fuller's conversations began in November, 1839, and were held consecutively for five winters. The subjects dealt with were Greek Mythology, Fine Arts, Ethics, Education, the Influence of Woman. The conversations were held as a rule at the end of the morning, twenty-five or thirty being the average number present. " Ten or a dozen, besides Miss Fuller," says Mr. Higginson, " usually took actual part in the talk. Her method was to begin each subject with a short introduction, giving the outline of the subject, and suggesting the most effective points of view. This done, she invited questions or criticisms: if these lagged, she put questions herself, using persuasion for the timid, kindly raillery for the indifferent. There was always a theme and a thread."[1]

[1] Higginson, 115.

The consideration of a further important aspect of transcendentalism, its relation to the anti-slavery agitation, may best be reserved for a later part of the discussion. Meanwhile, one question, suggested by this reference to slavery, belongs to the present chapter, the question: When did the transcendental period close? There can surely be little dissent from the proposition that the movement was at its height during the years 1835–1845; but to choose a date to mark its conclusion is just as impossible as to select one to designate its beginning. The results of a movement are often not less significant than its causes in explaining its real nature, and to obtain a true conception of transcendentalism it is as necessary in some cases to follow the lives of the transcendentalists even beyond the middle of the century, as it is to trace the early development of Unitarianism, or—as we shall attempt to do in the next chapter—to examine the intellectual and literary influences that moulded the thinking of these men.

CHAPTER II

Intellectual and Literary Influences Affecting the Transcendentalists

Their early environment; their reading and studies; their influence on one another; Emerson's and Parker's accounts of "the times."

What were the most potent intellectual and literary influences on the thoughts and lives of these leading transcendentalists? With a view to an answer to this question the present chapter is principally devoted to an account of their reading and studies. The emphasis naturally is on their early reading and on that done just prior to and during the height of the transcendental period. Oftentimes, however, their later studies are not without significance, and all reference to them has not been excluded. To throw light on this main discussion, and for the purpose of indicating briefly the relation of these men to the streams of tendency treated in Chapter I, there is prefixed to the account of each man's studies a paragraph or two concerning his early environment, especially the religious atmosphere within which he grew up. These sections will serve to show how far each came in contact with the Calvinistic spirit, and how far, negatively, that spirit was thus a stimulus to his activity. The influence of the transcendentalists on one another was, of course, great, through their conversation, their letters, their writings, and in many subtler ways. Especially pronounced was that of Dr. Channing. Doubtless they themselves would have been unable to tell just how much they owed to this source or to that. There are to be found in fact, in this connection, more than one pair of externally contradictory statements. Some incidental treatment of this matter of mutual influence will be made in the course of the chapter.

42

Channing[1]

I

The early religious environment of William Ellery Channing was Puritanical; Calvinistic, yet not illiberal. Both of his parents were orthodox in belief but tolerant in spirit. His father—who died when Channing was only twelve—was a man of high moral character, amiable and even temper, and engaging and affectionate manners. His attitude toward his children was, however, in accordance with the custom of the time, somewhat distant and austere. Channing's mother[2] was a woman who seems to have combined in a remarkable way traits of tenderness and severity. She had abundant common-sense and practical capacity, as well as a keen sense of humor, but above all an unfailing sincerity, and firmness in truth and

[1] William Ellery Channing (for the importance given to Channing in this study, see p. 27) was born in Newport, Rhode Island, in 1780. His father, William Channing, was a graduate of Princeton College, and a lawyer of considerable eminence. The son went to school in Newport until he was twelve, when he was sent to the home of his uncle in New London, Connecticut, under whom he prepared for college. He entered Harvard in 1794 and graduated four years later. Then for over a year he was tutor in the family of David Meade Randolph in Richmond, Virginia. This experience bred in him an extreme hatred for slavery. It was during this time too that by foolishly ascetic habits he permanently undermined his health. On his return from the South he began the study of theology, first at home, then in Cambridge, and in 1803 he became the minister of the Federal Street Society, Boston. This was his only pastorate, and he held it for nearly forty years. In 1814 Channing married his cousin, Ruth Gibbs. In 1822 and 1823 he traveled abroad for his health for more than a year, meeting, among other eminent men, Wordsworth and Coleridge. In the years 1825–1830 he wrote those articles, especially the essays on Milton, Fénelon, and Napoleon, which gained for him a considerable European fame (for his influence in France, see Renan's *Études L'Histoire Religieuse,* 361). In 1830 he took another trip in search of health, this time to the West Indies. Increasingly during the latter part of his life, his interest turned toward the questions of politics and social reform then being agitated. In 1835 he published his book on slavery; after this his part in the anti-slavery contest was prominent and courageous, though never extremely radical. He died in 1842.

[2] For a description of her by her son, see Channing, 9.

principle.   The son may be said to have inherited both a vigorous and a delicately sensitive constitution.

The way in which the atmosphere and sterner doctrines of Calvinism shocked this sensitive nature is well brought out in various anecdotes and reminiscences of Channing's youth, as, for instance, his description of Dr. Hopkins, exponent of the Hopkinsonian form of Calvinism, whose preaching he heard as a child and who was a frequent guest at his father's table: " My recollections of Dr. Hopkins go back to my earliest years. . . . Perhaps he was the first minister I heard, but I heard him with no profit. His manner, which was singularly unattractive, could not win a child's attention; and the circumstances attending the service were repulsive. The church . . . was literally ' as cold as a barn ' and some of the most painful sensations of my childhood were experienced in that comfortless building."[1] But the most familiar as well as the most illuminating anecdote is the one telling the mingled feelings of awe and despair with which, after listening to a sermon of the extreme Calvinistic type, the boy heard his father pronounce it " sound doctrine," and then his utter astonishment at beholding that same father return home undismayed and calmly resume the common round of life.   " Could what he had heard be true?   No! his father did not believe it; people did not believe it!   It was *not* true! "[2]

During Channing's college days—owing largely, we must believe, to skeptical influences in the air, born of the French Revolution—his early attitude of revolt was strengthened, and his seeking for intellectual independence encouraged.   It was then that his real consecration came to the work of the Christian ministry.   He writes: " In my senior year, the prevalence of infidelity, imported from France, led me to inquire into the evidences of Christianity, and then *I found for what I was made*.   My heart embraced its great objects with an interest which has been increasing to this hour."[3] With this new devotion of himself to the religious life, Channing retained,

[1] *Ibid.*, 15.
Ibid., 16.
Ibid., 39.

confirmed and re-enforced, his early feelings against the darker parts of Calvinism, especially against the doctrine of total depravity; and through his writings passage after passage[1] may be found showing the intensity of his aversion—an aversion which he describes as "a horror which we want words to express"—toward a teaching which he believed dishonored God and degraded human nature.[2]

II

While in college, the study of three, or possibly four authors seems to have had special influence on Channing. He "read the Stoics with delight," also Locke, Berkeley, Reid, Hume,[3] and Priestley.[4] But these were not the writers from whom he took the most. "Only three books that I read at that time were of any moment to me: one was Ferguson on 'Civil Society,' one Hutcheson's 'Moral Philosophy' and one was Dr. Price's 'Dissertations.'"[5] One day after reading Hutcheson, and under the stimulation of his thought, there came to Channing, in the form of a vivid spiritual experience, an intuition that forever after dominated his thinking, the idea of the dignity of human nature, of the beauty of disinterested love, of the significance of man's position in an order of eternal

[1] As fully and as well brought out as anywhere in the *Discourse at the Ordination of the Rev. Jared Sparks, Works,* iii, 85. See also Channing, 185, and *Works,* iv, 61.

[2] Under these circumstances his admiration for the genius of Jonathan Edwards (*Works,* v, 303) does credit to his liberality and breadth of view. See also his tribute to the greatness of Hopkins in his sermon on *Christian Worship,* and in *Note B* appended to that discourse, *Works,* iv, 303.

[3] See Channing, 55, and touching Hume's argument on miracles, *Works,* iii, 115.

[4] In 1841 he wrote: "With Dr. Priestley, a good and great man, who had most to do in producing the late Unitarian movement, I have less sympathy than with many of the 'orthodox.' . . . I am little of a Unitarian, have little sympathy with the system of Priestley and Belsham, and stand aloof from all but those who strive and pray for clearer light, who look for a purer and more effectual manifestation of Christian truth."—Channing, 427.

[5] Miss Peabody, *Reminiscences,* 368.

progression, and of the endless possibilities of his growth. In the reading of Ferguson he found and appropriated in his own way this same idea as applied to society, the whole conception of social progress. The writer who seems most to have influenced his strictly metaphysical thinking was Dr. Price. In 1840, when he was reading Jouffroy, Channing said:

"I have found here a fact which interests me personally very much. Jouffroy says that Dr. Price's Dissertations were translated into German at the time of their first appearance, and produced a much greater impression there than they did in England; and he thinks they were the first movers of the German mind in the transcendental direction. Now, I read Price when I was in college. Price saved me from Locke's Philosophy. He gave me the doctrine of ideas, and during my life I have written the words Love, Right, etc., with a capital. His book, probably, moulded my philosophy into the form it has always retained, and opened my mind into the *transcendental depth*. And I have always found in the accounts I have read of German philosophy in Madame de Staël, and in these later times, that it was cognate to my own. I cannot say that I have ever received a new idea from it; and the cause is obvious, if Price was alike the father of *it* and of *mine*."[1]

This—whatever Hume and Kant would think of Jouffroy's historical criticism—is interesting as containing the avowal by Channing that his philosophy was transcendental, that he did not get it directly from the Germans, and indeed that in 1840 he had never read their works. In the case of these three writers, Hutcheson, Ferguson, and Price, though there is no proof, it seems decidedly reasonable and probable that they served more to unlock latent tendencies in Channing's own nature than to transfer to his mind in any significant measure the detailed content of their own teachings.

A fourth writer whose influence on Channing was considerable was Shakespeare. There was, during the years when he was in college, a renascence of interest at Harvard in the

[1] Channing, 34, and Miss Peabody, *Reminiscences,* 369.

great dramatist,[1] and later in life when speaking of Words-worth's *Excursion* he declared that he " never read anything but Shakespeare more."[2]

Channing's studies and reflections while in Virginia[3] had deep influence on the course of his later development, and we may well agree with him in characterizing this period as " perhaps the most eventful " of his life. " I lived alone," he says, " too poor to buy books, spending my days and nights in an outbuilding, with no one beneath my roof except during the hours of schoolkeeping. . . . With not a human being to whom I could communicate my deepest thoughts and feelings, and shrinking from common society, I passed through intellectual and moral conflicts, through excitements of heart and mind, so absorbing as often to banish sleep, and to destroy almost wholly the power of digestion. I was worn well-nigh to a skeleton. Yet I look back on those days and nights of loneliness and frequent gloom with thankfulness."

Though his reading at this time was varied, including among other subjects a good deal of history, it is abundantly clear from his letters that his greatest inspiration was from writers whose ideas were of French Revolutionary kinship. In them he found confirmation of the views he had already begun to accept, for what appealed to him most was their trust in human nature and their hope for a state of social perfection. He reads Mrs. Wollstonecraft and pronounces her the greatest woman of the age ; he reads Rousseau's *Eloise* and exclaims, " What a writer! Rousseau is the only French author I have ever read, who knows the way to the heart ; " Godwin, too, he dips into with admiration, recommending to his friend Shaw, *Caleb Williams*. Just what he got from this one or from that cannot be said, but the general, if not the specific, source of his thinking is perfectly clear when we find him writing, " I derive my sentiments from the *nature of man*," or declaring his belief that it is necessary " to destroy all distinctions of

[1] See *Memoirs of the Buckminsters*, 92.

[2] Channing, 276.

[3] All the quotations in this and the following paragraph are from Chapter iv, Channing.

property . . . and to throw the produce of their [mankind's] labor into one common stock, instead of hoarding it up in their own garners." "You must convince mankind," he continues, "that they themselves, and all which they possess, are but *parts of a great whole;* that they are bound by God, their common Father, to *labor* for the good of this great whole. . . . *Mine* and *thine* must be discarded from his [man's] vocabulary. He should call everything *ours.*" Channing's native philanthropic tendencies were kindled by this conception to such intensity that his exhortations to his friends at the North would be laughable, were they not so sincere: "Rouse, then!" he cries out, ". . . we will beat down with the irresistible engines of truth those strong ramparts consolidated by time, within which avarice, ignorance, and selfishness have intrenched themselves." It is no wonder that his friends began to fear that in his Virginia environment he had been converted to Jacobinism, or that his brother wrote him, expressing apprehension lest he had become one of the "Illuminati." But Channing was, in reality, far enough from any such alliances. He remained both Federalist and Christian, and apparently found no difficulty in fusing his new views with his old. He indulged in the "melancholy reflection," to be sure, that so many of the writers whom he admired were deists, but for his own part he practically identified the Revolutionary doctrine of Fraternity with the Christian doctrine of love, and made at this time a new and deeper consecration of himself to the cause of Christianity.

On returning to Newport he plunged into his theological studies, making use, in this connection, of the Redwood Library, "a collection of books, extremely rare and valuable for the time." His preparation for the ministry was continued at Harvard. During these years, in addition to some of the men already mentioned, he seems to have been influenced to some extent by the writings of William Law,[1] by Butler's *Sermons on Human Nature,* and—both positively and negatively—by the works of Jonathan Edwards, whom later he called the "intensest thinker of the new world."[2]

[1] *Ibid.,* 87.
[2] *Works,* v, 303.

And now a word as to other somewhat later literary and philosophical influences.

If frequency of allusion affords any criterion, the perusal of Miss Peabody's *Reminiscences* of Channing would lead one to infer that during all the latter part of his life, Coleridge and Wordsworth were the most important influences of this kind on Channing. He speaks enthusiastically to Miss Peabody of Wordsworth's genius,[1] and reads to her frequently from his writings;[2] we find them together searching his works for all examples of a certain thought,[3] and hear of a copy of his poems "that lay on the table."[4] The references to Coleridge are hardly less frequent. Channing it was who first directed Miss Peabody's attention to Coleridge (from the latter she learned the meaning of *transcendental*[5]), lending her the *Friend,* and reading to her from his writings.[6] The whole impression which one gets is that Wordsworth and Coleridge were scarcely less than Channing's constant companions. "In the poetry of Coleridge and Wordsworth," he says, "I find a theology more spiritual than in the controversial writings of either Unitarians or Trinitarians."[7] He speaks of the Lake poets as being the prophets of a new moral world,[8] and of "the great poet of our times, Wordsworth, one of the few who are to live."[9] Of Wordsworth, says his nephew, "he always spoke with the most respectful affection, as of a benefactor by whom he felt that his heart and mind had been equally enriched. Shortly after the 'Excursion' appeared, he obtained a copy of it, which was sent over by a London house to a publisher who knew little of its worth. . . . But

[1] Miss Peabody, *Reminiscences,* 158.

[2] For a discussion of the Ode on the *Intimations of Immortality, Ibid.,* 127.

[3] *Ibid.,* 188.

[4] *Ibid.,* 134.

[5] *Ibid.,* 364.

[6] *Ibid.,* 72.

[7] *Ibid.,* 72.

[8] *Ibid.,* 80.

[9] *Works,* vi, 155. See this same passage also for a reference to Dickens.

5

to Channing it came like a revelation. He kept it constantly by him; and, as he once said, had 'never read anything but Shakespeare more.'"[1] The meeting of Channing and Wordsworth when the former went to England gave great mutual delight; Wordsworth read to him from *The Prelude*,[2] and Channing characterized himself at that time as one who professed "to be greatly in debt to Mr. Wordsworth's genius."[3] To the influence of Coleridge Channing also expressed his obligations, declaring that to him he "owed more than to the mind of any other philosophic thinker,"[4] and that the *Biographia Literaria* supplied the "wants left by the study of Locke,"—statements which are probably only superficially inconsistent with those already quoted about Dr. Price. Coleridge, as well as Wordsworth, Channing met when abroad,[5] and he had the pleasure of listening to one of the famous monologues,[6] in part at least an exposition of the Trinity.[7] Coleridge requested his visitor to read his essays on "Method."

Among other English writers of the day, Channing took delight in Shelley, speaking of him as "a seraph gone astray";[8] while concerning Carlyle this is, perhaps, sufficient: "When the 'Sartor Resartus' was put into his hands, he said to me that he scarce ever was so completely taken out of himself. 'Certainly it gave me no new idea, but it was a perfect quickener of *all* my ideas.'"[9]

Of French writers Madame de Staël and Cousin had probably as much effect, in his later life, as any. We find Miss Peabody reading[10] to him Cousin's *Introduction to Philosophy*,[11]

---

[1] Channing, 275.

[2] Miss Peabody, *Reminiscences*, 81.

[3] Channing, 342.

[4] Miss Peabody, *Reminiscences*, 75.

[5] Channing, 343.

[6] Miss Peabody, *Reminiscences*, 76.

[7] *Ibid.*, 70. Channing said afterward: "I have no objection to the formula of the Trinity as Coleridge explained it." *Ibid.*, 441.

[8] *Ibid.*, 339.

[9] *Ibid.*, 370.

[10] *Ibid.*, 351; and see also 9.

[11] For Channing's interest in and knowledge of the history of philosophy, see *Ibid.*, 140.

his *Examination of Locke,* and his *Plato.* Indeed Channing seems to have known Plato mainly if not entirely through Cousin's translation, and he dwells with satisfaction on the kinship which he finds between the Greek philosopher's and the Christian view of the world.[1]

It was through Madame de Staël's *Germany* that his interest was aroused in German philosophy;[2] and though we have heard his declaration that he probably never " received a new idea from it," the following may be quoted from his nephew's statement:

" It was with intense delight that he made acquaintance with the master minds of Germany, through the medium, first, of Madame de Staël, and afterward of Coleridge. He recognized in them his leaders. In Kant's doctrine of the Reason he found confirmation of the views which, in early years received from Price, had quickened him to ever deeper reverence of the essential powers of man. To Schelling's sublime intimations of the Divine Life everywhere manifested through nature and humanity, his heart, devoutly conscious of the universal agency of God, gladly responded. But above all did the heroic stoicism of Fichte charm him by its full assertion of the grandeur of the human will."[3]

Richter, Schiller, and Goethe were also among Channing's acquaintances;[4] and Margaret Fuller read Herder to him, and German theological criticism.

Finally, deserving at least of mention[5] are the facts of his contact with Quakerism,[6] and of his having read, about 1820, a manuscript essay of the Swedenborgian, Sampson Reed,[7]

---

[1] *Ibid.,* 175.

[2] *Ibid.,* 76.

[3] Channing, 275.

[4] Chadwick, 207. For Channing's condemnation of Goethe for lack of morals, see Miss Peabody, *Reminiscences,* 337.

[5] Channing's correspondence with Miss Aikin does not reveal much about his studies. He was apparently reading, among others, Hallam, Berkeley, Priestley, Mackintosh, Scott, Lake Poets, Hartley, Milman, and French philosophers.

[6] Miss Peabody, *Reminiscences,* 310; also 108 and 191.

[7] *Ibid.,* 186.

and later the same author's *The Growth of the Mind,* the book that Emerson so highly commended. Swedenborg himself[1] Channing did not read.

ALCOTT[2]

I

Alcott's parents were both Episcopalians. His father, in the words of Mr. Sanborn, " was a diffident, retiring man, and kept much at home, content with his simple lot, industrious, temperate, conscientious, honorable in all his dealing, and fortu-

---

[1] *Ibid.,* preface, iv, and 185.

[2] Amos Bronson Alcott was born in Wolcott, Connecticut, in 1799. His father, Joseph Chatfield Alcox (Alcott changed the spelling of the name), was a farmer and mechanic, and from early youth Bronson was accustomed to work on the farm. At the age of six he began going to the common school, and until he was ten he attended nine months a year. In 1813 he studied at the home of his uncle, Dr. Bronson, and in 1815 for three months in the school of Mr. Keys, the minister of the parish. For a time he thought of entering Yale College, but, mainly because his father could not afford the expense of such an education, he gave up this plan and went to the South, hoping to find a position as a teacher. Peddling, however, proved both more feasible and more remunerative than teaching, and he spent most of the next five years selling wares in Virginia and the Carolinas. His success financially was varied, but for the whole period, owing to illness and extravagance, was small. In 1825 he obtained the position of master in the village school at Cheshire, Connecticut. Common schools in the neighborhood had fallen into neglect. Alcott accordingly resolved on reform, and during his stay of two years at Cheshire, by the originality and success of his teaching, he attracted considerable attention. He anticipated, to a degree, kindergarten methods now in vogue, methods which later earned him the title of the American Pestalozzi. It was through the modest fame of his school that he made the acquaintance of Rev. S. J. May, whose daughter he married in 1830. After leaving Cheshire, Alcott taught for a time in Bristol, and then, over a period of more than ten years, in various schools in Boston and Philadelphia, where he carried out and further developed his radical educational theories. In 1834 he opened in Boston his " Temple School," the last and most famous of his children's schools. At first it flourished, having at one time as many as forty pupils, but various causes (see below, p. 154) operated to impair its prosperity and finally in 1839 it was given up. After this Alcott first tried his scheme of public " conversations." In 1840 he

nate in his domestic life."[1]   His mother was a woman of
sweet and kindly disposition, to whose beneficent influence
on his life her son paid more than one tribute.   He owed her,
he declared, not a little of his " serenity of mind, equanimity
of disposition, hope and trust in the future."[2]   It was the
special wish of his mother that he should take orders in the
church, and for a time he thought of entering Yale College.
He relinquished this plan, however, and spent four or five years
of his early manhood as a pedlar in the South.   This period
of his life brought him rich experience.   He seems, under
the influence of the society around him, to have yielded to the
temptation to spend money lavishly on himself (especially for
fine clothes), and to have indulged in the dream of living the
life of ease and luxury which he saw being led by a certain
class of idle Southern gentlemen.   But having gone too far in
his spendthrift habits he at length came to his senses.   He
wrote to his brother in 1822, " I have seen the folly of my
past extravagance, and hope you will take timely warning
by my example.   A young man at twenty-three should have
learned his lesson at less cost than I have."[3]   At the end of
these years in the South, Alcott came in contact with the
Quakers of North Carolina, and this experience seems to have

moved with his family to Concord and there for a time made an endeavor
to stick to farm work, but his interest in the thought-currents of the
day was too strong, and he again began holding conversations and giving
lectures. Sailing in 1842, he spent most of a year in England. On his
return he and his family removed to a farm in the town of Harvard,
Massachusetts, where with two English friends they instituted the small
community of " Fruitlands." This soon proved a failure, and after a
short stay at Still River, the Alcotts returned to Concord. There, and
later in Boston, they struggled against poverty, until finally the second
of the daughters, Louisa May, gained literary success and freed her
parents from financial embarrassment. Alcott continued his conversations and lectures, and in his later years saw realized, in the Concord
School of Philosophy, the long cherished dream of his life. He died
in 1888.

[1] Sanborn, 8.
[2] *Ibid.*, 20.
[3] Sanborn, 57.

had an important influence on his later development.[1] At any rate, from about this time his views of life assumed a much higher and more serious form. In March–April, 1823, he records, " The moral sentiment now supersedes peddling, clearly and finally."[2]

Travel is ever an enemy of provincial and traditional opinion and so a mother of philosophy; and to the total experience of this period in the South—we have dwelt on it here for this reason—must be attributed in no small degree the liberal and radical tendencies which Alcott exhibited on his return to New England. It was lack of orthodoxy more than anything else, apparently, that led to the giving up of his first school at Cheshire, Connecticut. When we read the following passage in his diary for June 10, 1827, we realize at once that among those who still held tenaciously to religion Alcott was an American pioneer in extreme theological radicalism—though the entry is given here, not for its positive significance but in order to show some of the beliefs against which he was revolting:

" I cannot but regard the popular doctrine of the Atonement by Jesus Christ as erroneous,—taking its rise from the uncertainty and obscurity of its history, and the fondness of the human mind to support as sacred, in matters relating to theology, whatever deviates from the ordinary course of human action. . . . Those who at the present day idolize the person of Jesus Christ, asserting him to be God, exhibit the disposition of man in ancient times to deify such of their fellow-men as performed great and magnanimous actions. Having little conception of the human mind, and the adaptation of mental causes to mental effects, they are at a loss to account for such actions upon any other supposition than divine agency. . . . I hold that the Christian religion is the best yet promulgated, but do not thence infer that it is not susceptible of improvement; nor do I wish to confound its doctrines with its founder, and to worship one of my fellow-beings. If my sentiments are

---

[1] How great this was, forms an interesting subject of speculation, especially since the Quaker doctrine of " Inner Light " is essentially transcendental.

[2] Sanborn, 59.

erroneous, I ardently desire to be conducted to truth, wherever it may lead."[1]

The following, written very much later in life, shows something of his feeling toward the older religion and theology[2] of New England: "Creeds, like other goods, pass by inheritance to descendants. Not every one of the present generation were [sic] so fortunate as to inherit a liberal and humane one. I, for my part, while acknowledging gratefully my indebtedness to whatsoever was humane and holy in the Puritan creed, have wished it had bequeathed to us some gleams of Jove's smiling Olympus to soften the terrors of its blazing Sinai. . . . Nor can it be denied that, dreary and doleful as it was, it has borne fruits that any faith might honor, has planted institutions still in advance of all others in our modern civilization, has nurtured heroic qualities of character, if not the gentler ones."[3]

II

Bronson Alcott early became a lover of books, and his mother, he tells us, encouraged his reading habits. Among the books of his youth were the Bible, Pilgrim's Progress, Hervey's Meditations, Young's Night Thoughts, Burgh's Dignity of Human Nature, Paradise Lost, Robinson Crusoe, and Thomson's Seasons.[4] The Pilgrim's Progress he made a habit of reading through once a year, "and this book more than any other," says Mr. Sanborn, "gave direction to his fancies and visions of life."

That Alcott's studies were not wholly neglected during his sojourn in the South is shown by entries in his autobiography. The following were written while he was among the Quakers of North Carolina:

"*March and April*, 1823. Have a good deal of intercourse with Friends in Chowan and Perquimans Counties. Read

---

[1] Sanborn, 98.

[2] His remarks in 1828 (*Ibid.*, 121) on a ritualistic Episcopalian service, and on a Calvinistic sermon by Dr. Lyman Beecher, show how his nature was revolting from the traditional forms and theology.

[3] *Table Talk*, 101.

[4] Sanborn, 16–17.

Penn's 'No Cross, No Crown,' Barclay's Apology, Fox's 'Journal,' Clarkson's 'Portraiture of Quakerism,' William Law's 'Devout Call,' and other serious books of like spirit. Copy passages into my diary. The moral sentiment now supersedes peddling, clearly and finally."[1]

"May. . . . I read Cowper's Poems, Hervey's Meditations, and the New Testament."

In 1827, after his return to the North, he writes of having read among other things, " Edgeworth's Practical Education, Dwight's Theology, Miller's Retrospect, Kitt's Elements, Reed [sic], Stewart and Locke on the Philosophy of Mind, Watts' Logic, etc.;"[2] while among the books bought for his Cheshire school library are "the works of Miss Edgeworth, Pilgrim's Progress, many books of travels, Adam Smith's Theory of the Moral Sentiments, Locke on the Understanding, Watts on the Mind, Cogan's Treatise on the Passions, Browne's Philosophy of the Human Mind, the newly estab-lished Journal of Education."[3]

Alcott opened his school in Philadelphia in 1831, and it was while there that he seems to have done a particularly large amount of reading and to have become acquainted with writ-ers of the transcendental type. His studies appear to have been predominantly philosophical and to have afforded meta-physical sanction for those views of education and life that he had already begun to form. He read "more or less of Aris-totle, Plato, Bacon, Sir James Mackintosh, Brougham, Car-lyle, Cogan, Bulwer's novels, Shelley's poetry, Sismondi, De Gerando, George Combe, and innumerable works on edu-cation, morals, and religion."[4]

It was at this time that he became personally acquainted with Dr. Channing. In his diary for 1833 he writes:

"I have seen Dr. Channing several times. Our conversa-tions have chiefly turned on intellectual subjects—Coleridge's character and writings, Sir James Mackintosh, Bentham,

---

[1] Ibid., 59.
[2] Ibid., 73.
[3] Ibid., 75.
[4] Sanborn, 165.

Early Education, Slavery, etc. His views are marked by a deep philanthropic spirit and a philosophic tendency. . . . On most topics connected with the nature, duties, and destiny of man, our opinions are analogous. They are the fruits of the same school of philosophy, a union of the Christian with the Platonic. He is, I conceive, the greatest man of his age. His mind is more purely philosophic than that of any other American divine; his speculations more profound and generous. His views are universal; they embody the infinite and spiritual. His heart has sympathized more deeply with his race than often happens to the philosophic genius, and the fruits of that genius will form a part of literature to remain in the treasury of America, long after he shall have departed. Another age will understand and adopt his views."[1]

This is but one of a number of appreciations of Channing, and as late as 1835, in a list of "prophets of the present time" arranged "according to their apprehension of the spiritual ideal," Alcott places Channing first and Emerson third, though a little later, of course, Emerson would have been given the first place. The seven line octave of one of Alcott's sonnets well sums up the influence of Channing on him:

> "Channing! my Mentor whilst my thought was young,
> And I the votary of fair liberty,—
> How hung I then upon thy glowing tongue,
> And thought of love and truth as one with thee!
> Thou wast the inspirer of a noble life,
> When I with error waged unequal strife
> And from its coils thy teaching set me free."[2]

A list of readings from his diary in 1835 (he was then in Boston) includes Plato, Coleridge, Hesiod, Boëthius, *Sartor Resartus*.[3] And the following, written in the same year, should be quoted, not merely for what is said of Plato but for the interesting reference to natural science, and as showing, too, how early Alcott had appropriated the main elements of his later philosophy, especially his doctrines of pre-existence and of the creation of finite things by lapse from perfection:

[1] *Ibid.,* 168.
[2] Cooke, *Poets of Transcendentalism,* 59.
[3] *Genius and Character of Emerson,* 42.

" My own conceptions of life are confirmed in the happiest manner in the Platonic theory. In Plato, as in Jesus, do I find the Light of the World, even the *supersensual* light, that lighteth every man who cometh into the world of sense, and essayeth to regain that spirit it seemeth to have lost by the incarnation of itself. The true study of man is man. When this is felt as it ought to be, natural science will receive an impulse that we cannot at present conceive of. Then we shall begin at the beginning, and not, as now, at the end; we shall trace things in the order of their production, see them in the process of formation, growth, consummation,—the only true way of apprehending them, the method of philosophy. Without this method all our boasted acquisitions are fragments. . . . As Man is my study,—universal as well as individual man,—man in his elements, embracing views of him in all stages of his career,—in his pre-existent life, his infancy, childhood, youth, manhood, decline, resumption in God,—so doth all Nature, in its manifold relation, present innumerable topics for consideration, as the framework and emblem of this same Being. Man, the Incarnate Spirit; God, the Absolute Spirit; Creation, the emblem of these two,—such are my topics of speculation and inquiry."[1]

And a little later in the same year, September 27, 1835, he writes in his diary:

" In 1833 I was a disciple of Experience, trying to bring my theories within the Baconian method of Induction, and took the philosophy of Aristotle as the exponent of humanity, while my heart was even then lingering around the theories of Plato, without being conscious of it. A follower of Aristotle was I in theory, yet a true Platonist in practice. . . . I was looking outward for the origin of the human powers, making more of phenomena than I ought; studying the concrete, without a sense of the grounds on which this was dependent for its form and continuance. It was Coleridge that lifted me out of this difficulty. The perusal of the ' Aids to Reflection,' the ' Friend,' and the ' Biographia Literaria ' at this time gave my mind a turn towards the spiritual. I was led deeper to

[1] *Ibid.*, 42.

seek the grounds even of experience, and found the elements of human consciousness not in the impressions of external nature, but in the spontaneous life of Spirit itself, independent of experience in space and time. Thus was I relieved from the philosophy of sense. Since that time I have been steadily pursuing the light thus let in upon me, and striving to apprehend, represent, and embody it, not only in theory but in practice."[1]

Mr. Harris, in his essay on Alcott's philosophy, suggests that it may have been some of Coleridge's quotations from Boehme and Plotinus that touched especially the chord of sympathy in Alcott. His nature and the subsequent development of his thought lend reasonableness to this view. At any rate he soon seems to have become interested in the mystical thinkers, and his philosophy rapidly assumed the form which was to be embodied in the *Orphic Sayings* of the *Dial,* and which he retained,[2] in its more fundamental principles unchanged, for the rest of his life. This fact renders quotations and inferences from some of his later publications more indicative of his earlier sources than they otherwise could be trusted to be.

The writers whom he seemed to enjoy the most, whom he found richest in suggestion, and with whom his own thought appears most in accord, were men like Pythagoras,[3] Plato, Jamblicus, Plotinus, Porphyry, Proclus, Boehme, Swedenborg: on the whole thinkers whose systems were predominantly Platonic, Neo-Platonic, or mystical.[4] His statement that " if Zoroaster, Pythagoras, Socrates, Behmen, Swedenborg, were to meet in this town, he should not be ashamed, but should be free of that company "[5] shows the type of mind with which he considered himself most in sympathy.

Among ancient thinkers, Plato he considered "pre-eminent in breadth and beauty of speculation,"[6] and his admiration of

[1] *Ibid.,* 47.

[2] Sanborn, 634. (Mr. Harris's essay.)

[3] *Ibid.,* 400.

[4] See the whole of Mr. Harris's essay in the Sanborn-Harris biography.

[5] *Ibid.,* 426.

[6] *Concord Days,* 230. See also *The Genius and Character of Emerson,* 42.

the Academic philosophy was so great that Emerson was accustomed to speak of him as " Plato's reader." Pythagoras, too, Alcott esteemed highly, declaring that of the educators of antiquity he was " the most eminent and successful."[1] The life of Pythagoras by Jamblicus was Alcott's favorite book;[2] he speaks of its author as an " admiring disciple, and a philosopher worthy of his master."[3]

Plotinus, and the other Neo-Platonists, Alcott read in the translations of Thomas Taylor. His ranking of Plotinus is conveyed when he speaks of Jacob Boehme as having " exercised a deeper influence on the progress of thought than anyone since Plotinus,"[4] while Boehme himself he characterizes as " the subtilest thinker on Genesis since Moses,"[5] and it was from him that he derived his doctrine of temperaments.[6] Of Swedenborg Alcott's knowledge seems to have been considerable, and his studies in this mystic were probably directly effective in inducing some of his own states of " illumination " to which reference will later be made.[7]

Beyond what he got from Coleridge it does not appear that Alcott, in his earlier years, went deeply into German philosophy, though later his knowledge and admiration of it were increased;[8] he never studied it, however, in the original, for he " read no language but his own and a little French."[9]

Among British philosophers, Berkeley, as might be expected, he singles out for especial praise, calling him England's " finest thinker since Bacon,"[10] and declaring that " his claim to the name of metaphysician transcends those of most[11] of his countrymen."[12]

[1] Concord Days, 88.
[2] Sanborn, 641.
[3] Concord Days, 88.
[4] Concord Days, 237.
[5] Tablets, 189.
[6] Sanborn, 628. He read Boehme in the translation of William Law.
[7] Page 129.
[8] Sanborn, 552–558.
[9] Sanborn, The Personality of Emerson, 69.
[10] Concord Days, 152.
[11] The following from Concord Days is interesting and not at all surprising: " Nothing profound nor absolute can be expected from minds of the type of Mill, Herbert Spencer, and the rest."
[12] Concord Days, 236.

Coleridge, whose influence on Alcott has already been mentioned, he finds "the most stimulating of modern British thinkers,"[1] and of him and Wordsworth he says that he recalls no other writer since Milton "whose works require a serene and thoughtful spirit, in order to be understood." Alcott's admiration of Wordsworth's ode on the *Intimations of Immortality*[2] is unbounded, and he quotes it over and over; of his literal application of it in his school teaching we shall have occasion to speak later on. Outside Wordsworth, and perhaps Milton, his taste in poetry is best represented by such names as Donne, Vaughan, Crashaw, Herbert, Quarles, and Cowley.

Even this short survey of Alcott's reading makes it possible to assert with some confidence that the men to whom he devotes separate sections in *Concord Days* include many, if not most of his masters—Pythagoras, Plotinus, Goethe, Carlyle, Plato, Socrates, Berkeley, Boehme, Coleridge; while a short list of some of the writers whom he quotes or refers to most frequently is equally in harmony with what we have already observed (those who appear most frequently are put first): Plato, Coleridge, Evelyn, Goethe, Aristotle, Plutarch, Wordsworth, Pythagoras, Berkeley, Glanvill, Montaigne, Milton, St. Augustine, Herrick, Plotinus, Proclus, Marcus Aurelius, *Bhagavad Gita,* Fuller, Henry More, William Law, Bacon, and Jacobi. With this list we may conclude our discussion of Alcott's studies, merely remarking, finally, that his general views on books and their function are nearly identical with Emerson's. "As with friends," so in the case of books, he says, a man "may dispense with a wide acquaintance. Few and choice. The richest minds need not large libraries. . . . I confess to being drawn rather to the antiques, and turn with a livelier expectancy the dingy leaves, . . . I value books for their suggestiveness even more than for the information they may contain, works that may be taken in hand and laid aside, read at moments."[3] It is partly a result of this literary creed,

[1] *Concord Days,* 246; see also *Ibid.,* 136.
[2] Sanborn, 199; *Concord Days,* 108; *Table Talk,* 57. For the analysis of the ode in his school, see Miss Peabody's *Record of a School,* 144.
[3] *Table Talk,* 5.

doubtless, partly owing to the native cast of his mind and the circumstances of his education that the reader of Alcott's works is inevitably left with the impression that his studies were conspicuously lacking in continuity and thoroughness, and his knowledge almost wholly without that quality which he, perhaps, considered its distinguishing feature—correlation.

EMERSON[1]

I

Emerson came of the best New England stock, and on the paternal side was descended from a long line of Puritan clergy-

[1] Ralph Waldo Emerson was born in Boston in 1803. His father, Rev. William Emerson, minister of the First Church, died early, and as a result the life of the Emerson family was for a number of years a struggle against poverty. There were four other sons beside Ralph Waldo, two of whom, Edward and Charles, young men of exceptional promise, died of consumption. Emerson received his early training at the grammar and Latin schools and at home under the supervision of his aunt, Mary Moody Emerson. He entered Harvard in 1817, and graduated, without taking conspicuous rank, four years later. On leaving college, after a short experience in school-teaching, he began the study of divinity, and was ordained in March, 1829, becoming assistant pastor and soon after pastor of the Second Church, Boston. In September of the same year he was married to Miss Ellen Tucker. She died soon after of consumption. In 1832 he resigned his pastorate, mainly on account of a difference of opinion which arose over the question of administering the Lord's Supper. In 1833 he went abroad, traveling in Sicily, Italy, France, and finally in England, where he met, among other eminent men, Coleridge, Wordsworth, and Carlyle. He returned to America in the fall of 1833 and the next summer began his residence in Concord. In 1835 Emerson was married to Miss Lydia Jackson. Already, before this, he had begun turning his attention to writing and lecturing, and in the years 1836, 1837, and 1838, respectively, came the publication of *Nature,* the delivery of the Phi Beta Kappa oration, *The American Scholar,* and the *Divinity School Address.* From this time on, his life of literary activity continued, its course marked rather by the delivery and publication of lectures and addresses than by events of external variety or significance. During the years 1842–1844 he was editor of the *Dial.* In 1847 he made a second visit to Europe, embodying some of the observations of his two trips in *English Traits,* published in 1856. In 1871 he visited California and the next year made a third trip abroad. His last years were marked by a gradual decline of his faculties, particularly of his memory. He died in 1882.

men. His father, who died while Waldo was still a small boy,
was a man of pleasing and affable personality and of marked
liberality of belief and spirit, " far from having any sympathy
with Calvinism."[1] Emerson's mother was a woman " of great
patience and fortitude, of the serenest trust in God, of a dis-
cerning spirit, and a most courteous bearing. . . . Both her
mind and her character were of a superior order, and they
set their stamp upon manners of peculiar softness and natural
grace and quiet dignity."[2] At the death of her husband she
struggled bravely to secure the education of her sons. The
loss of his father made Emerson's youth one of hard work,
with few opportunities for the usual sports and recreations of
boyhood. His early intellectual training was under the supervision of his aunt, Mary Moody Emerson,[3] a woman of noble,
though of stern character, and of exceptional mental power.
Her reading[4] was from the best authors, and both her attitude
toward the world and her literary style—as revealed in her
remarkable letters—show striking similarities with the philosophy and style of her nephew. To her influence on him he
bore testimony when he wrote later in life, " I have no hour
of poetry or philosophy, since I knew these things, into which
she does not enter as a genius."[5] To him and to his brothers
" their mother was a serene and ennobling presence in the
house; their aunt a spur, or better, a ferment in their young
lives."[6]

Emerson seems on the whole to have come less directly in
contact with Calvinism than did many of the transcendentalists.
Certainly we find in his works no such bits of fervid writing
on the subject as we find in Channing's and Parker's, and

[1] Holmes, 11. See also, on the next page of Holmes's biography, a
letter of Emerson concerning his father's theology.

[2] Ibid., 13.

[3] See Emerson's Works, Centenary Edition, x, 593.

[4] " Her early reading was Milton, Young, Akenside, Samuel Clarke,
Jonathan Edwards, and always the Bible. Later, Plato, Plotinus, Marcus
Antoninus, Stewart, Coleridge, Cousin, Herder, Locke, Madame de Staël,
Channing, Mackintosh, Byron." Emerson's Works, x, 376.

[5] Cabot, 30.

[6] Emerson in Concord, 9.

such allusions as he makes seem to have less of the element of
personal feeling[1] and more of a calm and even historical
judiciousness. He says, speaking of the old theology, " false-
hoods, superstitions, are the props, the scaffolding, on which
how much of society stands;"[2] and *apropos* of the heroism of
those who believe in fate, " Our Calvinists in the last generation had something of the same dignity."[3]   Again, in 1841,
he writes of the Puritans: " Great, grim, earnest men, I belong
by natural affinity to other thoughts and schools than yours,
but my affection hovers respectfully about your retiring footsteps, your unpainted churches, strict platforms, and sad offices;
the iron-gray deacon, and the wearisome prayer, rich with the
diction of ages."[4]   On the other hand, however, though it
was nominally with Unitarianism, it was really with the traditional New England spirit that Emerson came in conflict
when the dispute over the Lord's Supper led to his retirement
from the ministry. He thought that this rite, supported by
custom rather than by vital spiritual meaning, was a bit of
hollow formalism, and preferred to sever his connection with
the church rather than to continue to administer a sacrament
into which his whole heart could not enter.[5]   His resignation
was voluntary and there was no ill feeling on either side.

II

Of Emerson's earliest reading we know comparatively little,
but we can scarcely be wrong in inferring that it included some
of the favorite authors of his aunt, to whom reference has
already been made. We hear of his delight in Scott's poetry
and in Ossian;[6] but of the influences that first and most profoundly helped to shape Emerson's thought we know hardly
anything more interesting than the following, from a letter

[1] For his criticism of a church service, see *Works,* Centenary Edition,
vi, 413.

[2] Journal, 1834, Cabot, 303.

[3] *Works,* vi, 11. See also *Ibid.,* x, 107, and Cabot, 594.

[4] *Ibid.,* 304, and other entries in his journal corroborate the same
general contention.

[5] For the sermon preached to justify his attitude, see *Works,* xi, 9.

[6] *Works,* Centenary Edition, v, 337.

(1841) to Margaret Fuller: "I know but one solution to my nature and relations, which I find in remembering the joy with which in my boyhood I caught the first hint of the Berkeleyan philosophy, and which I certainly never lost sight of afterwards."[1] Even at the price of some violence to chronology it is worth while to place by this another passage. The contradiction,[2] highly typical of Emerson, is doubtless more seeming than real, but it helps to show how guardedly we must take his superlative statements. " In Roxbury in 1825 I read Cotton's translation of Montaigne. It seemed to me as if I had written the book myself in some former life, so sincerely it spoke my thought and experience. No book before or since was ever so much to me as that."[3]

While in college Emerson's retiring disposition did not lead him to make acquaintances rapidly. One of his class-mates writes: " By degrees, however, the more studious members of the class began to seek him out. They found him to be unusually thoughtful and well-read; knowing perhaps less than they about text-books, but far more about literature. He had studied the early English dramatists and poets, pored over Montaigne, and knew Shakespeare almost by heart."[4] He belonged during his sophomore year to a book-club that subscribed for the *North American Review* and the leading English periodicals and that spent many of its evenings in reading Scott's novels. His notebooks give " evidence of wide reading of a desultory kind, in which history, memoirs, and the English Reviews are prominent."[5] He knew something, too, of contemporary poets, Byron, Moore, Coleridge, and Wordsworth, though his opinion of the latter two was to undergo a radical change.

Among Emerson's teachers were George Ticknor and Edward Everett, who had just returned from abroad, bringing

[1] Cabot, 478.
[2] For surely we are not to escape it by insisting on the strict literalness of the word " book."
[3] *Emerson in Concord,* 29.
[4] Cabot, 59.
[5] *Ibid.,* 58.

6

with them an enthusiasm for German literature and German university methods. He appears to have given particular attention to their courses. We know too that he studied philosophy. Berkeley has been mentioned; of Bacon,[1] Locke, Hume,[2] and Stewart, Emerson also knew something; and his two Bowdoin prize dissertations on *The Character of Socrates* and *The Present State of Ethical Philosophy*[3] show his interest in metaphysical thought and a knowledge of its history.

Emerson's studies were continued after graduation:

". . . he early came to love Plato, and, after leaving college, seems to have studied him very closely. At this period Tillotson, Augustine,[4] and Jeremy Taylor were among his favorite authors. One of the earliest of the serious books he read was a translation of Pascal's *Pensées,* which he carried to church with him and read almost constantly."[5]

While studying divinity Emerson felt to some extent the influence of Dr. Channing, under whom he would have liked to have his preparation. Channing, unwilling to undertake this formally, conferred with him occasionally and recommended books for reading. Emerson wrote to his aunt in 1823: "Dr. Channing is preaching sublime sermons every Sunday morning in Federal Street,"[6] and though the two men never came into intimate contact, Emerson's characterization of Channing as "our Bishop"[7] is a clear recognition of indebtedness. After his trip abroad he spoke of him as "the King of preachers,"[8] saying that there were no such men in Great Britain. Of the other transcendentalists, Alcott doubtless had the most influence on Emerson. The practical cer-

[1] Bacon and Berkeley "have been friends to me." Woodbury, *Talks with Ralph Waldo Emerson,* 26.

[2] Cabot, 104.

[3] Both these are reprinted in Dr. Hale's *Ralph Waldo Emerson.*

[4] On Augustine and Thomas Aquinas, see *Works,* Centenary Edition, i, 414.

[5] Cooke, 22.

[6] Cabot, 105.

[7] Miss Peabody, *Reminiscences,* 371.

[8] Sanborn, *The Personality of Emerson,* 40.

tainty that the former was the orphic poet of *Nature,* together with Emerson's repeated high estimates[1] of his intellect, is evidence in this direction.

Before entering in more detail on an account of Emerson's reading, it may be well to say a word concerning his general attitude toward books and study. There is no doubt that Emerson loved books and that he read very widely. Indeed it would hardly be an exaggeration to affirm that a large part of his life was spent in reading. Yet his own writings— though such a book as *English Traits* might in itself be considered by some a refutation of the statement—scarcely give the impression of being the work of a learned man, nor does there seem to be evidence that Emerson deserves to be called a really careful or scholarly reader. He appears to have used books much more for imbibing the spirit of their writers and extracting felicitous quotations than for studying the details of their thought. " I read Proclus, and sometimes Plato, as I might read a dictionary, for a mechanical help to the fancy and the imagination. I read for the lustres."[2] In nearly all of the authors in whom he takes special delight there is at least a touch of mysticism, and in all of them there can be detected a kinship of some sort with Emerson's own nature—in Plato and Plotinus, in Goethe and Coleridge, in Swedenborg and the authors of the " Oriental Scriptures." This sympathy enabled him to comprehend, as it were, in a flash, their points of view. He could think in their ways and so he repeats their thoughts. He rarely gives us the impression of having laboriously or exhaustively studied another author.

He writes in his Journal for February 8, 1825 : " My cardinal vice of intellectual dissipation—sinful strolling from book to book, from care to idleness—is my cardinal vice still ; is a malady that belongs to the chapter of incurables."[3] And elsewhere he expresses a longing for the gift of continuity.[4] In

[1] See p. 159, n. 4.
[2] *Works,* iii, 222.
[3] Cabot, 111.
[4] *Ibid.,* 295 ; and see also *Works,* xii, 48.

the same connection a passage from the essay on *Experience* is illuminating: " Once I took such delight in Montaigne that I thought I should not need any other book; before that, in Shakspeare; then in Plutarch; then in Plotinus; at one time in Bacon; afterward in Goethe; even in Bettine; but now I turn the pages of either of them languidly, whilst I still cherish their genius."[1] We cannot help wondering how far Emerson is speaking out of his own experience, and how far by " reading " he means *careful* reading, when he says in his Journal for 1837, " If you elect writing for your task in life, I believe you must renounce all pretension to reading."[2]

Emerson's views on the function of books are given very vigorously in the *American Scholar:*

" Meek young men grow up in libraries, believing it their duty to accept the views which Cicero, which Locke, which Bacon have given, forgetful that Cicero, Locke, and Bacon were only young men in libraries, when they wrote these books."

" Books are the best of things, well used; abused, among the worst. What is the right use? . . . They are for nothing but to inspire."

" Man Thinking must not be subdued by his instruments. Books are for the scholar's idle times."

But it is in the essay on *Books* more than anywhere else that we find Emerson's ideas about the literature of the world and the place it should occupy in a man's life. Probably this essay reflects pretty accurately the place that that literature actually did fill and had filled in his life, for while recognizing his habit of speaking familiarly of writers of whom he had little or no knowledge, we are bound to admit that the impression obtained from this paper is that its author had at least a fair acquaintance with the more important works which he mentions.[3] And this view is corroborated by a study of the sources of Emerson's quotations. " There are books; and

---

[1] *Works,* Centenary Edition, iii, 55.

[2] Cabot, 291.

[3] His list of these best books is too long to transcribe here in detail. Its principal names will be included in the course of the discussion.

It is practicable to read them, because they are so few;" "Be sure then to read no mean books,"—these are the texts of the essay. It is a plea for the reading of the works " of rich and believing men who had atmosphere and amplitude about them." "I visit occasionally the Cambridge Library," he remarks, " and I can seldom go there without renewing the conviction that the best of it all is already within the four walls of my study at home."

What he says in this essay on the subject of translations reveals the transcendental tendency to exalt content above style, and shows how insensible he could be to the true significance of literary *form:*

" What is really best in any book is translatable, any real insight or broad human sentiment. . . . I rarely read any Latin, Greek, German, Italian, sometimes not a French book, in the original, which I can procure in a good version. . . . I should as soon think of swimming across Charles River when I wish to go to Boston, as of reading all my books in originals when I have them rendered for me in my mother-tongue."[1]

On turning to a more detailed discussion of the writers who apparently most influenced Emerson, we should bear in mind the incessant habit of exaggeration of this author of *The Superlative* (a transcendental habit concerning which we shall have more to say in another part of our discussion). It is quite unsafe in this matter to trust any single, isolated sentence; yet, after all, perhaps it is not so difficult to distinguish between the cases where he means his absolute statement and where it is a mere rhetorical mannerism.

Emerson's reading and love of Shakespeare early in life seem to have been real, not merely invented by his admirers as forming an indispensable part of the biography of a man of letters. We have seen the statement of a classmate that he knew Shakespeare almost by heart. The frequency with which Emerson quotes him gives ground for the evident purport of the exaggeration. It would be superfluous to transcribe passages showing the high esteem in which Emerson held Shakes-

---

[1] See, in this connection, George Ripley's statement, Frothingham, *George Ripley,* 268.

peare. He reiterates his inconceivable wisdom and "transcendent superiority"[1] over all other writers, and, as in the following, ascribes to him the most potent influence:

". . . he is the father of German literature: it was with the introduction of Shakespeare into German, by Lessing, and the translation of his works by Wieland and Schlegel, that the rapid burst of German literature was most intimately connected."[2]

Concerning Montaigne's influence on Emerson the quotation already given is sufficient.[3]

Of Plato Emerson made the acquaintance when in college,[4] first probably through the medium of Cudworth's *The True Intellectual System of the Universe*. He writes in his journal in 1845, referring to a period just after his graduation:

" I had read in Cudworth from time to time for years, and one day talked of him with Charles W. Upham, my classmate, and found him acquainted with Cudworth's argument and theology, and quite heedless of all I read him for,—namely, his citations from Plato and the philosophers. . . ."[5]

From Plato, too, we are told, Emerson got his earliest conception of the symbolism of nature,[6] and he once declared " that it was a great day in a man's life when he first read the *Symposium*."[7] Indeed, there seems to be considerable evidence for the belief that in the long run Plato forms the most continuously powerful influence on Emerson's thinking. It is only " sometimes " that he reads Plato " for the lustres "; he tells (1841) of taking away with him " Phædrus, Meno and the Banquet which I have diligently read,"[8] and the whole impression left by his various statements is that Emerson came as near really *studying* Plato as any writer he ever read. " Among secular books, Plato only is entitled to Omar's

[1] *Works,* vi, 137.
[2] *Ibid.,* iv, 195. See also xii, 180.
[3] See also *Works,* Centenary Edition, iv, 337.
[4] *Ibid.,* ii, 427.
[5] *Ibid.,* iv, 294.
[6] *Ibid.,* ii, 436.
[7] *Ibid.,* iv, 307.
[8] *Ibid.,* iv, 310; see also *Ibid.,* 311.

fanatical compliment to the Koran, when he said, 'Burn the libraries; for, their value is in this book,'"—so begins the essay on *Plato;* and these sentences are from that on *Books:* "Of Plato I hesitate to speak, lest there should be no end. . . . He contains the future, as he came out of the past. . . . Nothing has escaped him." These and dozens of other similar assertions appear somewhat less hyperbolic when we consider, what seems to have been true, that Emerson well-nigh identified the spiritual and ideal, with the Platonic way of looking at things. This alone could have allowed such a statement as, "How Plato came thus to be Europe, and philosophy, and almost literature, is the problem for us to solve,"[1] or can render less than absurd, "'Tis quite certain, that Spenser, Burns, Byron and Wordsworth will be Platonists; and that the dull men will be Lockists."[2] Emerson came near to believing that all the great spiritual truths "have a kind of filial retrospect to Plato and the Greeks."[3]

Another of Emerson's favorites is Plutarch, and the frequency with which he quotes him, together with the rather detailed section given to him in the essay on *Books,* proves that he is an author whom he had read extensively. "He required his son to read two pages of Plutarch's Lives every schoolday and ten pages on Saturdays and in vacation;"[4] and we are told that Emerson called Plutarch's *Morals*[5] "his tuning-key when he was about to write."[6]

Emerson took a marked interest in the Neo-Platonists. "In 1835 he began to study Plotinus, and other writers of the same class. The German mystics attracted his attention, as did the English idealists."[7] He read Plotinus, Porphyry, and

---

[1] *Works,* iv, 46.

[2] *Ibid.,* v, 228.

[3] *Ibid.,* 229.

[4] *Emerson in Concord,* 174.

[5] He wrote a preface to Prof. W. W. Goodwin's edition of the *Morals,* 1871. Reprinted in *Works,* x, 277.

[6] Mrs. Dall, *Margaret and Her Friends,* 139.

[7] Cooke, 39. The rest of the same passage may be appended, though, as has been and will be pointed out, he knew some of these authors much earlier than 1835, "The same year he was reading, with the keenest relish and enthusiasm, the poems of George Herbert, and the prose writings of Cudworth, Henry More, Milton, Coleridge, and Jeremy Taylor. As the result of these studies . . . he wrote . . . *Nature.*"

Synesius in Thomas Taylor's translations.[1]   In 1841 he writes,
"I have also three volumes new to me of Thomas Taylor's
Translations, Proclus, Ocellus Lucanus, and Pythagorean
Fragments."[2]   (In 1842 he was reading Jamblicus' *Life of
Pythagoras*.)[3]

His interest in mystical philosophy, however, was not confined to that of the Neo-Platonists.   Boehme[4] too he knew;
but better perhaps than any other, Swedenborg.[5]   Only a few
years after leaving college his attention was drawn in this
direction by Mr. Sampson Reed, a Boston Swedenborgian and
the author of *Observations on the Growth of the Mind*,[6] a book
which had attracted Emerson's favorable notice; and while
studying divinity he was dipping into the Swede.[7]   In the
third letter of the Carlyle correspondence he says of the followers of Swedenborg: "They are to me, however, deeply interesting, as a sect which I think must contribute more than
all other sects to the new faith which must arise out of all."
In his essay on Swedenborg occurs a passage on mysticism
in general in which, while he treats it sympathetically, he
condemns all its extreme manifestations and points out its kinship with pathological conditions of the mind.   To Swedenborg
he attributes profound insight into the spiritual constitution
of the world, but at the end he qualifies: "The entire want
of poetry in so transcendent a mind betokens the disease, and,
like a hoarse voice in a beautiful person, is a kind of warning.
I think, sometimes, he will not be read longer.   His great
name will turn a sentence.   His books have become a monu-
ment."[8]

Closely allied to these other mystical influences was that of
the poetry and sacred scriptures of the Orient, especially of
India and Persia.[9]   Though Emerson did not make their

[1] Cabot, 290; *Works*, Centenary Edition, i, 437 and 441–442; v, 400.
[2] *Ibid.*, iv, 310.
[3] *Ibid.*, ii, 296.
[4] *Works*, iii, 38 and 180; iv, 136; viii, 263.
[5] *Works*, Centenary Edition, iv, 321.
[6] *Emerson in Concord*, 37; Holmes, 80.
[7] *Works*, Centenary Edition, iv, 295.
[8] *Works*, iv, 138.
[9] See *The Genius and Character of Emerson*, 372.

acquaintance till later they may perhaps best be spoken of here. This interest in " Ethnical Scriptures " was widespread among the transcendentalists (Thoreau's liking for them is well known), and translations of the oldest ethical and religious writings were begun in the third volume of the *Dial*. His Journal for 1845 " shows that Mr. Emerson was reading, not only in the Koran and Akhlak-i-Jalaly, but in the East Indian scriptures, and he gives quotations. He writes, ' The East is grand and makes Europe appear the land of trifles.' "[1] This same admiration of the Orient is shown in the essay on Plato: " In all nations there are minds which incline to dwell in the conception of the fundamental Unity. . . . This tendency finds its highest expression in the religious writings of the East, and chiefly, in the Indian Scriptures, in the Vedas, the Bhagavat Geeta, and the Vishnu Purana. Those writings contain little else than this idea, and they rise to pure and sublime strains in celebrating it." And in his enumeration of the " Bibles of the world " in the essay on Books those just mentioned, together with several other Eastern scriptures, are included.

The little poem *Brahma* is worthy of mention in this connection. It would be hard to imagine a more condensed summary of Oriental pantheism than is contained in these sixteen short lines, and Mr. W. T. Harris has shown by passages cited from the *Bhagavad Gita* how *Brahma* is an epitome of that whole book.[2] The similarity even in the details of the expression proves that Emerson must have known his source intimately.

Besides the Indian, Emerson knew something of the Persian writers, mainly through the German translation of Baron Von Hammer-Purgstall; and he contributed to the *Atlantic Monthly* in 1858 a paper on *Persian Poetry*.[3] Hafiz and Saadi he knew best apparently, the former being first spoken of in his Journal for 1841.[4]

[1] *Works*, Centenary Edition, iv, 314.
[2] *The Genius and Character of Emerson*, 373.
[3] Reprinted, *Works*, viii, 225.
[4] *Works*, Centenary Edition, viii, 413.

" At the age of 23 Mr. Emerson had been interested in Coleridge and by him in German thought."[1]   Even before this, while in college, he had known something of Coleridge's poetry. We find him writing to his aunt December 10, 1829: " I am reading Coleridge's ' Friend ' with great interest. . . . He has a tone a little lower than greatness, but what a living soul, what a universal knowledge,"[2] and he continues through a long paragraph of high adulation.   Speaking of Carlyle's *Sartor Resartus,* Mr. Cabot says: " . . . when I tried, long afterward, to recall to him the stir the book made in the minds of some of the younger men, he hesitated, and said he supposed he had got all that earlier from Coleridge."[3]

From the passages devoted to him in *English Traits,*[4] we draw the conclusion that Emerson esteemed Wordsworth by far the greatest of the more modern English poets.   " The Ode on Immortality," he writes, " is the high-water-mark which the intellect has reached in this age ;"[5] and elsewhere, " the capital merit of Wordsworth is that he has done more for the sanity of this generation than any other writer."[6]   He speaks of having hung over the works of Wordsworth and Carlyle in his chamber at home,[7] and he once declared " that he still found himself unable to compare any early intellectual experience with the effect produced on his mind by the poet's description of the influence of nature upon the mind of a boy."[8] " The fame of Wordsworth," he wrote in the *Dial,* " is a leading fact in modern literature. . . . The Excursion awakened in every lover of Nature the right feeling. We saw stars shine, we felt the awe of mountains, we heard the rustle of the wind in the grass, and knew again the ineffable secret of solitude."[9]   We are told that " Emerson could quote almost

[1] *Ibid.,* v, 330.
[2] Cabot, 161.
[3] *Ibid.,* 241.
[4] *Works,* v, 21 and 279. See also *Works,* xii, 225.
[5] *Works,* v, 282.
[6] *Ibid.,* xii, 227.
[7] *Emerson in Concord,* 45.
[8] Conway, *Emerson at Home and Abroad,* 50.
[9] *Works,* xii, 187 (from the *Dial*).

entirely the 'Prelude' and 'Excursion' so much had he pondered them,"[1] and in *Parnassus,* his book of selections from the poets, Wordsworth (43 selections) stands next to Shakespeare (88).

For the poetry of Shelley Emerson had a rather marked distaste, declaring that he could never read it " with comfort."[2]

Landor he read in 1832, making transcripts from the *Imaginary Conversations.*[3]

Emerson's relations with Carlyle are so well known, through their remarkable friendship and the publication of their correspondence, that they do not need detailed restatement here. About the year 1828 Emerson began to be interested in the articles of Carlyle appearing at that time in the English and Scotch reviews.[4] Soon after, he read *Wilhelm Meister* in Carlyle's translation, passages from it being found in his " Blotting Book " for the fall of 1830.[5] The desire to see Carlyle himself was one of the hopes that attracted him to Europe in 1833. In 1836 he published an American edition of *Sartor* and in 1838 collected some of Carlyle's writings from the reviews and brought them out under the title of *Critical and Miscellaneous Essays.* Among others, one result of this acquaintance with Carlyle was the turning of Emerson's more careful attention to German and especially to Goethe. A few quotations may be given, from the Carlyle-Emerson correspondence, on this subject; but first let us notice what Dr. Hedge wrote of Emerson in 1828:

" I tried to interest him in German literature, but he laughingly said that as he was entirely ignorant of the subject, he should assume that it was not worth knowing. Later he studied German, mainly for the purpose of acquainting him-

---

[1] Woodbury, *Talks with Ralph Waldo Emerson,* 46. The temptation is to believe this an exaggeration, but it is interesting to compare the statement that Emerson knew Shakespeare almost by heart, and to remember how he recalled all of *Lycidas* except three lines, when unaware that he knew any of it. See *Works,* Centenary Edition, xii, 458.

[2] Woodbury, *Talks with Ralph Waldo Emerson,* 53.

[3] *Works,* Centenary Edition, ii, 389 ; see also *Ibid.,* v, 327.

[4] *Emerson in Concord,* 36.

[5] *Works,* Centenary Edition, iv, 295.

self with Goethe, to whom his attention had been directed[1] by Carlyle."[2]

And now from letter iii (1834), Emerson to Carlyle: " Far, far better seems to me the unpopularity of this Philosophical Poem[3] (shall I call it?) than the adulation that followed your eminent friend Goethe. With him I am becoming better acquainted, but mine must be a qualified admiration. . . . The Puritan in me accepts no apology for bad morals in such as *he*."[4]

From letter vi (1835), Emerson to Carlyle: ". . . we know enough here of Goethe and Schiller to have some interest in German literature. A respectable German here, Dr. Follen, has given lectures to a good class upon Schiller. I am quite sure that Goethe's name would now stimulate the curiosity of scores of persons."[5]

From letter xii (1836), Emerson to Carlyle: " I read Goethe, and now lately the posthumous volumes, with a great interest."[6]

From letter lii (1840), Carlyle to Emerson: " Do you read German or not? . . . Tell me. Or do you ever mean to learn it? I decidedly wish you would."[7]

Emerson answered a few weeks later: " You asked me if I read German, and forget if I have answered. I have contrived to read almost every volume of Goethe, and I have fifty-five, but I have read nothing else: but I have not now looked even into Goethe for a long time."[8]

Emerson wrote to Grimm in 1861: " I read German with some ease, and always better, yet I never shall speak it."[9]

And ten years later to the same: " I duly received from you the brochure on Schleiermacher, and read with interest, though

[1] Coleridge had probably introduced him to Goethe before he read Carlyle at all. *Ibid.*, iv, 295.

[2] Cabot, 139.

[3] *Sartor Resartus.*

[4] *Carlyle-Emerson Correspondence*, 29.

[5] *Ibid.*, 55.

[6] *Ibid.*, 100.

[7] *Ibid.*, 299.

[8] *Ibid.*, 311.

[9] *Emerson-Grimm Correspondence*, 60.

his was never one of my high names.   For Goethe I think I have an always ascending regard."[1]

Beside his treatment of him in *Representative Men*,[2] Emerson discussed Goethe at length in his *Thoughts on Modern Literature*[3] in the *Dial*, speaking of him as the man who in the most extraordinary degree united in himself the tendencies of the age, but always charging him with moral deficiences.   In 1844, writing of his great influence, he characterized him as " precisely the individual in whom the new ideas appeared and opened to their greatest extent and with universal application, . . ."[4]   Nearly all of Emerson's numerous discussions of Goethe contain the double elements of praise and blame—both oftentimes appearing in the same passage.   For example: " The old eternal Genius who built the world has confided himself more to this man than to any other. . . . Goethe can never be dear to men.   He has not even the devotion to pure truth ; but to truth for the sake of culture."[5]

To other German writers there are references here and there in Emerson's works which seem to imply at least a superficial, almost beyond doubt an indirect, knowledge.   This knowledge was attained too in some cases after the height of the transcendental movement.   Thus of Kant,[6] of Schelling, of Hegel, and of Schleiermacher,[7] of whom the last, as we have just heard, was not one of Emerson's high names.

In one of his earliest addresses[8] he speaks as if acquainted with Cousin's system.   His remarks are rather disparaging to the Frenchman's philosophy.   In *English Traits* he speaks of him again,—" whose lectures we had all been reading in Boston."

It remains to say just a word of Emerson's reading along one or two other lines.

[1] *Ibid.*, 85.
[2] *Works*, iv, 247.
[3] *Works*, xii, 189.
[4] *Works*, Centenary Edition, iv, 372.
[5] *Works*, iv, 270. See also *Ibid.*, iii, 230, and viii, 69.
[6] *Ibid.*, vii, 30 ; viii, 463 ; x, 240 and 310.
[7] *Carlyle-Emerson Correspondence*, 50.
[8] *Works*, i, 165.

He had dipped pretty widely into English literature—Elizabethan and seventeenth-century especially. He speaks himself of his " habit of idle reading in old English books," and tells how he made Margaret Fuller acquainted (about 1835) " with Chaucer, with Ben Jonson, with Herbert, Chapman, Ford, Beaumont and Fletcher, with Bacon and Sir Thomas Browne."[1] Mr. Conway puts it more emphatically: " Emerson went thoroughly into old English books, from Chaucer to Sir Thomas Browne and Burton, but valued more highly the earliest of these."[2]

One class of books, of which except in the case of Plutarch and Jamblicus almost no mention has been made, constituted a conspicuous part of Emerson's reading: biographies. The essay on Books in itself would make this clear, but we have other evidence: about the time he left the church, for instance, he was deeply interested in the life of George Fox;[3] and we hear too that he read all the available memoirs of Napoleon.[4] " Mr. Emerson's reading was largely in biographies. For novels and romances he cared little."[5]

This last statement receives corroboration,[6] for we are told that he did not care for Kingsley,[7] and he declared himself that he " never could turn a dozen pages in ' Don Quixote ' or Dickens without a yawn."[8] In favor of George Sand's *Consuelo* he seems to have made somewhat of an exception— probably on account of its mystical element.

Emerson was always enthusiastic over the advance of science, and some of his earliest lectures were on scientific subjects. This enthusiasm followed almost inevitably from his transcendental belief, for transcendentalism is itself a naturalistic interpretation of the world, is founded, we might almost say, on the conception of law, and welcomed, as if it were its

Memoirs of Margaret Fuller Ossoli, i, 204.

[2] Conway, *Emerson at Home and Abroad,* 105.

[3] *Works,* Centenary Edition, iii, 332.

[4] *Ibid.,* iv, 359.

[5] *Ibid.,* ii, 392.

[6] *Ibid.,* vii, 412.

[7] Sanborn, *The Personality of Emerson,* 41.

Woodbury, *Talks with Ralph Waldo Emerson,* 54.

own, every conquest of science in the diminishing domains of the supernatural. To this interest of his father in scientific topics, his son has borne witness: " Not only among the poets and prophets, but (perhaps with Goethe as a bridge) in the works of the advancing men of Science,—John Hunter, Lamarck, Lyell, Owen, Darwin,—he was quick to recognize a great thought."[1]

Before attempting any summary of Emerson's reading,[2] as an interesting commentary on our discussion, we may transfer from Holmes' biography his exhaustive study of Emerson's authorities :[3]

" The named references, chiefly to authors, as given in the table before me, are three thousand three hundred and ninety-three, relating to eight hundred and sixty-eight different individuals. Of these, four hundred and eleven are mentioned more than once ; one hundred and fifty-five, five time or more ; sixty-nine, ten times or more ; thirty-eight, fifteen times or more ; and twenty-seven, twenty times or more. These twenty-seven names alone, the list of which is here given, furnish no less than one thousand and sixty-five references.

Authorities.	Number of Times Mentioned.
Shakespeare	112
Napoleon	84
Plato	81
Plutarch	70
Goethe	62
Swift	49
Bacon	47
Milton	46

[1] *Emerson in Concord,* 65. See also the Biographical Sketch prefixed to the Centenary Edition of his Works (I, xxvi sq.).

[2] For further hints and discussion about Emerson's reading, see (to some of these reference has already been made in the foot-notes): Cooke, Chapter xix; Appendix F to Cabot; Emerson's Essay on Books; the notes of the Centenary Edition of the Works—among these notes, especially those under *Representative Men,* and a letter giving advice about reading, vii, 400.

[3] Holmes, 381.

The name of Jesus occurs fifty-four times."

Unless we attach great significance to his remark about Berkeley, it seems harder in the case of Emerson than in that of any of the other transcendentalists to tell just what and just whence were the most powerful influences that contributed to his transcendental views. Of writers of the ideal type, chronologically Berkeley came first. Of the rest we cannot be certain of the order; but Plato probably was next, and then, perhaps not many months apart, Swedenborg and Coleridge (and Wordsworth); somewhat later came Carlyle and Goethe; after them the Neo-Platonists, and still later the Oriental writers.[1] Of all of these except the last Emerson knew something when *Nature* appeared, a statement that discloses the difficulty of the problem. The many striking similarities, however, between Emerson's thought and Coleridge's—and so between Emerson's and Schelling's[2]—coupled with the former's

[1] This is the conjectural order of real influence, not merely of introduction. It neglects for instance Emerson's early knowledge of Coleridge's and Wordsworth's poetry. It should be noted too that Emerson speaks of taking supreme delight " in Plotinus; . . . afterward in Goethe."

[2] For Coleridge's confessed obligations to Schelling and his explanation of the similarities in their " systems " see *Aids to Reflection* (*Works*, New York, 1858, iii, 263).

remark to Dr. Hedge about getting "all that earlier from Coleridge" lead us to believe that Coleridge was a more vitally stimulating, even if a less continuous influence on Emerson than Plato or the Neo-Platonists. We should never forget finally, in discussing these transcendentalists, the remarkable affinity which seems to exist among nearly all thinkers of the mystical type, and especially in the case of Emerson we shall not be wrong in finding a considerable underived, original element in his thought.[1]

PARKER[2]

I

Theodore Parker's father, though a farmer and mechanic, was a man of intellectual power who, during the intervals of his manual toil, found time for wide reading. It is worth noting that with marked ability as a mathematician and a deep interest in political economy and history, he took his greatest

---

[1] Emerson once wrote: "He must be a superficial reader of Emerson who fancies him an interpreter of Coleridge or Carlyle." *Works,* Centenary Edition, v, 387.

[2] Theodore Parker, the youngest of eleven children, was born in Lexington, Massachusetts, in 1810. He was brought up on a farm and from early boyhood was accustomed to hard work. His schooling began at the age of six and for ten years he had a few months in the district school each year. When sixteen he attended the "Academy" at Lexington for a quarter. At seventeen he began teaching in district schools, continuing this for four years. In 1830 he entered Harvard College, but as he knew he could not be spared from his work at home, he tutored himself, merely going up for examinations, and so, as a non-resident, was not entitled to a degree. Beginning in March, 1831, he taught for a year in a private school in Boston. In the spring of 1832 he opened a private school of his own in Watertown. It was while here that he came under the influence of Dr. Convers Francis, and here too he met Miss Lydia D. Cabot, whom he married in 1837. In 1834 he entered Cambridge Divinity School, where he remained a little over two years. In 1837 he assumed, in West Roxbury, his first pastorate. Sailing in 1843, he spent a year in travel in Europe. In 1846 he accepted a call to the Twenty-eighth Congregational Society in Boston. The immense strain of his labors, especially those connected with the anti-slavery struggle, told on his strength, and in 1859 he was obliged to give up his ministry and go abroad in search of health. He died in Florence in the spring of 1860—an old man at fifty.

7

delight in the reading of philosophy. Theodore very probably inherited his liking for the metaphysical from his father. Parker's mother was of a profoundly religious nature. Her religion was not a perfunctory matter but one of deep personal experience. This is a part of what her son says of her in an autobiographical fragment written not long before his death:

"She was eminently a religious woman. I have known few in whom the religious instincts were so active and so profound, and who seemed to me to enjoy so completely the life of God in the soul of man. To her the Deity was an Omnipresent Father, filling every point of space with His beautiful and loving presence. She saw him in the rainbow and in the drops of rain which helped compose it as they fell into the muddy ground to come up grass and trees, corn and flowers. . . . The dark theology of the times seems not to have blackened her soul at all. She took great pains with the moral culture of her children—at least with mine."[1]

And again in a sermon: "Religion was the inheritance my mother gave me in my birth,—gave me in her teachings. . . . I mention these things to show you how I came to have the views of religion that I have now. My head is not more natural to my body, has not more grown with it, than my religion out of my soul and with it. With me religion was not carpentry, something built up of dry wood from without; but it was growth,—growth of a germ in my soul."[2]

At the close of his autobiography Parker relates an incident which occurred when he was only four years old, but of which, only a few months before his death, he declared, "I am sure no event in my life has made so deep and lasting an impression on me." That is the excuse for referring to it here.

One day on his father's farm he caught sight of a little spotted tortoise under a rhodora and started to stike it with a stick. "But all at once something checked my little arm, and a voice within me said, clear and loud, 'It is wrong!' I held my uplifted stick in wonder at the new emotion—the consciousness of an involuntary but inward check upon my

[1] Weiss, i, 23.
[2] Frothingham, 17.

actions, till the tortoise and the rhodora both vanished from my sight. I hastened home and told the tale to my mother, and asked what was it that told me it was wrong? She wiped a tear from her eye with her apron, and taking me in her arms, said, ' Some men call it conscience, but I prefer to call it the voice of God in the soul of man. If you listen and obey it, then it will speak clearer and clearer, and always guide you right; but if you turn a deaf ear or disobey, then it will fade out little by little, and leave you all in the dark and without a guide. Your life depends on heeding this little voice.' "[1]

Although, because of his parents' simple and liberal beliefs and their careful distinction " between a man's character and his creed," Parker escaped many of the prevalent theological " superstitions "[2] of the times, he did not, even in youth, fail to come in vital contact with some of them. This is well shown by his experiences on running across a copy of the Westminster Catechism: " I can scarcely think without a shudder of the terrible effect the doctrine of eternal damnation had on me. How many, many hours have I wept with terror as I laid [sic] on my bed and prayed, till between praying and weeping sleep gave me repose."[3] After reading the life of Jonathan Edwards and expressing admiration of his character but wondering how such a man could have assented to doctrines like total depravity and eternal damnation, he cries out, " Oh! if they wrung his soul as they have wrung mine, it must have bled."[4] But it was in his early youth that this struggle took place and he tells us that from his seventh year he had " no *fear* of God, only an ever-greatening love and trust."[5] For a whole year, while a student and teacher, he sat under the

[1] Weiss, i, 25. Cf. Jonathan Edwards' account of the conversion of a child of four. *Narrative of Surprising Conversions, Works,* iii, 265. Katherine Philips, " the Matchless Orinda," is said to have read her Bible through at four. Cf. DeFoe's " Family Instructor " for equally precocious religiosity in children.

[2] " I count it a great good fortune that I was bred among religious Unitarians, and thereby escaped so much superstition." Weiss, ii, 481.

[3] Weiss, i, 30.

[4] Weiss, i, 38.

[5] *Ibid.,* ii, 452.

preaching of Dr. Lyman Beecher, the well-known orthodox minister, a fact which speaks for his fairness of mind. He expressed great respect for Dr. Beecher, but of his theology he writes, " The better I understood it, the more self-contradictory, unnatural, and hateful did it seem,"[1] and looking back, later in life, he says of this time, " Dr. Channing was the only man in the New England pulpit who to me seemed great."

II

Of Theodore Parker's early reading he himself says : " Good books by great masters fell into even my boyish hands ; the best English authors of prose and verse, the Bible, the Greek and Roman classics—which I at first read mainly in translations, but soon became familiar with in their original beauty— these were my literary helps. What was read at all, was also studied, and not laid aside till well understood. If my books in boyhood were not many, they were much, and also great.

" I had an original fondness for scientific and metaphysical thought, which found happy encouragement in my early days ; my father's strong, discriminating and comprehensive mind also inclining that way, offered me an excellent help."[2]

Again he says : " Homer and Plutarch I read before I was eight ; Rollin's Ancient History about the same time ; and lots of histories, with all the poetry I could find, before ten. I took to metaphysics about eleven or twelve."[3]

Later among his companions are mentioned Shakespeare and Milton, and (now in the original) Homer, Xenophon, Demosthenes, and Aeschylus.[4] During his school teaching, in addition to his classical reading, he made the acquaintance of Cousin and Coleridge ;[5] and as the years go by the names begin to come thicker and faster and more bewildering in their range, until we are tempted to believe that Theodore

[1] *Ibid.*, i, 57.
[2] *Ibid.*, ii, 450.
[3] *Ibid.*, i, 43.
[4] *Ibid.*, 49.
[5] *Ibid.*, 64.

Parker read everything, though it should be remarked that he always seems to have read for substance rather than for form, a fact which helps to explain the enormous number of pages covered.

From almost the first he read in the original, books in other than the English language.   Early in life he mastered Greek and Latin.   French, Spanish, and German (this latter in 1831) were soon added to his accomplishments.   He learned a new language with wonderful facility.   It would be impossible to tell of just how many he really became master,[1] but here are a few which we know he studied: Italian, Portuguese, Dutch, Icelandic, Chaldaic, Arabic, Persian, Coptic, Swedish, Hebrew, Syriac, Anglo-Saxon, Modern Greek.[2]   This list in itself gives us a hint of what a plastic memory Parker had.   He literally remembered everything he read.   As a boy he could repeat a poem of 500 or 1000 lines after a single reading.   His biographers supply a large number of instances of his wonderful retention of even the minutest details of his studies.   At his death his home was more a library than an ordinary dwelling house, for he had about 13,000 volumes (of which less than one fourth were in English).[3]   James Freeman Clarke records a conversation in which he asked Parker, " Do you read all your books, and do you know what is in them? " " I read them all," he said, " and can give you a table of contents for each book."[4]   A complete account of Parker's reading, then, would evidently have to include, as one of its divisions, a catalog of these 13,000 books.   It is quite possible, however, without approaching the matter in this hopeless way, to gain a fair idea of the general character of the works read.

When, in 1832, Parker was teaching in Watertown, he made the intimate acquaintance of Rev. Convers Francis, minister

[1] Lowell, commenting on a sketch of Parker prepared for the *Atlantic* in 1860, writes to the author, Mr. Higginson, " Your *twenty* languages is a good many."   Mr. Higginson replies in his *Old Cambridge,* " My phrase ' twenty languages ' was an underestimate of those in which Parker had at least dabbled."

[2] Weiss, i, 72.

[3] Higginson, *Cheerful Yesterdays,* 93.

[4] *Memorial and Biographical Sketches,* 120.

of the First Parish.　Mr. Francis, a man of liberal, un-
dogmatic views, was one of the first persons in New England
to attain an appreciative knowledge of the German language,
and both he himself and his library, to which the young
teacher had access, were factors in giving Parker's mind its
bent at this critical period.　A few names indicating the scope
of his reading at this time are those of Cicero, Herodotus,
Thucydides, Pindar, Theocritus, Bion, Moschus (the last four
of whom he translated), Aeschylus, Cousin, Goethe, Schiller,
Klopstock, Coleridge, Scott, and Byron.[1]　Later, while in the
divinity school, he found " great help " from a study of the
Greek philosophers, and still later, during his residence at
West Roxbury (1837), his reading included De Wette, Jacobi,
Henry More, Bulwer, Fichte, Coleridge, Descartes.[2]　" Spinoza
I shall take soon as I get my copy. . . . The ' Iliad ' is a
part of almost every day's reading."　" I have got lots of new
books—upwards of one hundred Germans ! "[3]

His plans of work for a coming week or month at this
time are also illuminating.　Mere plans in the case of some
men would mean little ; not so with Parker.　Here is a sample :
1. Continue the translation of Ammon.
2. Continue the study of Plato.[4]
3. Read Tasso and Dante.
4. Iliad.
5. Greek Tragedies.
6. Aristophanes.
7. Goethe's Memoirs.
Another plan for a week's work includes De Wette, Jacobi,
Fichte, and Ammon.

The more we inquire into Parker's reading the more apparent it becomes that, in the vast field covered, the works
most frequently mentioned are those in philosophy, poetry, and
theology and Biblical criticism.　The first and second of these

[1] Frothingham, 39.
[2] Weiss, i, 100.
[3] *Ibid.,* 101.
[4] His first reading of Plato had an overpowering effect on him. " I shall
never forget that event in my life." Weiss, i, 111 ; see also *Ibid.,* ii, 61.

divisions include many if not most of the greatest of the world's philosophers and poets. The following, *apropos* of a new work of Agassiz', which the author had declared that only a handful of men in the world could understand, is significant as showing what Parker considered the strenuous element in his intellectual pabulum: " I suppose it would be presumptuous in a man brought up on Descartes, Bacon, Leibnitz, and Newton, and fed on Kant, Schelling,[1] and Hegel, not to speak of such babies as Plato and Aristotle, to think of comprehending the popular lectures of this Swiss dissector of mud-turtles."[2] Parker's studies in the realm of German theological criticism were very wide,[3] and his translation of De Wette's *Introduction to the Old Testament* was his greatest literary achievement.

But it would be futile to go on merely mentioning names.[4] The range of his reading was so great that we should be somewhat at a loss to select from the total array those books and men which were most influential on Parker's spiritual growth, had he not, fortunately, told us something about this himself.

When in 1859 he was obliged to give up his Boston pastorate, he wrote a letter to his people, a letter which gives an account of the religious experience of his life, and so affords consider-

[1] Parker heard Schelling lecture while abroad in 1844, and came into first-hand contact with Hegelianism. Frothingham, 201.

[2] *Ibid.*, 326.

[3] See *e. g.*, his article on " German Literature." *Dial*, i, 315.

[4] A sentence or two may be quoted from Frothingham's biography (p. 46) :

" Only by transcribing the journal, commenced in 1835, could any idea be obtained of the extent of his researches. The folio pages are crowded with lists of books read or to be read—analyses, summaries, comments on writers of every description, in every tongue. Only to name them would be a fatigue,—Eichhorn, Herder, Ammon, De Wette, Paulus, Philo, the Greek historians, the fathers of the Church, the Greek and Latin poets, Plato, Spinoza, the Wolfenbüttel Fragments. The succession is bewildering ; but there is the record in the private journal, the veracity whereof cannot be disputed,—a record showing acquaintance not with the names of the books merely, but with their contents. In two months, November and December, 1835, the names of sixty-five volumes are given as having been read in German, English, Danish, Latin, Greek. . . ."

For other lists of books read by Parker, see Chadwick, 71 ; Frothingham, 108–110 (" Plato is a constant companion ") ; and *Ibid.*, 177.

able information concerning the sources of his transcendental-ism.[1]   After speaking of his early education he tells of his decision to become a minister and of the gradual decay of his beliefs in many of the accepted doctrines even of the Unitarians. The conclusions he reached were much influenced, he says, by studies under four heads:

"I studied the Bible with much care" and "the latest critics and interpreters, especially the German."

"I studied the historical development of religion and theology amongst Jews and Christians."

"I studied the historical development of religion and theology amongst the nations not Jewish or Christian."

"I studied assiduously the metaphysics and psychology of religion."

Under this last head he says: "The common books of philosophy seemed quite insufficient; the sensational system, so ably presented by Locke in his masterly Essay, developed into various forms by Hobbes [who—if we may be permitted to interrupt the quotation so ruthlessly—died some ten or eleven years before the publication of Locke's Essay], Berkeley, Hume, Paley and the French Materialists, and modified, but not much mended, by Reid and Stewart, gave little help; it could not legitimate my own religious instincts, nor explain the religious history of mankind. . . . "

Nor could the views of ecclesiastical writers like Clarke, Butler, Cudworth, and Barrow solve his problems or offer him much aid.   Continuing, he remarks:

"The brilliant mosaic, which Cousin set before the world, was of great service, but not satisfactory.   I found most help in the works of Immanuel Kant, one of the profoundest thinkers in the world, though one of the worst writers, even of Germany; if he did not always furnish conclusions I could rest in, he yet gave me the true method, and put me on the right road.

[1] Reprinted in the appendix of Weiss's biography.   Those interested should consult the whole of this article.   It gives an excellent conception of the thought-ferment of the times.   A short summary of a part of it will be made at the end of this chapter.

"I found certain great primal Intuitions of Human Nature, which depend on no logical process of demonstration, but are rather facts of consciousness given by the instinctive action of human nature itself. I will mention only the three most important which pertain to Religion.

"1. The Instinctive Intuition of the Divine, the consciousness that there is a God.

"2. The Instinctive Intuition of the Just and Right, a consciousness that there is a Moral Law, independent of our will, which we ought to keep.

"3. The Instinctive Intuition of the Immortal, a consciousness that the Essential Element of man, the principle of Individuality, never dies.

"Here, then, was the foundation of Religion laid in human nature itself, which neither the atheist nor the more pernicious bigot, with their sophisms of denial or affirmation, could move or even shake. I had gone through the great spiritual trial of my life, telling no one of its hopes or fears, and I thought it a triumph that I had psychologically established these three things to my own satisfaction, and devised a scheme which to the scholar's mind, I thought, could legitimate what was spontaneously given to all, by the great primal Instincts of Mankind."

We perceive from these quotations that Parker's drawing from Kant was from the *Critique of Practical* rather than from the *Critique of Pure Reason.* Kant's writings, it is plain, did not offer Parker an entirely new point of view. He gained from them, rather, a basis for the belief, the first hint of which he had received from his mother and suggestions of which he had imbibed from various sources—among others from Channing and Emerson. Of his contemporaries, indeed, Channing probably had the most potent influence on Parker. What Channing's preaching meant to him we have already seen,[1] while the inspiration he was capable of receiving from Emerson is well attested by the following entry in his Journal after hearing the *Divinity School Address:* "My soul is roused, and this week I shall write the long-meditated sermons on the

[1] P. 84.

state of the Church and the duties of these times."[1] Both
Channing and Emerson will be mentioned again in this connection at the end of the chapter.

The early age at which Parker's reading was begun reminds
one of the still more extraordinary education of John Stuart
Mill—starting when he was three with a study of Greek—an
account of the first part of which he has given in the opening
chapter of his *Autobiography*. Parker's early studies were
evidently more purely voluntary, for he had no master standing over him comparable to the elder Mill. The voluminous-
ness of Parker's reading again reminds us of Mill, or of
Macaulay, especially of the latter's prodigious literary imbib-
ings when in India.[2] The mention of Macaulay's name and
the recollection of his wonderful memory suggests a question:
the question whether Parker is not himself open to the same
charge which has been brought against Macaulay—of devouring books simply because they were books. At first sight the
mere suggestion of such a thing in connection with Parker
seems the height of injustice, for, if he was anything, he was a
practical man, who intended to put everything he gained to use.
Yet one cannot but confess that the impression left by the story
of his reading is more that of intellectual omnivorousness than
of scholarly balance, and though one may be at a loss to put
his finger on the source of the conviction, one can not help
having the feeling that Parker regarded anything in the shape
of a book on a serious subject, *ipso facto,* something to be read
and made a part of his mental equipment. The truth seems to
be that he plunged into his reading with that same tremendous
energy with which he plunged into everything, and the paradox might not be entirely without meaning were we to assert
that if Parker had been a little less practical himself his reading
might have been more practically balanced. On the whole,
although there are plenty of historical considerations[3] to explain his attitude toward books (of any serious fault in which
he must himself have been quite unconscious), one may well

---

[1] Conway, *Emerson at Home and Abroad,* 175.

[2] See Chapter VI of Trevelyan's Life of Macaulay.

[3] Some of these will be mentioned at the end of this chapter and in the
concluding chapter of the essay.

hesitate, in spite of his really immense erudition, to call Parker a great scholar. To say what we have said of his reading is merely to apply specifically what may be remarked in a wider way of the whole man: although the conditions and circumstances of Parker's life may cause us to feel nothing but admiration for the intensity and strenuousness with which he lived, we cannot but feel that his nature would have been more fully rounded if it could have included a little of Emerson's serene repose.

Margaret Fuller[1]

I

On both the paternal and maternal sides Margaret Fuller came of Puritan blood. Her father, in the words of Mr.

[1] Sarah Margaret Fuller was born in 1810 in Cambridgeport, a part of Cambridge, Massachusetts. Until the middle of 1833 the Fuller home remained in Cambridge, and there Margaret spent her early years—except for what little time she was away at school—reading and studying widely, and forming many of those friendships that were to have vital influence on her spiritual growth. In 1833 the Fullers removed to Groton, Massachusetts, where to Miss Fuller's continued intellectual labors were added many family cares and duties. These were greatly increased by the death of her father in 1835, and her health became seriously impaired. She had been cherishing hopes of travel abroad, but relinquishing these she began teaching school to support herself and to help pay for the education of her brothers and sisters. She first taught in Bronson Alcott's school in Boston, and after that in an academy in Providence. These experiences were in 1837–1838. Miss Fuller then returned home, and beginning early in 1839 the family resided for three years at Jamaica Plain, and later at Cambridge. These years were in a special sense her transcendental period; she was editor of the *Dial,* and for five winters held her famous " conversations." Toward the end of 1844, at the invitation of Horace Greeley, she went to New York to write literary criticism for the *Tribune,* making her home in the Greeley family. While in New York she became widely interested in many works of practical philanthropy and social reform. Finally, in 1846, her early dream was realized, and she sailed for Europe in August of that year. She traveled in England, Scotland, and France, where she met many men and women of note. From France in February, 1847, she went to Italy and there in December she was married to the Marquis Ossoli. Owing to the revolutionary troubles in which her husband was involved, the union was a secret one. A son was born to them the next year. In 1850, when returning to America, father, mother, and child were lost in a shipwreck off Fire Island.

Higginson, was "a man of some narrowness and undue self-assertion, very likely; but conscientious, vigorous, well-informed, and public-spirited. His daughter Margaret always recognized, after all his mistakes, her great intellectual obligations to him; and his accurate habits of mind were always mentioned by her with admiration."[1] Her mother was a woman of marked personal beauty and refinement, of humility and sweetness, a true example of New England piety. The trace of her nature is to be discerned doubtless more in the emotional than in the intellectual tendencies of her daughter.

Margaret Fuller, like Parker and Alcott, has left an autobiographical fragment, written in 1840 and covering the first years of her life. In this she tells the story of her early education. Her father had sole charge of her training, and under his supervision she began the study of Latin at six,[2] taking up English grammar at the same time. This was but the beginning of a long process[3] which, developing her intellectual powers far too early in life, strained her delicately nervous organization and impaired her health. "Poor child!" she exclaims in the autobiography. "Far remote in time, in thought, from that period, I look back on these glooms and terrors, wherein I was enveloped, and perceive that I had no natural childhood."[4]

Just how directly Margaret Fuller came in contact early in life with Calvinism and the stricter Puritan spirit is a matter about which there appears to be little evidence. In the autobiographical sketch she gives a hint of the way Sunday was spent in the Fuller household, showing that it must have been, in many respects at least, not unlike the typical New England home. "This day was punctiliously set apart in our house. We had family prayers, for which there was no time on other days. Our dinners were different, and our clothes. We went

---

[1] Higginson, 16.

[2] See, for remarks on this, *Ibid.*, 22.

[3] A note by the editor, Miss Fuller's brother, on page 352 of *Woman in the 19th Century* should be consulted, in which he asserts that too much emphasis has been put upon this sternness of his father's nature and on his unwise treatment of Margaret as a child.

[4] *Memoirs*, i, 16.

to church.   My father put some limitations on my reading, but—bless him for the gentleness which has left me a pleasant feeling for the day!—he did not prescribe what was, but only what was not, to be done.   And the liberty this left was a large one."[1]   For the rest, we are forced to judge of these matters, so few are her allusions to them, mainly from mere phrases and sentences dropped here and there in her letters and journals, though usually the proper inference is unmistakable.   For example: "Cambridge, July 11, 1825.—Having excused myself from accompanying my honored father to church, which I always do in the afternoon, when possible . . . ."[2]   Or again: "It was Thanksgiving day (November, 1831), and I was obliged to go to church, or exceedingly displease my father.   I almost always suffered much in church from a feeling of disunion with the hearers and dissent from the preacher."[3]   Such remarks as these, and various longer passages,[4] while constituting no very voluminous evidence, show clearly enough that even though the older doctrines and forms were not entirely without meaning and attractiveness for her,[5] in the main Miss Fuller early fell into open dissent from the Puritan religious customs and theology.

II

The earliest literary influences that touched the life of Margaret Fuller were the works of the writers of Rome and Greece, especially of Rome.   She devotes considerable space in the autobiographical fragment to an analysis of the Roman genius and its effects on her own character.   How much in her later years she read into these early experiences we cannot tell, but this is what she says:

[1] *Ibid.,* 26.

[2] *Ibid.,* 52.

[3] *Ibid.,* 139.

[4] See *Memoirs,* i, 136, and ii, 91.   And in this connection the following is of interest: "Margaret . . . said that when she was first old enough to think about Christianity, she cried out for her dear old Greek gods.   Its spirituality seemed nakedness.   She could not and would not receive it. It was a long while before she saw its deeper meaning." *Margaret and Her Friends,* 161.

[5] *Memoirs,* i, 197, and ii, 85.

"I steadily loved this ideal in my childhood, and this is the cause, probably, why I have always felt that man must know how to stand firm on the ground, before he can fly. In vain for me are men more, if they are less, than Romans. Dante was far greater than any Roman, yet I feel he was right to take the Mantuan as his guide through hell, and to heaven."[1]

Continuing the account of her childhood she says it was her fortune to make the early acquaintance of three great authors, Shakespeare,[2] Cervantes, and Molière, and she tells something of what she owed to each. "They taught me to distrust all invention which is not based on a wide experience. Perhaps, too, they taught me to overvalue an outward experience at the expense of inward growth; but all this I did not appreciate till later."[3]

In a letter to a former teacher, written from Cambridge in 1825 (she was then fifteen) we get a glimpse of her early studiousness. After saying that she is taking the time for the letter from Ariosto and Helvetius, she goes on:

"I rise a little before five, walk an hour, and then practise on the piano, till seven, when we breakfast. Next I read French,—Sismondi's 'Literature of the South of Europe,'— till eight, then two or three lectures in Brown's Philosophy. About half-past nine I go to Mr. Perkins's school and study Greek till twelve, when, the school being dismissed, I recite, go home, and practise again till dinner, at two. Sometimes, if the conversation is very agreeable, I lounge for half an hour over the dessert, though rarely so lavish of time. Then, when I can, I read two hours in Italian, but I am often interrupted." She continues with the account of the rest of her day, and concludes, "Thus, you see, I am learning Greek, and making acquaintance with metaphysics, and French and Italian literature."[4]

From other letters: "Cambridge, May 14, 1826.—I am studying Madame de Staël, Epictetus, Milton, Racine, and

[1] *Memoirs*, i, 20.

[2] Emerson remarked of her about 1835, "She was little read in Shakspeare," *Ibid.*, i, 204.

[3] *Ibid.*, 30.

[4] *Ibid.*, 52.

Castilian ballads, with great delight. There's an assemblage for you."[1] Such an "assemblage" is typical of transcendentalism, and highly significant. "Cambridge, January 10, 1827.— As to my studies, I am engrossed in reading the elder Italian poets, beginning with Berni, from whom I shall proceed to Pulci and Politian. I read very critically. Miss Francis and I think of reading Locke, as introductory to a course of English metaphysics, and then De Staël on Locke's system."[2]

There is proof that always from these early years, but especially while in Groton,[3] Margaret Fuller read widely and voluminously; at a rate like Gibbon's, Emerson said. She began the study of German in 1832 and at that time she was already acquainted with masterpieces of French, Italian, and Spanish literature. It would be as useless as it would be impossible to make a complete catalog of the works she read; but a few names, and here and there extracts from her letters and journals, will indicate the range of interest.

She tells of reading Godwin,[4] some of the later Elizabethan dramatists[5]—Ford, Shirley, Heywood—"all Jefferson's letters,[6] the North American, the daily papers, etc., without end."[7]

"American History! Seriously, my mind is regenerating as to my country, for I am beginning to appreciate the United States and its great men. . . . Had I but been educated in the knowledge of such men as Jefferson, Franklin, Rush! I have learned now to know them partially."[8]

She refers to a course of study laid out for the winter of 1834, which she mentions as nearly completed, "the History and Geography of Modern Europe, beginning the former in the fourteenth century; the Elements of Architecture; the works of Alfieri, with his opinions on them; the historical and

[1] *Ibid.,* 55.

[2] *Ibid.,* 55.

[3] Higginson, 45.

[4] *Memoirs,* i, 110.

[5] *Ibid.,* 115.

[6] See Mr. Higginson's remarks on the significance of Miss Fuller's reading Jefferson; Higginson, 4 and 308.

[7] *Memoirs,* i, 124, from an entry headed "Groton."

[8] *Ibid.,* 149.

critical works of Goethe and Schiller, and the outlines of history of our own country."[1] The enthusiasm she felt for her studies is shown by an entry in 1836 (?) : " I am having one of my ' intense ' times, devouring book after book.   I never stop a minute, except to talk with mother, having laid all little duties on the shelf for a few days."[2] Then she goes on to speak of Mackintosh and Shelley.[3] Again (1836) : " I have ventured on a book so profound as the Novum Organum."[4] And still again : " 1836.—I have, for the time, laid aside *De Staël* and *Bacon,* for *Martineau* and *Southey*. . . . I have finished Herschel, and really believe I am a little wiser.   I have read, too, Heyne's letters twice, Sartor Resartus once, some of Goethe's late diaries, Coleridge's Literary Remains, and drank [*sic*] a great deal from Wordsworth. . . . I find my insight of this sublime poet perpetually deepening."[5] Later she wrote of Wordsworth as her " beloved friend and venerated teacher."[6]

In May, 1837,[7] she returned to Emerson a borrowed copy of Coleridge's *Literary Remains,* " ' ransacked pretty thoroughly,' " and of *The Friend* " with which she ' should never have done.' "   She subscribed[7] at about the same time for two copies of Carlyle's *Miscellanies;* and in 1839 had evidently borrowed Tennyson,[8] for she wrote, " I thought to send Tennyson next time but cannot part with him."   Of Coleridge her opinion, uttered somewhat later, was :

" I have little more to say at present except to express a great, though not fanatical veneration for Coleridge, and a conviction that the benefits conferred by him on this and future ages are as yet incalculable.   Every mind will praise him for what it can best receive from him.   He can suggest to an infinite degree ; he can *in*form, but he cannot *re*form and

[1] *Ibid.,* 150.
[2] *Ibid.,* 164.
[3] See Higginson, 42, note.
[4] *Memoirs,* i, 166.
[5] *Ibid.,* 166.
[6] *Papers on Literature and Art,* i, 89.
[7] Higginson, 69.
[8] See *Memoirs,* ii, 66.

renovate. To the unprepared he is nothing, to the prepared, everything."[1]

A number of extracts from letters in 1839 show that Miss Fuller was reading fairly extensively in French authors at that time. Molière,[2] George Sand,[3] De Vigny,[4] and Béranger[5] come in for special mention. Of Rousseau, the following is of interest as showing how early she read him and how great his influence was; but when, before or since, has the epithet " stately " been bestowed on Rousseau, and what a light the word sheds on her own mental condition!—" Blessed be the early days when I sat at the feet of Rousseau, prophet sad and stately as any of Jewry! Every onward movement of the age, every downward step into the solemn depths of my own soul, recalls thy oracles, O Jean Jacques! "[6]

About this same time, too, she appears to have been taking great interest in art and the history of art.[7]

So far, we have purposely omitted all but incidental reference to what made up Miss Fuller's most extensive and thorough study, works in the Italian and in the German language. Concerning the German, an entry in her diary only a few months before she moved to Groton in 1833 is of interest:

" I have settled the occupations of the coming six months. Some duties come first,—to parents, brothers, and sisters,— but these will not consume above one sixth of the time. . . . All hopes of traveling I have dismissed. All youthful hopes, of every kind, I have pushed from my thoughts. I will not, if I can help it, lose an hour in castle building and repining, —too much of that already. I have now a pursuit of immediate importance: to the German language and literature I will give my undivided attention. I have made rapid progress for one quite unassisted.[8]

[1] *Papers on Literature and Art* (1846), i, 88.
[2] *Memoirs,* i, 244.
[3] *Ibid.,* 248.
[4] *Ibid.,* 250.
[5] *Ibid.,* 258.
[6] *Ibid.,* 251 ; see also ii, 206.
[7] *Ibid.,* i, 265.
[8] Higginson, 41.

8

James Freeman Clarke gives this description of Miss Fuller's German studies:

"Of Margaret's studies while at Cambridge, I knew personally only of the German. She already, when I first became acquainted with her, had become familiar with the masterpieces of French, Italian and Spanish literature. . . .

"Margaret began to study German early in 1832. Both she and I were attracted towards this literature, at the same time, by the wild bugle-call of Thomas Carlyle, in his romantic articles on Richter, Schiller, and Goethe, which appeared in the old Foreign Review, the Edinburgh Review, and afterwards in the Foreign Quarterly.

"I believe that in about three months from the time that Margaret commenced German,[1] she was reading with ease the masterpieces of its literature. Within the year, she had read Goethe's Faust, Tasso, Iphigenia, Hermann and Dorothea, Elective Affinities, and Memoirs; Tieck's William Lovel, Prince Zerbino, and other works; Körner,[2] Novalis, and something of Richter; all of Schiller's principal dramas, and his lyric poetry. Almost every evening I saw her, and heard an account of her studies. Her mind opened under this influence, as the apple blossom at the end of a warm week in May."[3]

And Emerson writes: "When she came to Concord,[4] she was already rich in friends, rich in experiences, rich in culture. She was well read in French, Italian, and German literature. She had learned Latin and a little Greek. But her English reading was incomplete; and, while she knew Molière, and Rousseau, and any quantity of French letters, memoirs, and novels, and was a dear student of Dante and Petrarca, and knew German books more cordially than any other person, she was little read in Shakspeare; and I believe I had the pleasure of making her acquainted with Chaucer, with Ben Jonson, with Herbert, Chapman, Ford, Beaumont and Fletcher, with Bacon and Sir Thomas Browne."[5] . . .

[1] See *Woman in the Nineteenth Century*, 359.
[2] *Memoirs*, i, 169. "I trust you will be interested in my favorite Körner."
[3] *Ibid.*, 112.
[4] He met her in 1835.
[5] *Memoirs*, i, 204.

"Dante, Petrarca, Tasso, were her friends among the old poets,—for to Ariosto she assigned a far lower place,—Alfieri and Manzoni, among the new. But what was of still more import to her education, she had read German books, and, for the three years before I knew her, almost exclusively,—Lessing,[1] Schiller,[2] Richter,[3] Tieck, Novalis,[4] and, above all, Goethe."[5]

Beside the authors mentioned in Clarke's and Emerson's lists, she read somewhat of Uhland, Heine, Eichhorn, Jahn, De Wette and Herder.[6] These last two she translated one evening a week to Dr. Channing.[7] This was after she had begun teaching school in Boston. Here, among other subjects, she had classes in German and Italian. The Italian class read from Tasso, Petrarch, Ariosto, Alfieri, and "the whole hundred cantos of the Divina Commedia."[8] With her advanced German class she read in Schiller, Goethe, Lessing, Tieck, and Richter.[9]

Of her German acquaintances it seems to have been Goethe who attracted her especially. In 1833 she wrote to Dr. Hedge: "I have with me the works of Goethe which I have not yet read, and am now engaged upon 'Kunst und Alterthum,' and 'Campagne in Frankreich.' I still prefer Goethe to anyone, and, as I proceed, find more and more to learn."[10] And the year before she had made this confession: "It seems to me as if the mind of Goethe had embraced the universe. . . . I am enchanted while I read. He comprehends every feeling I have ever had so perfectly, expresses it so beautifully; . . .

[1] *Ibid.*, 121.

[2] *Ibid.*, 117 and 148.

[3] *Ibid.*, 147 and 130. "How thoroughly am I converted to the love of Jean Paul."

[4] *Ibid.*, 118 and 169.

[5] *Ibid.*, 242.

[6] Higginson, 45.

[7] *Memoirs*, i, 175.

[8] *Ibid.*, 174.

[9] *Ibid.*, 174. Beside her regular classes she had private pupils, with one of whom she speaks of reading "the History of England Shakspeare's historical plays in connection."

[10] *Ibid.*, 147 ; cf. *Ibid.*, 117.

I persevere in reading the great sage, some part of every day, hoping the time will come, when I shall not feel so over-whelmed, and leave off this habit of wishing to grasp the whole, and be contented to learn a little every day, as becomes a pupil."[1]

Soon after learning German she had translated Goethe's *Tasso,* and her interest in Goethe became so great that later (in 1837), at the suggestion of George Ripley, she seriously contemplated writing his life.[2] *Apropos* of this and showing the spiritual stimulation she was receiving from her studies, she declared:

"It will be long before I can give a distinct, and at the same time concise, account of my present state. I believe it is a great era. I am thinking now,—really thinking, I be-lieve; certainly it seems as if I had never done so before. If it does not kill me, something will come of it. Never was my mind so active; and the subjects are God, the universe, im-mortality. But shall I be fit for anything till I have abso-lutely re-educated myself? Am I, can I make myself, fit to write an account of half a century of the existence of one of the masterspirits of the world? It seems as if I had been very arrogant to dare to think it; yet will I not shrink back from what I have undertaken,—even by failure I shall learn much."[3]

Emerson's estimate of the influence of Goethe on Miss

[1] *Ibid.,* 119.

[2] Some of her remarks on the subject of this contemplated work are of special interest as showing that Miss Fuller's plans for collecting materials included the consultation of original sources, books being actually sent her from Europe (*Memoirs,* i, 175), and that, as far as this undertaking went at least, she was not open to that charge of superficiality that could have been justly brought against much of the scholarship of the time. Her accuracy in this respect was revealed in early youth in a newspaper answer to an article in the *North American* by George Bancroft on the character of Brutus.

Miss Fuller was obliged, for domestic reasons, to give up her plan of a life of Goethe. (*Memoirs,* i, 177.) In 1839, however, she published a translation of Eckermann's *Conversations.* (*Ibid.,* 243.) Her paper on Goethe in the *Dial* (Vol. ii, p. 1) is one of the best of her critical essays.

[3] *Memoirs,* i, 128.

Fuller is undoubtedly exaggerated when he says that her study of him had left room in her mind for no other teacher.[1] This is what he wrote of her to Carlyle in 1846:

" She is, I suppose, the earliest reader and lover of Goethe in this Country and nobody here knows him so well. Her love too of whatever is good in French and specially in Italian genius, give her the best title to travel. In short, she is our citizen of the world by quite special diploma."[2]

Thus far nothing in particular has been said of Miss Fuller's more technical philosophical reading. In 1825 we found her reading " Brown's Philosophy," and a little later contemplating Locke and trying Bacon. A letter on returning the book in 1833 shows she had delved extensively in a French version of Plato, with delight if not always with logical conviction. She gives criticisms of various dialogues:

" June 3, 1833. I part with Plato with regret. I could have wished to ' enchant myself,' as Socrates would say, with him some days longer.

" ' Crito ' I have read only once, but like it. I have not got it in my heart though, so clearly as the others.

" The ' Apology ' I deem only remarkable for the noble tone of sentiment, and beautiful calmness. I was much affected by Phaedo, but think the argument weak in many respects."[3]

In September, 1832, she thus expresses herself on the question of the value of philosophical studies:

" Not see the use of metaphysics? A moderate portion, taken at stated intervals, I hold to be of much use as discipline of the faculties. I only object to them as having an absorbing and anti-productive tendency. . . . Time enough at six-and-twenty to form yourself into a metaphysical philosopher. The brain does not easily get too dry for *that*."[4]

Somewhat later (" Groton ") she writes: " I have long had a suspicion that no mind can systematize its knowledge, and carry on the concentrating processes, without some fixed

[1] See *Memoirs*, i, 242.
[2] *Carlyle-Emerson Correspondence*, ii, 141.
[3] *Memoirs*, i, 116.
[4] *Ibid.*, 123.

opinion on the subject of metaphysics. But that indisposition, or even dread of the study, which you may remember, has kept me from meddling with it, till lately, in meditating on the life of Goethe, I thought I must get some idea of the history of philosophical opinion in Germany, that I might be able to judge of the influence it exercised upon his mind. . . . When I was in Cambridge, I got Fichte and Jacobi; I was much interrupted, but some time and earnest thought I devoted. Fichte I could not understand at all; though the treatise which I read was one intended to be popular, and which he says must compel (*bezwingen*) to conviction. Jacobi I could understand in details, but not in system. It seemed to me that his mind must have been moulded by some other mind, with which I ought to be acquainted, in order to know him well,—perhaps Spinoza's. Since I came home, I have been consulting Buhle's and Tennemann's histories of philosophy, and dipping into Brown, Stewart, and that class of books."[1]

These last two quotations, together with the one earlier given about the " great era " when she was " really thinking," probably illustrate pretty fairly the evolution of her opinion on philosophy. The total impression left by an investigation of her studies is that Miss Fuller read less of the technically metaphysical[2] and on the whole had less of a liking for it than any of the other leading transcendentalists. Yet her interest in the problems and mysteries of life seems to have been hardly less on that account. She merely imbibed her philosophy more from other sources than from the professional metaphysicians.

In concluding this consideration of Margaret Fuller's reading, two brief passages should be quoted, the first of which constitutes a confession of what our investigation has already suggested—that her mind, namely, possessed somewhat of

[1] *Ibid.,* 127. *Apropos* of this experience and of Sir James Mackintosh she writes, " It is quite gratifying, after my late chagrin, to find Sir James, with all his metaphysical turn, and ardent desire to penetrate it, puzzling so over the German philosophy, and particularly what I was myself troubled about, at Cambridge,—Jacobi's letters to Fichte." *Ibid.,* 165.

[2] *E. g.,* that she did not know Berkeley, see Mrs. Dall, *Margaret and Her Friends,* 82.

that vagrant quality so often characteristic of the transcendental temperament:

" Margaret said she could keep up no intimacy with books. She loved a book dearly for a while; but as soon as she began to look out a nice Morocco cover for her favorite, she was sure to take a disgust to it, to outgrow it. She did not mean that she outgrew the author, but that, having received all from him that he could give her, he tired her. That had even been the case with Shakespeare! For several years he was her very life; then she gave him up. . . . It was the same with Ovid, . . . She regretted her oddity, for she lost a great solace by it."[1]

The second passage, on the other hand, shows one of the purposes behind her reading, and affords at least a partial refutation of the charge, so frequently brought against her, that the only object of her studies was self-culture:

" It has been one great object of my life to introduce here the works of those great geniuses, the flower and fruit of a higher state of development, which might give the young who are soon to constitute the state, a higher standard in thought and action than would be demanded of them by their own time. . . . I feel with satisfaction that I have done a good deal to extend the influence of the great minds of Germany and Italy among my compatriots."[2]

A word may here be added concerning the influence on Margaret Fuller of the other transcendentalists. It has been seen that she taught in Alcott's[3] school and that she came in close contact with Channing.[4] But it was the influence of Emerson that was earlier and stronger. The following refers to a time before she was personally acquainted with him: " You question me as to the nature of the benefits conferred upon me by Mr. E's preaching. I answer, that his influence has been more beneficial to me than that of any

[1] Mrs. Dall, *Margaret and Her Friends*, 139.

[2] *Papers on Literature and Art*, preface, vii.

[3] See *Memoirs*, i, 171, for the mutual impressions of each other of Alcott and Miss Fuller.

[4] *Ibid.*, 175.

American, and that from him I first learned what is meant by an inward life. Many other springs have since fed the stream of living waters, but he first opened the fountain. That the 'mind is its own place,' was a dead phrase to me, till he cast light upon my mind. Several of his sermons stand apart in memory, like landmarks of my spiritual history. It would take a volume to tell what this one influence did for me. But perhaps I shall some time see that it was best for me to be forced to help myself."[1]   After listening to this it would evidently be superfluous to seek the ultimate source of Margaret Fuller's transcendentalism in Goethe or Coleridge or indeed anywhere beyond the Atlantic.

Before attempting any summary of these sections on the reading of the transcendentalists, it may not be out of place to insert a few extracts and summaries from the discussions by two of them, Emerson and Parker, of the influences which in their opinions contributed to the breaking up of tradition in New England during the first half of the nineteenth century. Emerson's discussion occurs in his paper, *Historic Notes of Life and Letters in New England.*[2]

He emphasizes first the growth of the modern idea (so opposite from that earlier prevalent) that the nation exists for the sake of the individual. "The most remarkable literary work of the age has for its hero and subject precisely this introversion; I mean the poem of Faust.[3] In philosophy, Immanuel Kant has made the best catalogue of the human faculties and the best analysis of the mind." Emerson then enumerates some of the forces and men that undermined the traditional religion in New England: the Arminians; the English theologians—followers of Locke in philosophy—Hartley, Priestley, and Belsham; the life and writings of Swedenborg; "the powerful influence of the genius and character of Dr. Channing." "Germany," he continues, "had created criticism in vain for us until 1820, when Edward Everett returned from

[1] *Ibid.,* 194.
[2] *Works,* x.
[3] Emerson did not like *Faust*; see *Works,* Centenary Edition, x, 573.

his five years in Europe." He then gives an extended account of the wide influence of this " master of elegance." " It was not the intellectual or the moral principles which he had to teach. It was not thoughts. . . . His power lay in the magic of form; it was in the graces of manner; in a new perception of Grecian beauty, to which he had opened our eyes." After mentioning Dr. Frothingham, " an excellent classical and German scholar," and Professor Andrews Norton, Emerson asserts his belief that " the paramount source of the religious revolution was Modern Science." He explains especially the disintegrating effect of the new astronomy and geology, and has somewhat to say of Goethe's innovations in optics and botany, and of the agitation over phrenology and mesmerism. Continuing, he speaks of Hegel, of Schelling, Oken, Combe's *Constitution of Man,* Dickens' novels, the essays of Channing, even the caricatures in *Punch.* The discussion then turns to personal recollections of the transcendental group, an account of the *Dial* and of Brook Farm. One sentence occurring among his allusions to Fourier should be quoted: " Our feeling was that Fourier had skipped no fact but one, namely Life."

Parker's discussion[1] is in some ways more specific and confined more immediately to the years just preceding the transcendental outburst. Of the spiritual influences most potent in his time, he mentions Garrison, Channing, Pierpont, and Emerson. Of the last he says, his brilliant genius " rose in the winter nights, and hung over Boston, drawing the eyes of ingenuous young people to look up at that great, new star, a beauty and a mystery, which charmed for the moment, while it gave also perennial inspiration, as it led them forward along new paths, and towards new hopes. America has seen no such sight before; it is not less a blessed wonder now." Then, after a word about the phrenologists, he continues:

" The writings of Wordsworth were becoming familiar to the thoughtful lovers of nature and of man, and drawing men to natural piety. Carlyle's works got reprinted at Boston, dif-

[1] A part of letter to his church, above referred to, reprinted in the appendix to Weiss's biography.

fusing a strong, and then also, a healthy influence on old and young. The writings of Coleridge were reprinted in America, all of them 'Aids to Reflection,' and brilliant with the scattered sparks of genius; they incited many to think, more especially young Trinitarian ministers; and, spite of the lack of both historic and philosophic accuracy, and the utter absence of all proportion in his writings; spite of his haste, his vanity, prejudice, sophistry, confusion, and opium—he yet did great service in New England, helping to emancipate enthralled minds. The works of Cousin, more systematic, and more profound as a whole, and far more catholic and comprehensive, continental, not insular, in his range, also became familiar to the Americans,—reviews and translations going where the eloquent original was not heard—and helped free the young mind from the gross sensationalism of the academic Philosophy on one side, and the grosser supernaturalism of the ecclesiastical Theology on the other.

"The German language, hitherto the priceless treasure of a few, was becoming well known, and many were thereby made acquainted with the most original, deep, bold, comprehensive, and wealthy literature in the world, full of theologic and philosophic thought. Thus, a great storehouse was opened to such as were earnestly in quest of Truth."

With a reference to Strauss' *Life of Jesus*,[1] he passes on to a long description of the religious turmoil of the times.[2]

Into the wilderness of names with which this survey of the reading of these transcendentalists has surrounded us, how will it be possible to bring any meaning? This very difficulty is replete with a meaning of its own, perhaps the most instructive thing of all.

[1] See Chadwick's *Parker*, 83.

[2] To these discussions of Emerson and Parker may be appended a line or two from Dr. Hedge's account of the formation of the Transcendental Club:

"The writings of Coleridge, recently edited by Marsh, and some of Carlyle's earlier essays, especially the 'Characteristics' and the 'Signs of the Times,' had created a ferment in the minds of some of the young clergy of that day. There was a promise in the air of a new era of intellectual life." (Cabot, 245.)

Select at random a handful of names from those that we
have come upon most often: Plato, Pythagoras, Plotinus,
Shakespeare, Rousseau, Godwin, Kant, Coleridge, Goethe,
Richter, Swedenborg. What is the significance of such a
list? Or again, consider the influences which these men tell
us were responsible early in life for first affording them their
newer vision, or, that vision once gained, for finding them a
firmer basis for their thought: Channing affirms that his earliest
insight into the transcendental conception of the world came
after reading Hutcheson, and that later the writings of Dr.
Price helped him to formulate his metaphysical thinking.
Alcott says that Coleridge lifted him out of his philosophical
difficulties and gave his mind a turn toward the spiritual, while
he speaks of Channing as his mentor when his thought was
young. Emerson declares that he knows " but one solution
to " his " nature and relations," the hint toward idealism—
never afterward lost—which Berkeley gave him in his youth;
he attributes to Montaigne an influence scarcely consistent
with the remark about Berkeley, and his early debt to Coleridge too is plain. Parker tells us it was Kant in whom he
found the real basis for his newer views. Margaret Fuller
says that it was Emerson who first taught her what the inward
life is, though many other springs afterward fed the stream.
Once more, what is the meaning of all this?

Surely these things show how various were the influences at
work, how organically transcendentalism was a part of the
thought currents of its own day, and how inseparably, like those
currents themselves, it was linked with the thought of earlier
times. Indeed, though it may seem equivalent to abandoning
the inquiry as hopeless to say that the real origin of the movement was " influences in the air," to put it so would doubtless
leave an impression much nearer the truth than to assign any
one writer or group of writers as its source. Transcendentalism was the product of the spirit of its age—like that spirit
itself a function of many and complex forces, and, like that
spirit again, to be understood only in relation to the history and
temper of the scarcely less complex age from which it took its
rise. Hence it is that transcendentalism seems from one point

of view a gradual outgrowth and culmination of Unitarianism; that it is deeply and vitally intermingled with French Revolutionary influences; that it connects at a score of points with English literary romanticism; that it appears almost an offshoot of German philosophical idealism; that it is intimately bound up with the growth of the scientific spirit; that it is by no means unaffected by contemporary currents of social unrest. Indeed there is hardly an important radical movement of the time, political, social, scientific, literary, theological, or philosophical, to which transcendentalism can be shown to be essentially unrelated.

Furthermore, the facility with which the transcendentalists found congenial food for reflection, not merely in Eastern scriptures, in Greek philosophy, and mediaeval mystics, but in a large part of all the greatest literature of the world, is highly significant, indicating that transcendentalism—in many ways even more than those larger European movements of which it was an aspect—was in no inconsiderable measure a renaissance.

Our study of their reading has tended to show that these transcendentalists share in common this interest in many of the great thinkers and much of the great literature of the world.[1] Perhaps the most marked of all transcendental mannerisms is the startling collocation of names from all ages, all countries, all walks of life, names which the writer often treats with the utmost familiarity, although of the men themselves he could have known but little. This, it will be recognized, is particularly characteristic of Emerson: " Plato, Plotinus, Archimedes, Hermes, Newton, Milton, Wordsworth."[2] Such a list is of course in some ways exceedingly funny, and this sort of thing has been provocative of not a little scoffing. But he who is ready only to laugh has not begun to understand transcendentalism. This practice is much more than a mere

[1] This utterance of Parker is typically transcendental: " I would rather not waste my time on mean authors; I would study the masters of poetry before I played with the *apprentices* and still more before I played with the lackeys of the apprentices." Frothingham, 296.

[2] *Works*, vi, 150; see also e. g., *Ibid.*, xii, 179, and *Dial*, i, 375.

mannerism of style; it is symbolic of an attitude of thought;
it is the counterpart, in the literary product, of certain habits
of the transcendental mind, dangerous habits, perhaps, yet
habits, under the circumstances, perfectly natural and intelligible.[1]   Finding many of the same ideas in men separated
by the widest distances in time and space—Orientals, Plato,
Jesus, Plotinus, Spinoza, Kant, Goethe, Coleridge—these transcendentalists became imbued with a feeling of the identity
rather than the diversity of the great thought of the world,
with a belief that all religions are aspects of one religion, all
philosophies of one philosophy.   In other words they had
awakened, possibly to a somewhat crude, but to a very real
and sincere cosmopolitanism.   They differed radically in the
thoroughness with which they had investigated the grounds
of their belief, in their actual knowledge of world literature;
but they agreed quite definitely in the belief and enthusiasm
itself:

"A marked aspect of our day is its recovery and recognition of past times and great names,—of Plato, Aristotle, Con-
fucius, Behmen, Shakespeare, Goethe; and some moderns are
becoming of new account."[2]

"The more liberal thought of intelligent persons acquires a
new name in each period or community; and in ours, by no
very good luck, as it sometimes appears to us, has been desig-
nated as transcendentalism.   We have every day occasion to
remark its perfect identity, under whatever new phraseology
or application to new facts, with the liberal thought of all men
of a religious and contemplative habit in other times and
countries."[3]

"Any history of philosophy fortifies my faith, by showing
me that what high dogmas I had supposed were the rare and
late fruit of a cumulative culture, and only now possible to
some recent Kant or Fichte,—were the prompt improvisations
of the earliest inquirers; of Parmenides, Heraclitus, and
Xenophanes.   In view of these students, the soul seems to

[1] For further discussion of this point, see the concluding chapter.
[2] Alcott, quoted in Sanborn, 414.
[3] Emerson, in the *Dial*, ii, 382.

whisper, ' There is a better way than this indolent learning of another. Leave me alone; do not teach me out of Leibnitz or Schelling, and I shall find it all out myself.' "[1]

" A great deal of the profoundest thinking of antiquity, which had become as good as obsolete for us, is now reappearing in extracts and allusions, and in twenty years will get all printed anew."[2]

But now from this insistence on the complexity of the sources of transcendentalism and on the impossibility of assigning absolutely their respective importance, it is nevertheless proper to recur to an acknowledgment of the large element of truth in the widely accepted theory that New England transcendentalism was a German importation. The extent of the admissible generalization seems to be this. The *original stimulus* to the *strictly metaphysical* part of transcendental thought came fairly largely (but by no means exclusively) from Germany. Of the various channels which brought this thought from Germany to America, England was considerably the most important, and France next.

Of the English writers who helped in this transference, Coleridge[3] on the whole seems to have been the most immediately and widely influential. Merely to place side by side a few facts from our study is sufficient to show that—though others meant more to this or that transcendentalist—in really significant influence on the whole group no other writer can be ranked higher than Coleridge, and probably none so high as he. To Coleridge, Channing said that he " owed more than to the mind of any other philosophic thinker." Coleridge helped Alcott out of his philosophic difficulties. Emerson " got all that earlier from Coleridge." Parker read Coleridge back in his school-keeping days and bore testimony to his great service to New England in helping emancipate enthralled minds. Margaret Fuller read Coleridge early, and later pronounced the benefits he had conferred upon the age " as yet incalculable." The widespread influence of Coleridge

[1] Emerson, *Works,* i, 156.

[2] *Ibid.,* 261. See also Frothingham's *Parker, 296.*

[3] See article on Coleridge, *Christian Examiner,* March, 1833.

meant that indirectly many of the elements of the philosophy of Schelling were broadly disseminated, and New England transcendentalism, in so far as it is a metaphysical system, has probably a closer affinity to his philosophy than to that of any of the other German idealists. After Coleridge, Wordsworth and Carlyle must be given the next rank. Wordsworth's influence was more subtle than Coleridge's, and may possibly have been just as pervasive. The seeds, at least, of transcendentalism were pretty thickly sown before Carlyle appeared, but his contribution too was great.[1]

Of French writers who helped to carry German thought, the most important were probably Mme. De Staël, Cousin, and Jouffroy, and of these the second seems to have been the most widely read.[2]

So much then for the incentive supplied from Germany. But now, this original stimulus once imparted, these transcendentalists drew from such widely different springs that all attempts at generalization must break down, except such as emphasize the very variety of their sources. Alcott's fountain of inspiration after the first seems to have been mainly the Greek philosophers, the Neo-Platonists, and the mystical writers of all time. The German influence on him during the transcendental period was probably less than in the case of any of the other leaders of the movement. Emerson dipped into at least a little of almost everything from the Orientals and Plato down. Parker read voluminously in practically all

[1] See article on the influence of Carlyle in the *Dial*, ii, 131.

[2] An article in the *Princeton Review*, xi, 37, reviewing several translations from Cousin, and Emerson's Divinity School Address, shows the wide influence Cousin was exerting and gives the views of a writer who deprecated this influence.

The following is from an article in the *North American Review* of July, 1841, also reviewing three translations from Cousin, one of which was a part of Ripley's *Specimens of Foreign Standard Literature:*

"The writings of Cousin form the popular philosophy of the day. Their success in this country is attested by the appearance of the three translations, of which the titles are given above, one of which has already passed to a second edition and has been introduced as a text book in some of our principal colleges."

See also *Orestes A. Brownson's Life*, Vol. 1, Chap. xix.

literatures and in many schools of philosophy. Margaret Fuller's reading seems to have been predominantly poetical and literary, and to have included less of the technically metaphysical than that of the others. Germany had a large direct influence upon her, Goethe coming as near as anyone to being her great name. It should be remarked, especially, that all these transcendentalists whom we have been considering knew and took delight in Plato.

Finally, the mutual influence of these men on one another was strong, and, above all, must the very great effect of Channing's thought and personality be given its due significance. If we may trust his statement that German philosophy never gave him a new idea, we perceive—and this gives us an opportunity to sum up our discussion—that he drew much of his inspiration from a point fairly high up in the stream of eighteenth century tendency, at a place where, or close to where, the current of influence was still predominantly from England to the continent rather than in the reverse direction. Through Unitarianism then, and through Channing, who diverted a part of the Unitarian stream into a new channel, we may trace an essentially direct English current ending in transcendentalism. Into this perhaps relatively slender stream was turned the turbulent, but congenital volume of German and other continental waters, and into that united river the thought of former ages dropped—not, in the image of Emerson's poem, like ordinary rain, but like veritable cloudbursts.

CHAPTER III

THE TRANSCENDENTALISTS AND PRACTICAL LIFE, I

The popular meaning of *transcendental;* some of the absurdities of the movement; mysticism and sentimentalism; transcendental and prophetic pride; the transcendentalists and practical life.

On September 26, 1840, Carlyle wrote to Emerson: " The *Dial* No. 1 came duly: of course I read it with interest; it is the utterance of what is purest, youngest in your land; pure, ethereal, as the voices of the Morning! And yet—you know me—for me it is *too* ethereal, speculative, theoretic: all theory becomes more and more confessedly inadequate, untrue, unsatisfactory, almost a kind of mockery to me! I will have all things condense themselves, take shape and body, if they are to have my sympathy."[1]

In this quotation, a single example from many similar utterances of Carlyle, is embodied—as was indicated at the beginning of our discussion in what was said of the popular use of *transcendental*—the most frequent and at the same time most definite of the adverse criticisms which have been brought against the New England transcendentalists, the charge that they were out of touch with the concrete things of the practical world, in a word that they were " lost in the clouds." These sentences then, which Carlyle applies here merely to the *Dial,* may be selected as an excellent expression (in temperate form, to be sure!) of the general criticism.

This general criticism took several more specific shapes. The transcendentalists, it was declared, were idle dreamers, lovers of solitude, the slaves and victims of their own emotions, of a mysticism that, whatever beautiful visions it might bring, unfitted them, hopelessly, for any practical contact with the world or any useful service to mankind; this mystical iso-

[1] *Carlyle-Emerson Correspondence,* i, 330.

lation bred in them, it was asserted, intellectual self-sufficiency and pride, individualism pushed to a well-nigh insane extreme; this intellectual self-centralization, again, blinded them to facts, to the evil, the ugliness, and sin within the world; the very absurdities of which they were guilty, finally, were sufficient to show their lack of a really balanced view of life. These—all of them variations on a single theme—are grave charges. Each demands its own consideration.

It is clear that the final appeal in this whole matter must be simply to the facts—in the widest sense—of these men's *lives*. That is the logical court of last resort. Our trial of the transcendentalists before that bar, however, is reserved for the next chapter. In this, meanwhile, it is proposed to consider several of these specific charges just enumerated, to examine in a way the evidence on which they rest, with an aim more immediately to understand than to pass judgment—though the postponement of the larger discussion does not mean of course the exclusion of all biographical material from the present more restricted one.

Let us proceed at once then to a consideration of one of the counts of the indictment. We shall take up the last one first —the question of the absurdities of which the transcendentalists are alleged to have been guilty—confining our attention mainly, in this chapter, to their "conversations" and their published writings.

I

The currency of the term "transcendental" in the popular sense, and indeed the whole humorous aspect which for the public the movement took on, were due in good measure to men and events apart from those now being treated, whether they were the vagaries of some "Come-outer," some perhaps apocryphal anecdote about the poet Jones Very,[1] whom the inmates of the Somerville Insane Asylum are said to have thanked for the good he had done them, or stories of plowing poets and dish-washing philosophers at Brook Farm. But even the leading transcendentalists were thoughtful enough,

[1] For an account of his "timeless" existence, see Sanborn, 295.

upon some occasions, to supply useful evidence to those who seemed to regard transcendentalism as simply a huge joke.

Alcott beyond question was the most prominent contributor. The methods adopted in his Temple school and the publication of the *Conversations with Children on the Gospels,* his experiences at Fruitlands, his later "conversations," all did their share; but doubtless, most of all, his *Orphic Sayings* in the *Dial.* It will surely be no exaggeration to say that these, more than all the other contributions to the *Dial* combined, served to bring down the ridicule of the community without discrimination on its pages. Margaret Fuller's "conversations" took their place in this respect beside Alcott's, while the material for the wits supplied by Emerson was perhaps certain passages in some of his earlier essays. (In Channing and Parker, as far as the writer is aware, there is nothing of this sort.)

By way of a few illustrations of these points, we might, to begin with, call attention to a little book, *Margaret and Her Friends,* reporting the conversations (1841) of Miss Fuller on Greek mythology. In its pages among other things are mentioned the sad consequences resulting from long gazing on the moonlight—or sleeping in it—and of a town where sixteen persons were bewildered in this way. If to some future age this document alone should descend to tell the story of the transcendental movement in New England, we can imagine some far-off reader wondering whether the town referred to might not have been Boston and whether the number of the moonstruck had not been underestimated. In fact in reading it one is maliciously reminded of Theodore Parker's remark about the transcendental nonsense "twaddled" by Margaret Fuller. To say this is not to infer that there was not much serious, even deep thought in these conversations, nor that those of others of the five years during which they were conducted[1] were necessarily as ethereal as those on mythology, the report of which we have; least of all is it to imply that they were not of real benefit and inspiration to those who attended them. We have personal testimony on the contrary that they were. Behind the mist of absurdly forced symbolism was always sincerity, always pure aspiration.

It is manifestly impossible to make extracts from these conversations without on the one hand failing to do justice to their serious intentions, or on the other, decreasing, from the lack of context, the humorous effect. A few short specimens, however, may be set down:

" R. W. E. thought every man had probably met his Jupiter, Juno, Minerva, Venus, or Ceres in society!

" Margaret was sure she never had!

" R. W. E. explained: ' Not in the world, but each on his own platform.'

" William Story objected. The life of an individual was not universal (!)

" Sophia Ripley repeated, ' The inner life.'

" William Story claimed to be an individual, and did not think individual experience could ever meet all minds, . . . like the story of Ceres for example. . . .

" Emerson said that we all did sundry graceful acts, in our caps and tunics, which we never could do again, which we never wanted to do again.

" Margaret said, at last we had touched the point. . . .

" Margaret . . . declared that . . . Æsculapius bore two [serpents] on his staff, Mercury two on his divining rod, and the cock was also sacred to Æsculapius.

" I asked if this did not indicate a certain subjection of these Gods to Wisdom?

" Some questions written on paper were here read. One asked why Minerva was born of the stroke of Vulcan, and why she was the patroness of weavers, and what that had to do with the story of Arachne.

" Margaret replied with ill temper to the first, that it was because Vulcan held the hammer—and to the second, that she did not know.

" Ida Russell thought that when Mechanic Art was married to Beauty, it might charm even Wisdom."

It is only fair to remark that all the participants in these conversations were not unconscious of the fun—Emerson and Margaret Fuller herself among others—but this fact cannot suffice as an explanation, for the tickets for ten sessions cost twenty dollars.

Alcott's conversations of the transcendental period, as far as we know them, appear to have had even more of the naively humorous element than Miss Fuller's, as, for instance, that on *Enthusiasm* as reported—from the notes of a member of the class—in *Concord Days*. This, with its "insights" concerning "temperaments" and "complexions"[1] is sufficiently described by the phrase which Alcott himself in this very conversation, with deliciously unconscious irony, applies to the method of the seer, "thought a-bed, or philosophy recumbent." While the discussion of Alcott's Temple school and his conversations with children is reserved till later, a single quotation here from one of these conversations will be sufficient to show how well they justified the popular smiles, even if not the lack of popular sympathy. The following are the animadversions of a child under seven years of age:

Josiah: " Mr. Alcott, we think too much about clay. We should think of Spirit. I think we should love Spirit, not Clay. I should think a mother now would love her baby's Spirit; and suppose it should die, that is only the Spirit bursting away out of the Body. It is alive; it is perfectly happy. I really do not know why people mourn when their friends die. I should think it would be matter of rejoicing. [This, we are constrained to believe, is the *ne plus ultra* of transcendental optimism.] For instance: now, if we should go out into the street and find a box—an old dusty box—and should put into it some very fine pearls, and by and by the box should grow old and break, why, we should not even think about the box; but if the pearls were safe, we should think of them and nothing else. So it is with the Soul and Body. I cannot see why people mourn for bodies."

[1] " The celestial man was composed more largely of light and ether. The demonic man combined more of fire and vapor. The animal man more of embers and dust." *Concord Days,* 192.

Mr. Alcott: " Yes, Josiah; that is all true and we are glad to hear it.[1] Shall some one else now speak beside you? "[2]

Josiah: " Oh, Mr. Alcott! then I will stay in the recess and talk."[3]

This is said to be a verbatim record.[4] Evidently Josiah had caught the true transcendental loquacity.

The presence in not inconsiderable degree in Alcott's writings, especially in their more speculative portions, of phrases and sentences that inevitably provoke a smile is to be accounted for much less by the character of the thought than by the simple fact that Alcott was very far from being a master of expression.[5] When Wordsworth writes:

> " Thou, over whom thy immortality
> Broods like the day, a master o'er a slave,
> A presence which is not to be put by;
> Thou little child, yet glorious in the might
> Of heaven-born freedom, on thy being's height,"

whether we give intellectual assent or not, we feel that this is great and serious poetry. But when one reads in Alcott, " Children are illuminated text-books, breviaries of doctrine, living bodies of divinity, open always and inviting their elders to peruse the characters inscribed on the lovely leaves,"[6] though the thought is well-nigh the same, good manners deter us from making comments in public. And dozens of other examples of this sort of thing could be picked out from Alcott's writings. We take a single specimen from *Tablets:* " Pursuing our peregrinations, we plunge suddenly into the abyss of origins, transformed for the moment into slumbering umbilici, skirting the shores of our nativity; or ascending spine-wise, traverse the hierarchy of gifts."[7] The *Orphic Sayings* are frequently in a style quite similar to this.[8]

[1] If "Josiah" was, as is presumable, Josiah Quincy, then a remark of Emerson would lead us to believe that he gave assent to this sort of thing.
[2] Josiah had been usurping the conversation.
[3] *Concord Days,* 106.
[4] See note 2, p. 119.
[5] It is true that late in life his powers of expression were increased.
[6] *Table Talk,* 57.
[7] *Tablets,* 202.
[8] See p. 131, where one of these *Sayings* is quoted in full.

The same element appears in Emerson, but much less frequently. We find distinct traces of it in *Nature,* as for instance where his orphic poet (supposedly Alcott) " sings ": " ' Man is the dwarf of himself. . . . Out from him sprang the sun and moon; from man the sun, from woman the moon,' " or where he says on his own account, " I became a transparent eyeball." The point again is that such a statement as this last is ridiculous quite apart from its truth or falsity. We may agree entirely or we may disagree with the philosophic thought, but we must surely admit that the sentence is grossly unpoetic[1] and wholly deserving of the cartoons it called forth.

The Scylla and the Charybdis of criticism on this whole matter are on the one hand to feel that the thought is true and thence to infer that the expression of it cannot be ridiculous, and on the other to perceive the ridiculousness of the expression and thence to infer that there can be no serious or worthy thought beneath it. Emerson—with some few lapses—is both poet and philosopher. Alcott made the mistake of attempting the untechnical, poetical method of philosophizing, without possessing the poet's power of expression.[2] This fact in itself is sufficient to prevent his writings from having great influence on the world.

Even this brief glance at some of the unconsciously humorous aspects of transcendentalism ought to be sufficient to show that there was more than a grain of justification in the popular attitude, and that while the public was wrong in its wide and promiscuously applied generalizations from little things, it was right in perceiving that the ridiculous element was there. The criticism which has failed to find it is obviously one-sided. Our short survey would seem to indicate too that more than in any other way (in their writings) these men laid them-

[1] Contrast *e. g.,* with *Brahma,* where the mystical thought and imagery are fused with high poetic art. *Brahma* in turn may be contrasted in this respect with Alcott's analogous lines beginning:

" He omnipresent is,
All round himself he lies."
(*Tablets,* 167.)

[2] See Sanborn, 259, for Emerson's criticism of Alcott's style.

selves open to well-grounded satire through a tendency to indulge in absurdly expressed utterances of a symbolic or highly figurative nature. What the significance of this tendency was, we may best consider at the end of the chapter. Meanwhile the fact of its existence is clear. That it is an inevitable attendant of the transcendental point of view is disproved by its absence in Channing and Parker. While it is infrequent in Emerson's writings, the reports of Miss Fuller's conversations make clear that he was quite capable of entering into the spirit of those meetings and even contributing his share; and his long intimacy with Alcott shows that he must have much more than merely tolerated the sort of thing to which we refer. The records of her conversations leave us in no doubt as to the presence of this element in Margaret Fuller, though, as with Emerson, it is found, at the most, very infrequently in her published writings. Of Alcott alone can it be said that it is present in a fairly conspicuous degree in his publications. On the whole, then, this quality cannot be set down as a primary transcendental characteristic, but is one, however, that did show a marked tendency to emerge in connection with the thoughts and spirit of these men.

II.

How far, we next ask, were the transcendentalists victims of over-emotionalism? Of sentimentalism? Of mysticism? A consideration of simply this last question, How far were the transcendentalists mystics? will perhaps, incidentally, suggest answers to the other two.

Professor William James in his Gifford Lectures, *The Varieties of Religious Experience*, proposes "four marks which, when an experience has them, may justify us in calling it mystical for the purpose of the present lectures." Though, as the last phrase indicates, Professor James makes no claim that his analysis involves a final definition of mysticism, we surely cannot do better than to adopt it for our present discussion. His four criteria are these:

" 1. *Ineffability*.—The handiest of the marks by which I

classify a state of mind as mystical is negative. The subject of it immediately says that it defies expression, that no adequate report of its contents can be given in words. It follows from this that its quality must be directly experienced; it cannot be imparted or transferred to others. In this peculiarity mystical states are more like states of feeling than like states of intellect. No one can make clear to another who has never had a certain feeling, in what the quality or worth of it consists. One must have musical ears to know the value of a symphony; one must have been in love one's self to understand a lover's state of mind. Lacking the heart or ear, we cannot interpret the musician or the lover justly, and are even likely to consider him weak-minded or absurd. The mystic finds that most of us accord to his experiences an equally incompetent treatment.

" 2. *Noetic Quality.*—Although so similar to states of feeling, mystical states seem to those who experience them to be also states of knowledge. They are states of insight into depths of truth unplumbed by the discursive intellect. They are illuminations, revelations, full of significance and importance, all inarticulate though they remain; and as a rule they carry with them a curious sense of authority for after-time.

" These two characters will entitle any state to be called mystical, in the sense in which I use the word. Two other qualities are less sharply marked, but are usually found. These are :—

" 3. *Transiency.*—Mystical states cannot be sustained for long. . . .

" 4. *Passivity.*— . . . the mystic feels as if his own will were in abeyance, and indeed sometimes as if he were grasped and held by a superior power. . . ."[1]

(As does Professor James, we shall put emphasis upon the first two marks.)

With this analysis of mysticism before us, we see at once why its appearance among the transcendentalists might in advance be reasonably predicted. If its nature be indeed ineffable emotion attended with intellectual illumination, its

[1] *The Varieties of Religious Experience,* 380.

very essence then is a blending, in some sort, of thought and feeling. But we have pointed out repeatedly that the whole revolutionary age in Europe was characterized by a vital and widespread fusion of just these elements; such a fusion indeed we have already declared transcendentalism itself— in part at least—to be, and the portion of our discussion on which we are now entering will supply not a little confirmation of this claim. Union of thought and feeling may take place of course in a wide variety of ways, but in the case of this New England movement there was more than one condition that favored the appearance of mysticism. That the transcendentalists were without exception of highly developed emotional natures is beyond question[1]—to read even the briefest stories of their lives is to perceive this; that they were all of a religious temperament is almost equally beyond denial; and that they came to maturity at a time and in a place where a strictly active indulgence of high emotion received little encouragement, our earlier chapters, we trust, have rendered plain. Here already are ingredients enough for making mystics. But more may be said. The philosophy of these men led in the same direction. (We will come in a moment to the objection which someone will raise that here we are getting the cart before the horse.) A natural corollary of the transcendental philosophy, with its belief in the immanence of God in man, is a belief in the possibility of the direct communion of the human soul with the divine. Aspiration is the reaching of the soul up to God; inspiration is the flowing of God into the soul; and these are one. It is easy to see how such a purely theoretical conception, if touched with emotion, might result in at least a degree, and where deeply tinctured with feeling, in a high degree, of mysticism. But this is not all. Not only does the content of the transcendental philosophy readily permit a mystical inference; its very method brings it even more closely into touch with states of rapture. All the transcendentalists adopted—in whatever varying degrees and kinds—the intuitional method of philosophizing; in other

---

[1] Emerson is by no means an exception to this statement in spite of the tranquil, sometimes even cold, element in his nature.

words they all accepted as authoritative, individual insights into spiritual truth. But the kinship between these insights and the " noëtic " quality of mysticism is on the very face of things apparent.

The moment a metaphysic sanctions an intuitional way of gaining truth, it has thrown open the doors into the deep world of feeling and mysticism. The very *Critique of Practical Reason* of Immanuel Kant holds within itself—whatever else it may contain in germ—the promise of a whole school of mystics. Philosophies of the transcendental type and certain forms of religious ecstacy have always shown a remarkable proneness to flourish together, and at the touch of emotion or in the heart of a fervid nature a belief of this sort stands always ready to put forth mystical blossoms. How far the philosophy nourishes the mysticism, how far the mysticism creates the philosophy—which one of us shall say? Each will answer according to his own philosophy of life. The two things are congenial, and he will be a bold judge indeed who attempts to cast up between them a final reckoning of causes and effects.

Does not transcendentalism present this very problem? It surely does. To untangle its intellectual and emotional strands is hopelessly impossible. Let this at once be fully recognized, for to recognize and admit it is to transform an obstacle into an explanation. We come then to take up these men in turn, knowing at the outset that because of their highly emotional, religious natures and because of both the content and spirit of their philosophy, in all of them we have potential mystics. And here, perhaps, is the best place to remark, that so far as the popular charge against the transcendentalists means that they did not go to the facts of the external world for the basis of their beliefs, it stands confirmed at once and forever. The intuitional method in their own eyes, however, was not an abandoning of experience for theory but rather a shifting of emphasis to another sort of experience, that of the inner as contrasted with the outer world.

The hyper-emotional, mystical temperament was Channing's

by nature. A bit of autobiography from a discourse delivered in his native town in 1836 will in itself render this clear:

" No spot on earth has helped to form me so much as that beach [at Newport]. There I lifted up my voice in praise amidst the tempest. There, softened by beauty, I poured out my thanksgiving and contrite confessions. There, in reverential sympathy with the mighty power around me, I became conscious of power within. There struggling thoughts and emotions broke forth, as if moved to utterance by nature's eloquence of the winds and waves. There began a happiness surpassing all worldly pleasures, all gifts of fortune, the happiness of communing with the works of God."[1]

The following from a letter of self-confession to his friend Shaw shows the intensity of his emotional nature and at the same time his own determination to overcome it:

" My whole life has been a struggle with my feelings. Last winter I thought myself victorious. But the earth-born Antaeus has risen stronger than ever. I repeat it, my whole life has been a struggle with my feelings. . . . I can remember the days when I gloried in the moments of rapture, when I loved to shroud myself in the gloom of melancholy. You may remember them too. But I have grown wiser as I have grown older. I now wish to do good in the world."

Speaking of " feeling," in this same letter he says: " I then went on to consider whether there were not many persons who possessed this boasted feeling, but who were still deficient in *active* benevolence. A thousand instances occurred to me. I found myself among the number. ' It is true,' said I, ' that I sit in my study and shed tears over human misery. I weep over a novel. I weep over a tale of human woe. But do I ever relieve the distressed? Have I ever lightened the load of affliction?' My cheeks reddened at the question; a cloud of error burst from my mind. I found that virtue did not consist in feeling, but in *acting from a sense of duty*."[2]

[1] See the whole of the discourse on *Christian Worship,* from which this quotation is taken, *Works,* iv, 303. Also Channing, 41—" Thus I am either borne to heaven on ' rapture's wing of fire,' or else I am plunged into the depths of despair."

[2] *Ibid.,* 60.

Advising a young friend late in life, he wrote: " Do anything innocent, rather than give yourself up to *reverie*. I can speak on this point from experience. At one period of my life I was a dreamer, castle-builder. Visions of the distant and future took the place of present duty and activity. I spent hours in reverie. I suppose I was seduced in part by physical debility ; but the body suffered as much as the mind."[1] And in another place : " I wasted a good deal of my early life in reverie, and broke the habit only by painful self-conflict. I felt that my powers were running wild, and my religious principles were infinitely important to me in giving me the victory."[2]

These quotations show distinctly that Channing, in early life at least, was far from being free from sentimentalism. Only the first of them, however, contains a reference to anything approaching an attendant spiritual illumination, and even this suggests rather than proves the presence of genuine mysticism. But another experience of Channing, to which we made an earlier allusion,[3] may well have been more truly mystical—we mean the one which came to him after reading Hutcheson. The account we have is not sufficiently detailed to warrant a really confident judgment, but it is clear that it was at least this : an experience of high emotional exaltation attended with what was believed to be a vivid and profound perception of spiritual truth.

It is clear that there was less of the mystical in Theodore Parker than in any of the other leading transcendentalists. Indeed, his active, fact-loving temperament was in not a few respects the exact opposite of that of the mystic. In him there was no tendency—to use the words he himself employed in warning another—to " dwell amid the sentimental flowers of religion, charmed by their loveliness and half bewildered by their perfume." But he did have, what we have said these men possessed in common, a highly emotional nature, and

[1] *Ibid.,* 58.
[2] *Ibid.,* 59.
[3] P. 45.

confidence in the validity of spiritual intuitions; and his belief in the possibility of the soul's immediate communion with God yields to that of few mystics in sincerity and fervor, as his prayers are in themselves enough to show.

There can be no doubt of the existence of genuine mysticism in Emerson's nature. A number of passages in his essays are plain attempts to convey something of the ineffableness of experiences he has undergone, and the very way in which he refers to mysticism reveals that the sentences were written by a man who had himself known states of the same general sort. "Ineffable is the union of man and God in every act of the soul. The simplest person, who in his integrity worships God, becomes God; yet for ever and ever the influx of this better and universal self is new and unsearchable. It inspires awe and astonishment." Passages like this are of far from infrequent occurrence in Emerson's writings.

In our discussion of his reading—of his interest in the Orientals, the Neo-Platonists, Boehme, and Swedenborg—his deep mystical sympathies have been already to some extent set forth. It is especially in the essay on *The Over Soul,* also in certain passages in *Nature,* in the address on *The Method of Nature,* and in some of the poems, that Emerson's capacity for ecstacy and his praise of it as "the law and cause of nature"[1] are manifested; and a very marked and undeniable capacity it is. In the essay on *Books,* after his enumeration of the great bibles of the world, he characterizes them as "majestic expressions of the universal conscience . . . more to our daily purpose than this year's almanac or this day's newspaper. . . . they are for the closet, and to be read on the bended knee. Their communications are not to be given or taken with the lips and the end of the tongue, but out of the glow of the cheek, and with the throbbing heart." But none of his writings show his kindred feeling for this "Infinitude of the Asiatic Soul" more completely than the little poem *Brahma.*[2]

[1] *Works,* i, 204.
[2] See p. 73.

The essay on *Swedenborg, or the Mystic* gives perhaps the best idea of Emerson's own views on mysticism :[1]

" All religious history contains traces of the trances of saints—a beatitude, but without any sign of joy ; earnest, solitary, even sad ; . . . The trances of Socrates, Plotinus, Porphyry, Behmen, Bunyan, Fox, Pascal, Guyon, Swedenborg, will readily come to mind. But what as readily comes to mind is the accompaniment of disease. This beatitude comes in terror, and with shocks to the mind of the receiver.

' It o'er informs the tenement of clay,'

and drives the man mad ; or gives a certain violent bias which taints his judgment. In the chief examples of religious illumination somewhat morbid has mingled, in spite of the unquestionable increase of mental power."[2]

These various passages reveal that Emerson had a deep sympathy with this class of writers, and that his own nature was, to say the least, deeply tinged with the mystical. They show too that he felt that these things held a danger within them. There is no evidence that he himself ever experienced any extreme degree of mystical ecstacy, but to show how far he was capable of carrying, not the rapturous, but the purely contemplative mood, an entry in his Journal for November 9, 1841, may be quoted :

" I read little, I write little. I seek, but with only my usual gipsy diligence, to drive my loitering troops metaphysical into phalanx, into line, into section ; . . . Gray clouds, short days, moonless nights, a drowsy sense of being dragged easily somewhere by that locomotive Destiny, which, never seen, we yet know must be hitched on to the cars wherein we sit—that is all that appears in these November weeks. Let us hope that, as often as we have defamed days which turned out to be benefactors, and were whispering oracles in the very droning nurses' lullabies which soothed us to sleep, so this may prove a profitable time."[3]

[1] See also *Works,* iii, 37 ; viii, 250.
[2] *Ibid.,* iv, 95.
[3] Cabot, 468.

The presence of Professor James' "mark" of "passivity," the abeyance of the individual will, is conspicuous here.

The emotional element in Margaret Fuller's nature was excessive. In the account of her early life we see her intense capacity for feeling. In the story of her school days at Groton in the romance *Mariana*,[1] Mariana represents Margaret herself;[2] and in some of the incidents of the tale we catch glimpses of the high-strung nature of the girl, as, for instance, where Mariana goes into convulsions as the result of a practical joke, or again where, discovered in falsehood and unable to defend herself, she "threw herself down with all her force against the iron hearth, on which a fire was burning, and was taken up senseless." But, although much of the over-emotional tendency of Miss Fuller—as in the case of Channing's early life—must be called mere sentimentalism, it is clear that there was genuine mysticism in it too. At least once in her life, Thanksgiving Day, 1831, she had an experience which seems to have approached the "union" of the Neo-Platonists and old mystics. Her description—far too long to quote in full—leaves no possible doubt as to the nature of this experience. We select merely two sentences: "I was for that hour taken up into God. In that true ray most of the relations of earth seemed mere films, phenomena."[3] From this hour she dates—and apparently with truth—a radical change in her own character. Another experience in 1840[4] appears to have been somewhat similar.[5]

In hardly anything she has left is the intensity of the emotional side of Miss Fuller's nature so completely embodied as in a letter addressed to Beethoven,[6] written after an evening at the Boston Academy of Music. One must read it all to obtain the real effect, but even a few lines show how in the

[1] Included in *Summer on the Lakes*.

[2] Higginson, 198.

[3] *Memoirs*, i, 141; a longer passage from her description is quoted below, p. 136.

[4] *Ibid.*, 308.

[5] See on this whole subject, *Ibid.*, ii, 94.

[6] *Ibid.*, i, 232.

pure emotion of music she found the truest utterance of this
" ineffable " element within her :

" Thou art to me beyond compare, for thou art all I want.
No heavenly sweetness of saint or martyr, no many-leaved
Raphael, no golden Plato, is anything to me, compared with
thee. The infinite Shakespeare, the stern Angelo, Dante,—
bitter sweet like thee,—are no longer seen in thy presence.
And, beside these names, there are none that could vibrate in
thy crystal sphere. Thou hast all of them, and that ample
surge of life besides, that great winged being which they only
dreamed of."

It is to be noticed that, especially as she grew older, she
recognized the danger of this high emotionalism, regretted it,
and struggled consciously and bravely against it :

" . . . the thoughts I had, with the swell of their religion,
kept me awake all night, and thus I was unfit to meet a very
fatiguing day, and last night, tired and with headache, could
not write. Thus it so often is. Feeling keeps from doing
what should show it."[1]

" I am in danger of giving myself up to experiences till
they so steep me in ideal passion that the desired goal is forgotten in the rich present. Yet I think I am learning how
to use life more wisely."[2]

Highly as the ecstatic temperament was developed in Margaret Fuller, it is Bronson Alcott who remains the true representative of mysticism among the leading transcendentalists.
He it was who had read most deeply in the ancient and modern mystics, and who had openly embraced their peculiar form
of transcendental philosophy. His experiences show all the
marks of genuine mysticism.

Mr. Harris gives an account of Alcott's trances ; surely none
of the other leading transcendentalists was capable of anything approaching this :

" I think Mr. Alcott has not preserved in written form the

[1] *Love Letters of Margaret Fuller,* letter xxiii. This whole book is an
excellent revelation of her emotional nature.
[2] *Memoirs,* ii, 94.

10

insights which he had at the time of his illumination. As he intimated to me, that period was one of such long-continued exaltation that his bodily strength gave way under it; and his visions of truth came to have mingled with them spectres which he perceived to be due to physical exhaustion. He saw the entire world as one vast spinal column. . . . He told me that when he had become almost deranged in his mind through this long-continued period of exaltation and insight into the spine as the type of all nature, and when he had begun to see spectres, his wife ' packed him up and sent him down to visit Mr. Emerson.' I therefore conceive this insight into the symbolic significance of the spine to be directly connected with his studies in Swedenborg."[1]

After this, it may seem that nothing can remain to be said, and surely nothing does—toward proving Alcott's mysticism. The world will not weep at his failure to record his insights concerning the spine. But it is easy to carry the inference too far, to suppose that all Alcott said or wrote was the product of similar excessively exalted states, tainted therefore with a sort of insanity, and worthless. This was not the case; and furthermore it does not dispose of a belief merely to call it mystical—as works like that of Professor James amply demonstrate.

The readiness with which not a few critics of transcendentalism have adopted practically this attitude of supposing that the slightest tinge of mysticism is sufficient to reduce a man or a belief to the realm of the ridiculous justifies a word in general on this point.

That element in human nature which the word " mystical " hints at, but only partially conveys, is one that even the life around us in a practical age proves we cannot neglect. Much more does the history of philosophy and religion and the whole voice of the East proclaim this truth. If we wish to be narrowly occidental, we may content ourselves with laughing at these things, but has that man the right to judge such utterances as Alcott's *Orphic Sayings* who comes to the task openly priding himself on the fact that his nature has never been

---

[1] Sanborn, 556.

stained with such illusions? Let us admit that these *Sayings*
are just as unsuited to the needs of the everyday American
world as they have been considered; that there is reason for
much of the ridicule that has been heaped upon them. But let
us not declare, as has been so often done, that no one ever
understood them, probably not even Alcott himself. For anyone who has not at least in some degree appreciated Neo-
Platonism and the "lapse" explanation of evil and finite
things, almost all of the *Orphic Sayings* are nonsense; but let
one gain even a momentary insight into this philosophy, and
nearly all of them become intelligible, and not a few much
more than that.

Let us take a single example. The following may be the
work of a mystic, but surely it is not mere fancy to see in its
latter sentences the doctrine of the Unmoved Mover of as
empirical a philosopher as Aristotle:

"XLIII. Genesis.—The popular genesis is historical. It
is written to sense, not to the soul. Two principles, diverse
and alien, interchange the Godhead, and sway the world by
turns. God is dual. Spirit is derivative. Identity halts in
diversity. Unity is actual merely. The poles of things are
not integrated: creation globed and orbed. Yet in the true
genesis, nature is globed in the material, souls orbed in the
spiritual firmament. Love globes, wisdom orbs, all things.
As magnet the steel, so spirit attracts matter, which trembles
to transverse the poles of diversity, and rest in the bosom of
unity. All genesis is of love. Wisdom is her form; beauty
her costume."[1]

Whether one agrees or disagrees with the thought of this
saying, one can hardly fail to smile; and this suggests that we
have here another case of what we noticed at the beginning
of the chapter, and that what provokes the mirth may lie less
in the thought than the expression.

It is clear, then, as we look back, that mystical elements
appear fairly conspicuously in the transcendentalists. With
Parker alone we may hesitate to connect the term—even

[1] *Dial*, i, 96.

though we remember the sincerity and fervor with which he believed in spiritual intuition and in the soul's immediate communion with God in the act of prayer. In Channing a proneness toward reverie was marked—especially in youth. It was largely mingled then with mere sentimentalism, but verged at times probably on the truly mystical. In Emerson this element was considerable, but in him it consisted especially in an intellectual sympathy with the mystical philosophers, and more in a tendency to excess of contemplation than to rapture. Margaret Fuller's nature was through and through ecstatic, and she experienced states of mystical illumination; but with her too, as with Channing, this element especially in youth was blended with a more ordinary sentimentalism. Alcott went further even than Miss Fuller, and among those under discussion is the extreme type of transcendental mysticism, in whom the temperament seems once, at the very least, to have induced a state closely verging on the pathological. It should not fail to be remarked that in the cases of Channing and Miss Fuller certain of these experiences appear to have been intimately connected with critical moments in their moral development.

But all the evidence bearing on this subject has not yet been presented. It has been deemed best to consider part of it under another heading, and the relation to mysticism and especially to the "noetic" quality of mysticism of what is now to be said of "transcendental and prophetic pride" cannot fail to be easily perceived.

III

How far were the transcendentalists guilty of intellectual self-sufficiency? How far was their individualism so aggressive as to arouse a natural antagonism?

The belief of these men in the immanence of divinity in humanity gave rise to a sense of "the sufficiency of man for all his functions" and consequently to a doctrine of self-reliance. This philosophy perhaps, or perhaps even more the kind of character on which it was grafted (the implied question we may waive at present), resulted in a certain quality which, though its manifestation in different natures varied greatly, was so fundamentally the same in all that we may almost be justified in calling it "transcendental pride." (Perhaps "pride" is an unsatisfactory word, but there seems to be no better.) These men all believed—and believed with high sincerity—that more than in anything else the amelioration of mankind lay in its gaining their own philosophical attitude toward the world and then in its carrying over that attitude into religion and life. Was it not natural, therefore, that they should have become imbued, just as they did, with a conviction of their important, in some cases almost prophetic mission to the world? Yet concerning the genuine and fundamental modesty of three of those whom we are treating, Channing, Emerson and Parker, there can certainly be nothing but agreement.

It would be superfluous to call to mind the almost painful self-effacement of Channing which, in his youth, was carried so far as seriously to undermine his health. Of his whole life in this respect the remark of his brother may stand as typical: "Never did I know him to be guilty of a selfish act, and he shrank from any mention of his incessant kindness, as if the least allusion to it gave him pain."[1] Yet in spite of his humility, Channing had a deep-rooted self-respect and self-reliance, flowing from his "one sublime idea," an idea summed up in the words, "I have no fear of expressing too strongly the connection between the divine and the human mind."[2] "Never suffer your opinions to be treated with scorn in social intercourse, any more than you would your characters; . . . Always feel yourself standing on the ground of equality with every sect and party, and countenance none by your tameness, or by shrinking from your convictions, to assume toward you a tone of dictation, superiority, or scorn. . . . One of the great lessons taught me by experience is, that self-respect, founded, not on outward distinction, but on the essential power and rights of human nature, is the guardian of virtue, and itself among the chief of virtues."[3]

[1] Channing, 111.
[2] *Works*, 295 (ed. 1877).
[3] Channing, 423; see *Works*, v, 313.

But another passage will come much nearer an explanation of what were the grounds of Channing's self-reliance, and of what, we cannot but believe, he considered his own mission in life. The spirit and thought of these words underlie a large number of his utterances:

" No man can be just to himself—can comprehend his own existence, can put forth all his powers with an heroic confidence, can deserve to be the guide and inspirer of other minds—till he has risen to communion with the Supreme Mind; till he feels his filial connection with the Universal Parent; till he regards himself as the recipient and minister of the Infinite Spirit; till he feels his consecration to the ends which religion unfolds; till he rises above human opinion, and is moved by a higher impulse than fame."[1]

On Emerson's modesty again it is unnecessary to linger; the evidence and the witnesses agree in declaring that he was, what Matthew Arnold called him, the " most modest and least self-flattering of men." " Do not charge me with egotism and presumption," writes Emerson in his Journal (1837), " I see with awe the attributes of the farmers and villagers whom you despise."[2] He was the last man, too, to try to force his opinion on another. Yet he was the author of the essay on *Self Reliance,* the preacher of individualism, and often wrote in a style of Delphic finality, which, impersonal as it was, if we did not know the man outside his essays, might lead us to think that he was sublimely self-sufficient. " For no man," he once declared, " can write anything who does not think that what he writes is for the time the history of the world."[3] It would be idle to contend that he who could enter the following in his Journal did not feel the importance—many will be inclined to say the exaggerated importance—of his mission to the world: "I have . . . slaves to free, . . . imprisoned spirits, imprisoned thoughts . . . which, important to the republic of man, have no watchman or lover or defender but I [*sic*] ;"[4] though on the other hand it should be remembered

[1] *Ibid.,* 136 (ed. 1877).
[2] *Emerson in Concord,* 98.
[3] *Works,* iii, 181 ; see also *Ibid.,* 180.
[4] *Emerson in Concord,* 78.

that Emerson had too keen a sense of humor to be unconscious of the misunderstanding and ridicule to which his own
prophetic role must necessarily subject him: " Empedocles
undoubtedly spoke a truth of thought, when he said, ' I am
God '; but the moment it was out of his mouth it became a
lie to the ear; and the world revenged itself for the seeming
arrogance by the good story about his shoe. How can I hope
for better hap in my attempts to enunciate spiritual facts? "[1]

Parker, though he was a veritable warrior in his aggressive-
ness, unafraid of any opposition, " our Savonarola " as Emerson called him, had a beautiful simplicity and humility of
character which it would be hard to overstate. In the pulpit
he could thunder against whole communities, but below the
pulpit he could go away in tears when a single man called him
" impious." Possibly in none of the transcendentalists was a
more active self-confidence united with a truer simplicity and
modesty. Yet even in Parker's case pride is surely not too
strong a word to describe the spirit with which he stated and
upheld his radical intellectual and religious views; and it is
clear that *his* self-confidence too rested on a belief in the divine
origin of his ideas.

So far there can be only agreement; but when we come to
the discussion of this element in Margaret Fuller and Alcott
difference of opinion is sure to appear.

Margaret Fuller has been considered by many not only one
of the proudest, but one of the vainest women that ever lived.
That her nature was proud, even haughty—if anyone had
any motive for denying it—it would be useless to deny.[2] She
had a queenliness of bearing amounting almost to imperious-
ness. She seemed conscious of her intellectual superiority.[3]
There are in her own utterances on this subject such confusion
and even absolute contradiction that one is led to suspect some

---

[1] *Works*, i, 190.

[2] *Memoirs*, i, 234, and ii, 110; Higginson, 303.

[3] Yet her admission, already quoted, of inability to understand a popular
work of Fichte is not indicative of the intellectual braggart; neither are her
fears of incapacity on undertaking the biography of Goethe, nor the reverence with which she approached the *Novum Organum*.

subtlety of character that has at first escaped him; for each of her apparently most egotistical remarks can be matched by one of well-nigh as striking and quite as sincere humility. Emerson is authority for the statement that Miss Fuller made this declaration, " I now know all the people worth knowing in America, and I find no intellect comparable to my own."[1] Place beside this interesting claim the following (1840), and which are we to believe?—". . . since I have had leisure to look at myself, I find that, so far from being an original genius, I have not yet learned to think to any depth, and that the utmost I have done in life has been to form my character to a certain consistency, cultivate my tastes, and learn to tell the truth with a little better grace than I did at first."[2]

The difficulty is partly, not wholly, cleared away when we remember that a distinct change is observable between the early and the late periods of Margaret Fuller's life. In a " credo " embodied in a letter written at nineteen she declares, " I believe in Eternal Progression. I believe in a God, a Beauty and Perfection to which I am to strive all my life for assimilation. From these two articles of belief, I draw the rules by which I strive to regulate my life." But in the same letter we find the avowal, " My pride is superior to any feelings I have yet experienced: my affection is strong admiration, not the necessity of giving or receiving assistance or sympathy."[3] Only a year or two later, on Thanksgiving Day, 1831, Margaret Fuller had that experience (already referred to) which seems to have been a critical hour in her spiritual development, and which, though giving utterance to an essentially unchanged belief, uttered it this time with humility rather than with pride. The whole account as given in the *Memoirs* should be read.[4] Suffice it here to say that for fear of displeasing her father she had attended church against her will. There the joyful nature of the services had jarred upon her own gloomy feelings, and wounded by what she

[1] *Memoirs*, i, 234. Emerson quotes this as a perfectly serious statement on Miss Fuller's part.
[2] *Ibid.*, ii, 26.
[3] *Ibid.*, i, 136.
[4] *Ibid.*, 139.

believed to be the world's failure to recognize her worth, she walked alone far out over the fields, and, after a period of struggle and anguish, under the influence of nature fought her way back to serenity. " I saw there was no self; that selfishness was all folly, and the result of circumstance; that it was only because I thought self real that I suffered; that I had only to live in the idea of the All, and all was mine. . . . My earthly pain at not being recognized never went deep after that hour. . . . Since that day, I have never more been completely engaged in self; but the statue has been emerging, though slowly, from the block. Others may not see the promise even of its pure symmetry, but I do, and am learning to be patient. I shall be all human yet; and then the hour will come to leave humanity, and live always in the pure ray."[1] There is evidence that there is truth in these words, and the years of Margaret Fuller's life, as one follows another, show her increasing humility and humanity. She is always conscious, however, of the inherent pride of her nature, and over and over we find her striving to overcome it: " It is I, who by flattering myself and letting others flatter me that I must ever act nobly and nobler than others, have forgot that pure humility which is our only safeguard. I have let self-love, pride and distrust creep upon me and mingle with my life-blood."[2] " I am ' too fiery ' . . . I never promised any one patience or gentleness, for those beautiful traits are not natural to me; but I would learn them. Can I not? "[3] The change in her own nature which Margaret Fuller, by sheer power of will, effected, is the most admirable aspect of her life; but even this can be looked on as only a partial explanation of the paradox of her pride and humility.

Quotations showing these two qualities could be multiplied almost indefinitely, but the few already given are enough to show at least one thing, her astonishing frankness of utterance. Concerning the fundamental truthfulness of her nature all her biographers are agreed, but it remained for Mr. Higginson to point out that this in itself serves in large measure to ex-

[1] *Ibid.,* 141 (from a journal).
[2] *Love Letters of Margaret Fuller,* letter xx (1845).
[3] *Memoirs,* ii, 96.

plain what was popularly considered her superlative vanity, that Margaret Fuller merely said about herself what other people often think of themselves but do not utter. Toward all things, herself included, she was the inexorable critic.[1] Of this element in her nature Horace Greeley is witness:

"But, one characteristic of her writings I feel bound to commend,—their absolute truthfulness.[2] She never asked how this would sound, nor whether that would do, nor what would be the effect of saying anything; but simply, 'Is it the truth? Is it such as the public should know?' And if her judgment answered 'Yes,' she uttered it; no matter what turmoil it might excite, nor what odium it might draw down on her own head. Perfect conscientiousness was an unfailing characteristic of her literary efforts. Even the severest of her critiques,—that on Longfellow's Poems,—for which an impulse in personal pique has been alleged, I happen with certainty to know had no such origin. When I first handed her the book to review, she excused herself, assigning the wide divergence of her views of poetry from those of the author and his school, as her reason. She thus induced me to attempt the task of reviewing it myself. . . . At length I carried the book back to her in utter despair of ever finding an hour in which even to look through it; and, at my renewed and earnest request, she reluctantly undertook its discussion. The statement of these facts is but an act of justice to her memory."[3]

There can be no question that Margaret Fuller could at times use her tongue sharply and sarcastically, and one can suspect that her victims may have been doubly incensed because her cutting sentences were keenly and truly critical. Doubtless it has been the handing down of anecdotes illustrating this unhappy failing and the transmission of revengeful feelings in the form of unwarranted prejudice that has helped to create that considerably prevalent idea of Miss Fuller which seems to consist of a personification of this single

---

[1] *Ibid.*, i, 128 and 295; ii, 210.
[2] See, on this point, *Ibid.*, 7.
[3] *Ibid.*, 158.

trait. Anything more unjust cannot readily be imagined. Margaret Fuller had the unfortunate combination of a temper and a tendency to utter the truth. But she had not a particle of petty meanness in her nature.

The qualities we have been discussing, together with her almost incredible lack of tact, do their full share in accounting for the disagreeable first impression that we know Miss Fuller frequently made on people. This absence of tact amounted sometimes, in her own phrase, to "childish petulance and bluntness." Mr. Higginson relates a story[1] of how, at some social gathering in Cambridge, when the cake was passed she at first took a piece and then, suddenly replacing it, remarked, " I fear there will not be enough to go round." And Horace Greeley's amusing account[2] of how he tried to offer her advice on the use of tea and coffee illustrates the same point.

But now do these different elements which we have been considering, when combined in the proper proportions, offer a final explanation of the original problem? They can hardly be said to do so. Does not the following—Miss Fuller's conversational brilliancy is well known—come nearer than anything hitherto quoted to showing the fundamental essence of her pride, at least as it appeared during the transcendental period?—

" There is a mortifying sense of having played the Mirabeau after a talk with a circle of intelligent persons. They come with a store of acquired knowledge and reflection, on the subject in debate, about which I may know little, and have reflected less; yet by mere apprehensiveness and prompt intuition, I may appear their superior . . . I should despise myself, if I purposely appeared thus brilliant, but I am inspired as by a power higher than my own."[3]

This is the pride and confidence of the prophet, the true transcendental pride if there be any, quite identical with the Delphic self-assurance of Emerson's essays and the *Orphic*

[1] Higginson, 305.
[2] *Memoirs,* ii, 153.
[3] *Ibid.,* 22.

Sayings of Alcott. Beyond dispute there is in it an element of the ridiculous; beyond dispute it shows some lack of humor; but it is vain to deny it also a certain grandeur. It is no mere posing; it is sincere. So though we may smile we must also ask: Was not Margaret Fuller really more proud of her aspirations[1] than of herself, of the truth she felt speaking through her than of what she actually was? Even prophetic pride may be unlovely enough; but the point is that it is also quite above a crude egotism. It is apparent how easily this woman may have been misinterpreted. We must not minimize any of the unpleasing, overbearing qualities of her nature; but it should be remarked in conclusion that, were there no other arguments to disprove it, the years of her married life, and, for a far longer period, the craving of her heart for human love, could leave against her no final charge of self-sufficiency.

Of Alcott it is more difficult to speak. The facts seem clear, and yet one fears to do injustice to a man so possessed with the sense of his mission to the world. The other transcendentalists took themselves seriously, but none so seriously as Alcott. He lacked completely the sense of humor.[2] He had drunk deep of the cup of "unity," saw the salvation of the world only in his philosophy, and believed in the Platonic conversation as a method of disseminating it. Transcendental and prophetic pride possessed him completely. Writes Emerson to Carlyle:

"He is a great man and was made for what is greatest, but I now fear he has already touched what best he can, and through his more than prophet's egotism, and the absence of all useful reconciling talents, will bring nothing to pass, and be but a voice in the wilderness."[3]

Alcott writes thus in *Concord Days:* "May we not credit New England with giving the country these new Instrumentalities for Progress, viz:—Greeley, the Newspaper; Garrison,

[1] *Ibid.,* i, 312.

[2] See Sanborn, 358, footnote, concerning the caricatures and parodies of the *Dial.*

[3] *Carlyle-Emerson Correspondence,* II, 14.

a free Platform; Phillips, a free Convention; Beecher, a free Pulpit; Emerson, the Lecture? The Conversation awaits being added to the list."[1]

Perhaps the reader is expected to associate no name with this last "instrumentality"; but the association is inevitable, and it seems hard to acquit Alcott of the charge of vanity. In this connection the following complaint of Alcott to Emerson is at once so startling and so illuminating that it leaves little to be said: "You write on the genius of Plato, of Pythagoras, of Jesus; why do you not write of me?"[2] Mere vanity was never responsible for that; for however much vanity we may be disposed to find in it, a more important ingredient was an extreme quality and an excessive quantity of transcendental pride. In a word Alcott was not free from what Mr. Higginson has well called "a certain high souled attitudinizing." The Concord School of Philosophy, which made him the American Plato and brought "plenty of talk to swim in," was the realization of a long-cherished hope. But it will be more charitable and probably at the same time more just to bear in mind what was observed in the case of Margaret Fuller, and when we are disposed to censure, to remember that Alcott was capable of writing such words as these: "Certainly men need teaching badly enough when any words of mine can help them. Yet I would fain believe that not I, but the Spirit, the Person, sometimes speaks to revive and spare."[3]

In all the transcendentalists, then, in varying degrees and kinds, we may observe a common transcendental pride, somewhat of the function of the prophet. All had had what they deemed a spiritual revelation, and all felt called on to preach it to the world. Alcott and Emerson wrote very frequently in the omniscient style; Margaret Fuller, and even Parker and

[1] *Concord Days*, 177.

[2] Sanborn, 543. Orestes A. Brownson is authority (to be accepted with hesitation perhaps under the circumstances) for the statement that Alcott "boasts of being to the nineteenth century what Jesus was to the first." Brownson's *Works*, iv, 420.

[3] Higginson and Boynton, *A Reader's History of American Literature*, 180.

Channing, were not free from a positiveness of utterance sometimes approaching it; while Alcott and Miss Fuller employed
it largely in their "conversations." They all showed, in
widely different ways, somewhat of the feeling that through
them an Absolute Truth greater than themselves was speaking. Now such a feeling when exposed to the world—even
though unaccompanied, as here, with any attempt to force
beliefs on others—was simply bound to call forth ridicule and
bitter opposition.

But we must analyze this matter a little further. It is clear
that we are considering simply an aspect of the self-reliance
and individualism of the transcendentalists, and a word should
be said in this connection concerning the meaning of those
phrases they so frequently employ—"rely on your instincts,"
"trust your intuitions." When Emerson, for instance, declares in the *American Scholar,* "If the single man plant himself indomitably on his instincts, and there abide, the huge
world will come round to him"—why is not such a doctrine,
it may be asked, the very height of lunacy, and the proposal
of it as a moral precept the opening of the very floodgates of
anarchy? Is this not indeed individualism run mad? Perhaps it is. But we should be careful to understand Emerson
before we judge him; and many who have censured this part
of his doctrine most severely, as we observed in our opening
chapter, show they have taken him entirely amiss. They
assume that he uses the word "instinct" in its ordinary sense.
He uses it of course in no such way, but in a way which can
be understood only in the light of his whole philosophy. Suppose he had said "conscience" instead of "instincts" (he
would have meant nothing different in kind, only something
less comprehensive in its application)—then the majority of
mankind would have been willing to assent, for the majority
of mankind believe—however they explain it—in the existence
of some reality corresponding to the former word. But when
Emerson goes further, and makes this inner sense not merely
a guide to conduct, but a diviner of spiritual truth, then the
great majority will not follow, then they say to him, "Your
words are jargon to us; you proclaim a thing that does not

enter our experience." And who can doubt that the great majority, so speaking, tell the truth? The question then for us is not so much, How far is Emerson's position true? as it is rather, How far by resting his beliefs upon an experience that most of mankind does not share, does he show himself thereby impractical? We know what his own answer to that question would have been. But meanwhile for the present we must leave the subject.

IV

One point remains for consideration in this chapter, the charge that the transcendentalists were blind to the facts of sin and evil in the world. A few quotations will make clear what their conceptions on these matters were.

Of the origin of evil Channing says, " I cannot hope to explain what the greatest minds have left obscure. In truth, I do not desire to remove obscurity from Providence. . . . The darkness of God's providence is to me an expression of its *vastness,* its immeasurable grandeur. . . . Of much that is evil in human life I see the cause and the cure. Many forms of human suffering I would not remove, if I could; for I see that we owe to them all the interest and dignity of life. . . . I do not see how sin and suffering can be removed, but by striking out from our nature its chief glories."[1] In his sermon on *The Evil of Sin,*[2] where he considers the question from the moral rather than from the philosophical point of view, he exhibits no tendency to emphasize the negative nature of evil: " I wish to guard you against thinking lightly of sin. No folly is so monstrous." This sermon, however, is not one, in its subject, typical of Channing, and sin and evil in his preaching as a whole are conspicuous by their absence.

Alcott's position is thus embodied:

> "'Evil no *nature* hath: the loss of good
> Is that which gives Sin its livelihood.'

" A check on itself, evil subserves the economies of good, as it were a condiment to give relish to good;" etc.[3]

[1] Channing, 455; see also 629.

[2] *Works,* iv, 151; see also v, 243.

[3] *Table Talk,* 167. See also Sanborn, 190, for a similar view written in his diary in 1835.

Margaret Fuller writes in her "Credo": "Whatever has been permitted by the law of being must be for good, and only in time not good. We trust, and are led forward by experience, . . . The moment we have broken through an obstruction, not accidentally, but by the aid of faith, we begin to interpret the Universe, and to apprehend why evil is permitted. Evil is obstruction; Good is accomplishment."[1]

And Emerson: "Good is positive. Evil is merely privative, not absolute: it is like cold, which is the privation of heat. All evil is so much death or nonentity," etc.[2]

"Sin, seen from the thought, is diminution, or *less;* seen from the conscience or will, it is pravity or *bad.* The intellect names it shade, absence of light, and no essence. The conscience must feel it as essence, essential evil. This it is not; it has an objective existence, but no subjective."[3]

And finally Parker: " . . . in estimating the phenomena of evil, my own faith says there is a perfect system of optimism in the world; that each man's life is to him an infinite good. Of course all his physical evils must be means of progress, all his errors likewise unavoidable steps in his course to happiness. But to legitimate this in the court of the understanding where all other truths are legitimated, I find difficult."[4]

"I think sin makes little mark on the soul; for, 1, much of it is to be referred to causes exterior even to the physical man; and 2, much to the man's organization. I think 99/100 of sin are thus explicable—the result of the man's limitation—A, the result of his circumstances; B, of his organization."[5]

In these brief quotations is exhibited on the whole remarkable unanimity—Channing, as usual, being less radical than the rest. Transcendentalism was a system of unflinching optimism. With this theory a tendency appears in the writ-

[1] *Memoirs,* ii, 289.

[2] *Works,* i, 123, *Divinity School Address,* 1838.

[3] *Ibid.,* iii, 80. See also vi, 241; and Cabot, 354-6. Practically the whole of the essay on *Compensation* is a discussion of this theme.

[4] Weiss, i, 148.

[5] *Ibid.,* 149. See also Parker's sermons on the *Economy of Pain* and the *Economy of Moral Error.*

ings of these men—varying, however, in different cases very greatly—to minimize, to soften, or simply leave out of account the ugly facts of life. In Alcott and Emerson this was most marked. The question of a corresponding neglect in the lives of the transcendentalists is not one for the present portion of our study.

And now, one by one, we have passed in review the counts of the indictment that began our chapter. And, after all, have not the discussions of these various topics been in reality— what we at first suggested that the different charges were themselves—but variations on a single theme? What, it is asked, has that theme been? It has been, we shall not say real mysticism, but surely something closely approaching it in nature. We have already emphasized the impossibility of separating the intellectual and emotional elements of transcendentalism, and this " something " akin to mysticism that has formed the essence of our chapter has ranged, in unbroken continuity, all the way from a genuine mysticism on the one hand to a fervidly felt and mystically related philosophy on the other. To see whether this suggested unity has any real existence, let us review briefly the topics we have taken up.

First we discussed some of the humorous aspects of the movement. And among these, what one, by far, was the most striking? A fantastic and absurd use of figure and symbolism. But a mere glance at the works of the great mystics of the world (of Boehme, for instance, or of Swedenborg) is sufficient to show that something of this sort—not always indeed so crude or so lacking in literary power—comes nearer perhaps than anything else to being the outward mark of mysticism, of the attempt of the seer to convey in words his " ineffable " experience. And what a remarkable confirmation of the contention is lent by the fact that in Alcott, the one unquestioned mystic of the group, this symbolism is most prominent; that in Margaret Fuller and Emerson there is some of it, but less; while in Channing and Parker there is none at all!

Mysticism itself we treated next, and here accordingly no comment is required.

11

Then we considered "transcendental pride"—and found each of these men assuming somewhat of the role of a prophet, speaking with somewhat of the finality of an oracle, exhibiting an unshakeable confidence in the veracity of his insights. Here—as we hinted before—do we not perceive a remarkable resemblance between the revelations of this prophetic spirit and the illuminating, "noetic" quality of mysticism; and has not the assurance with which these intuitions are affirmed a manifest relation to the sense of authority which the visions of the mystic carry with them? Surely it is something more than a coincidence that the intensity with which this prophetic pride appears in each of these persons is almost exactly proportional to his mystical intensity. Alcott and Margaret Fuller, in both cases, head the list; Channing and Parker[1] are at the other end. But one point is worthy of emphasis. The transcendentalists were not content to keep their revelations to themselves; they must publish and preach them from the housetops; and so, though their "pride" be in part the self-assurance of the mystic—already it is hinted—it may be something more.

Finally what of the transcendental attitude toward sin and evil? Has that too a link with mysticism? It has, beyond a doubt; though here, conspicuously, it is difficult to estimate the relative parts played by emotion and intellect in determining belief. An optimistic view of the universe, with a tendency to grant to evil only a relative or negative existence, is not an invariable, but it is a strikingly frequent attendant of the mystical nature,[2] and, it need hardly be added, of idealistic, transcendental philosophies. We have the union here of several forces, making together toward a single end. These men were in a way theologians, and, revolting from Calvinism with its intense and overwhelming conviction of the reality of sin, they went to the other extreme. They were philosophers seeking a principle of unity in the world, and finding it, as

[1] Parker of course exhibited one kind of pride intensely; but we refer especially to this distinctly prophetic pride.

[2] " . . . the mystic range of consciousness . . . *is on the whole pantheistic and optimistic, or at least the opposite of pessimistic.*" James, *The Varieties of Religious Experience,* 422.

they believed, in the ideal, they denied to the enemy of the ideal, essential existence. Lastly, they were men of mystical tendencies, and just as far as their emotional experiences lifted them out of the ordinary world, in so far the facts of that world became illusions and phenomena and their faith in an optimistic order was confirmed.

Even this hurried summary is sufficient, we trust, to show that if we use the term mysticism somewhat elastically, we were right in saying that our chapter has had, essentially, one theme; and as far as we have considered it, the popular charge against the transcendentalists might be said to simmer down, pretty largely, to this: that they were mystics.

And how of this charge, of the question with which we began? The purpose of the chapter, as was said, has been more to understand than to pass judgment. Yet certain conclusions perhaps suggest themselves. Just because our present position is tentative, however, is open to revision, let us put them not as conclusions at all, but mainly in the form of questions.

If it be true, as it surely is, that the very essence of mysticism is an individual and largely incommunicable experience, and if it be true, as again it surely is, that the practical element in human nature always involves some social aspect of man's being, then is not the conclusion inevitable that the very essence of mysticism is something impractical, that it is its very nature to be out of touch with everyday life? Just as far, then, as these transcendentalists were real mystics, just as far as they dwelt in a realm of ineffable and incommunicable experience, were they not in a very real sense "beyond the clouds"? Just as far as their philosophy—whether true or false is not the question—rested on an individual standard and they themselves relied on intuitions which humanity as a whole could neither appreciate nor share, were they not isolated from the world of common men and in so far unable to affect it? Just as far as the intensity of their individualism and the pride of their assurance repelled mankind—whether justly or not is not the question—did they not cut themselves off from effective service? Just as far as their belief in the non-reality of

sin and evil—whether true or false, again, is not the question
—led them to neglect or to gloss over the ugliness of the
world, were they not guilty of " transcending common-sense? "
These, we think, are pertinent inquiries. And everyone of
these men had in him something at least of the practical defi-
ciencies at which they hint. The popular criticism of the
transcendentalists has beyond doubt a basis in real fact.

But all this is unsatisfactory and not final. The vital question has not yet been asked. That question is not, How far
would it seem that these men *must* have been out of touch with
practical life? but rather, How far *were* they out of touch with
it? To attempt to answer this is our next task. But meanwhile what we have already seen is fertile in perplexities.
What is the meaning, we are constrained to ask, of these
struggles of Channing and Margaret Fuller against the mysticism and over-emotionalism of their natures? And this is
but one of the unanswered problems. We feel ourselves on
the verge of a deep contradiction. There is suggested already a paradox, the resolution of which (if such a thing be
possible) will bring us nearer perhaps than anything else to
the heart of what this curiously complex thing, New England
transcendentalism, really was.

CHAPTER IV

THE TRANSCENDENTALISTS AND PRACTICAL LIFE, II

I

William Ellery Channing, we have seen, was by birth of an emotional and contemplative rather than of an active disposition, exhibiting a marked inclination toward reverie and sentimentalism. But the passages quoted to illustrate these tendencies show not less strikingly another thing: that Channing believed this proneness to excess of thought and feeling full of danger and that he struggled manfully to give these inner elements practical expression. And so successfully did he struggle that it would hardly be an exaggeration to affirm that he devoted his whole mature life, both in the large things and in the small, to the service of others. To justify such a statement his brother's tribute to his unselfishness, previously quoted, is in itself almost sufficient. This unselfishness and the desire to *serve,* help not a little in accounting for one of Channing's most conspicuous traits—conservatism. Conservatism is, on the whole, the characteristic that puts him in most marked contrast with the later transcendentalists, with such a man, for instance, as Theodore Parker. Yet conservatism in Channing, strangely enough, seems to illustrate exactly what radicalism is witness to in Theodore Parker —the fundamentally utilitarian, philanthropic, practical spirit of the man. It was this element in the nature of the former that Hazlitt so keenly seized on:

"We never saw anything more guarded in this respect than Dr. Channing's 'Tracts and Sermons'—more completely suspended between heaven and earth. He keeps an eye on both worlds; kisses hands to the reading public all round; and does his best to stand well with different sects and parties. He

149

is always in advance of the line, in an amiable and imposing attitude, but never far from succor."[1]

This is a distortion of the truth. The bare fact may be correct, but there is an unjustifiable insinuation of a deliberately politic motive. Channing desired to serve the world. While he seems to have acted under the conviction that extreme radicalism cannot accomplish the best practical results, there is no evidence that he ever consciously sacrificed truth to utility.

His constantly increasing interest in the practical led him to write and speak very widely on varied topics of political and general public concern, and to have an active share in the agitation of social reforms[2] before the country. His part in the anti-slavery struggle, though his conservatism excited the animosity of the extreme abolitionists, was prominent and influential. To give details in this connection would be merely to summarize or repeat the chapters on that subject in his biographies or that on *The Anti-Slavery Movement in Boston* in Winsor's *Memorial History*. The mere enumeration of some of his acts in this agitation will accordingly be sufficient: his letter of protest against the anti-Garrison meeting in 1835, the publication of his *Slavery* in the same year, his open letter *The Abolitionists* to James G. Burney (1836), another open letter to Henry Clay on the *Annexation of Texas,* his prominent part in the demonstration after the murder of Lovejoy in 1837, and from this time till his death in 1842, various letters, essays, and addresses. Throughout, though he always displayed intellectual cautiousness and deliberation, there was never evidence of moral cowardice. The following from Samuel J. May, an abolitionist, and at one time among Channing's severest critics, is sufficient testimony to the boldness and heroism of Channing's attitude:

" We look back with no little admiration on one who, enjoying as he did, in the utmost serenity, the highest reputation as a writer and as a divine, put at hazard the repose of the rest of his life, and sacrificed hundreds of the admirers

---

[1] Chadwick, 203.

[2] Chadwick, chapter ix.

of his genius, eloquence, and piety, by espousing the cause of the oppressed, which most of the eminent men of the land would not touch with one of their fingers."[1]

Channing's part in the anti-slavery cause is an illustration of only one of numerous similar interests in matters of public concern. Prison discipline, temperance, pauperism, child labor, the condition of the working classes, educational questions[2] of a wide variety, these and many others received his attention and enlisted his sympathies, so that his name, not merely in this country but in Europe, came to be associated with many other than purely theological matters.[3] By not a few he was looked on as the apostle of freedom in the widest sense. The fact that Hazlitt and Brougham deemed him worthy of notice in the *Edinburgh Review* shows how much more than most Americans he had attracted attention abroad. In France, articles on Channing appeared in the *Journal des Débats* and many of his works were translated into French. Renan's essay on Channing in his *Études d'Histoire Religieuse* may be summed up in these words: " His theology . . . lays itself open to very easy attack; but his ethics may be praised without reserve."[4] Renan deprecated Channing's failure to adjust his theology to the most recent criticism, but he paid a high tribute to the worth and inspiring influence of his character.

To repeat, then, Channing became a man of action in spite of, not because of, his native disposition. As Alcott wrote of him in his diary, " His heart has sympathized more deeply with his race than often happens to the philosophic genius."[5] On the whole, especially when we bear in mind that he was a clergyman and hence quite properly interested first in religious matters, we may say that, so far from being out of relation to

---

[1] Chadwick, 276, note.

[2] Concerning his relations with Horace Mann, see Miss Peabody, *Reminiscences,* chapter xxiv.

[3] On Channing's reputation abroad, see *Life, Letters and Journals of George Ticknor,* i, 479.

[4] " Sa théologie . . . est très-facilement attaquable ; quant à sa morale, on peut la louer sans réserve."

[5] Sanborn, 168.

the world of cold facts about him, he was conspicuous for the breadth and practical character of his interests.

II

Bronson Alcott's relation to the practical world may best be considered perhaps in connection with certain characteristic events of his life.

For nearly fifteen years after his return from the South, Alcott devoted himself in the main to school-teaching. On the one hand his spirit was progressive and he made many admirable reforms, but on the other his theories were so radical as to arouse inevitable antagonism in the various communities where he taught and seriously to interfere with the practical success of his methods. What some of those methods were a glance at the last and most famous of his schools will show. This, the Temple School on Tremont street, Boston, opened most auspiciously, in September 1834, with thirty pupils. Miss Elizabeth Peabody, who later gave an account of this enterprise in her *Record of a School,* was Alcott's assistant; and Margaret Fuller too was connected with it for a time.

Alcott's fundamental educational theory was Platonic—and he certainly exhibited an astonishing consistency in carrying into practice his most radical philosophical ideas. He believed in the plenary inspiration of childhood. Emerson recorded in his Journal (1838) Alcott's contention that "from a circle of twenty well-selected children he could draw in their conversation everything that is in Plato."[1] The function of the teacher, as he saw it, was merely to touch this potentiality into life, to preserve the child's native divinity by striving to keep off the weight of custom and the inevitable yoke. His school was indeed an attempt to realize in practice the thought of Wordsworth's *Ode on the Intimations of Immortality.*[2] The fact that Alcott put in print some of these conversations with his school-children is proof, doubtless, of his courage and

[1] *Ibid.,* 185.
[2] He knew this ode well, and paraphrased it in his diary, 1834 (*Ibid.,* 199), and elsewhere.

deep faith in his own theories; but it is not less an indication
of deficient practical insight. These published conversations
are, from certain points of view, highly interesting reading;
but unfortunately some persons—wholly aside from any dis-
belief in pre-existence—may be inclined to discover in the
precocious answers of the pupils at least as much evidence
that A. Bronson Alcott was their teacher as that they had
spent their ante-terrestrial days in sporting upon the shore of
the immortal sea. The utterances of young Josiah—already
quoted—on clay and spirit and the death of babies, may possibly be deemed sufficient warrant for this view.

Miss Peabody, who was a transcendentalist herself, and in
agreement with Alcott's theories in many respects, believed
that he pushed them too far. Her criticism is doubly valuable: " I think you are liable to injure the modesty and uncon-
sciousness of good children by making them reflect too much
on their actual superiority to others." And she adds, bringing out a trait of Alcott's character, " I do not suppose you
will ever change your mind thro' the influence of another."[1]
Margaret Fuller criticized him adversely, also, putting in his
mouth the ironical exclamation: " O for the safe and natural
way of Intuition! I cannot grope like a mole in the gloomy
passages of experience."[2]

As time went on, various causes, mainly the opposition created by the publication of *Conversations with Children on the
Gospels,* contributed to impair the prosperity of his school,
and Alcott was plunged in financial embarrassments. He
writes in his diary these revealing words:

" I am involved in debt, arising from the unsuccessful issue
of previous experiments in human culture. What I earn is
all pledged by obligations to others, and I have already anticipated the earnings of the next two or three years, even should
I be successful. And so the claims of my family are to be
set aside for the claims of others. . . . Yet will I go on; great
results are to spring from the little seed that I shall sow."[3]

[1] *Ibid.,* 188.
[2] *Memoirs,* i, 171.
[3] Sanborn, 205.

His school struggled on, and the incident which ultimately caused its closing is as significant, in a very different way, as the quotation just given. In 1838 he received a colored child into his school. The parents of his pupils, with one exception, protested, and when Alcott refused to dismiss the negro girl, withdrew their own children. It was about this time that Mrs. Alcott wrote in a letter: " You have seen how roughly they have handled my husband. He has been a quiet sufferer, but not the less a sufferer because quiet. He stands to it, through all, that this is not an ungrateful, cruel world. I rail; he reasons, and consoles me as if I were the injured one. I do not know a more exemplary hero under trials than this same ' visionary.' He has more philosophy than half the persons who are afraid he is thinking too much."[1]

After the failure of his school, Alcott first ventured a trial of his scheme of public conversations. In these years, too, he showed an interest in many of the reform movements of the day, the temperance cause, woman's rights, the anti-slavery struggle. Though here again his part was mainly speculative, it was not wholly so. His connection with the famous Burns affair shows the moral and physical courage of which he was capable, and although this incident did not occur till some years later (1854), we may quote here a few sentences from Mr. Higginson's description. An attack on the court house, where Burns, the fugitive slave, was confined, had been repulsed, owing to the failure of the crowd to give assistance to the handful of abolitionists who led it.

" Meanwhile the deputy marshals retreated to the stairway, over which we could see their pistols pointing, the whole hall between us and them being brightly lighted. . . . Then followed one of the most picturesque incidents of the whole affair. In the silent pause that ensued there came quietly forth from the crowd the well-known form of Mr. Amos Bronson Alcott, the Transcendental philosopher. Ascending the lighted steps alone, he said tranquilly, turning to me and pointing forward, ' Why are we not within?' ' Because,' was the rather impatient answer, ' these people will not stand by us.'

[1] *Ibid.*, 231.

He said not a word, but calmly walked up the steps—he and
his familiar cane. He paused again at the top, the centre of all
eyes, within and without; a revolver sounded from within, but
hit nobody; and finding himself wholly unsupported, he turned
and retreated, but without hastening a step. It seemed to me
that, under the circumstances, neither Plato nor Pythagoras
could have done the thing better; and the whole scene brought
vividly back the similar appearance of the Gray Champion in
Hawthorne's tale."[1]

In 1840 the Alcotts moved to Concord. There were three
daughters then and a fourth was born during this year. In
Concord for a time Alcott made a brave effort to stick to farm
work and support his family; but his interest in the thought-
currents of the day was too strong, and he again began holding conversations and giving lectures. His knowledge of reform and reformers in England meanwhile was increasing,
and through the efforts of Emerson he was enabled, sailing in
1842, to spend most of a year in England. He came back
enthusiastic with new schemes for the application of radical
thought. During his stay in England he had met Carlyle, and
the latter's description of him, though it has often been quoted,
should be given again:

" The good Alcott: with his long, lean face and figure, with
his gray worn temples and mild radiant eyes; all bent on sav-
ing the world by a return to acorns and the golden age; he
comes before one like a kind of venerable Don Quixote, whom
nobody can even laugh at without loving!"[2]

In 1843 Alcott and his family (though Mrs. Alcott's heart
was not in the affair) moved out to a farm in the town of
Harvard, Massachusetts, about twenty miles from Concord,
where, with several " revolting friends," they instituted the
small community known as Fruitlands. The nature of the
experiment was thus proclaimed in the *Dial* by Alcott and his
English friend Lane:

" We have made an arrangement with the proprietor of an

---

[1] *Cheerful Yesterdays,* 157. Parker, too, had an active share in the Burns
incident. See the account in Frothingham's Parker, 425.

[2] *Carlyle-Emerson Correspondence,* ii, 8.

estate of about a hundred acres, which liberates this tract from human ownership. . . . Here we prosecute our effort to initiate a family in harmony with the primitive instincts in man. . . . The inner nature of every member of the family is at no time neglected. . . . Pledged to the spirit alone, the founders can anticipate no hasty or numerous accession to their numbers."[1]

This last indicates wherein the Fruitlands differed from the Brook Farm experiment. It was individualistic, not collectivistic. It was therein far more truly transcendental.

The community was strictly vegetarian; even milk and eggs were tabooed. Water was the only beverage. The "aspiring" vegetables, those which grow into the air like the fruits, were allowed, but the baser ones, like potatoes and beets, which grow downward, were forbidden. When cold weather came, the experiment had proved itself, materially at least, a complete failure. This was too much for Alcott. He lost his accustomed serenity, turned his face to the wall, and giving way to grief, refused to be comforted. For a while he seemed to want only to die. But he had a brave wife, and eventually he was brought to his senses and made to accept his fate.[2]

After a short stay at Still River, the Alcotts returned to Concord. Here they struggled against poverty, and it would appear that Mrs. Alcott did as much as her husband (probably more than he) toward supporting the family. A little money left her at the death of her father, together with five hundred dollars from Emerson, had enabled them to purchase a house, but there was not enough to supply their other wants, and when in 1848 they removed to Boston it was apparently mainly because Mrs. Alcott thereby found employment that contributed materially to the support of the family. She became a visitor among the poor for various benevolent societies and later she kept an intelligence office. Mrs. Alcott afterward declared: " I have labored, hand and brain, for the support of my family. The conditions of our life have been com-

---

[1] *Dial*, June, 1843.

[2] See, for a realistic account of this experiment, in the form of a story, Miss Alcott's *Transcendental Wild Oats*, included in her *Silver Pitchers*.

plicated, and difficult to understand; but we have submitted to no mean subterfuge, no ignoble surrender."[1]

During this time, Alcott was holding conversations, and had considerable spiritual but little financial success. He tried his luck in the West. The following entry in Miss Alcott's diary gives us a living glimpse into the " pathetic family "—and it is worthy of remark that the events recorded occurred in the very year of the Burns affair:

" 1854.—Pinckney Street.—I have neglected my journal for months, so must write it up. School for me month after month. Mother busy with boarders and sewing. Father doing as well as a philosopher can in a money-loving world. Anna at S.

" I earned a good deal by sewing in the evening when my day's work was done.

" In February Father came home. Paid his way, but no more. A dramatic scene when he arrived in the night. We were waked by hearing the bell. Mother flew down, crying ' My husband!' We rushed after, and five white figures embraced the half-frozen wanderer who came in hungry, tired, cold, and disappointed, but smiling bravely and as serene as ever. We fed and warmed and brooded over him, longing to ask if he had made any money; but no one did till little May said, after he had told all the pleasant things, ' Well, did people pay you?' Then, with a queer look, he opened his pocketbook and showed one dollar, saying with a smile that made our eyes fill, ' Only that! My overcoat was stolen, and I had to buy a shawl. Many promises were not kept, and travelling is costly; but I have opened the way, and another year shall do better.'

" I shall never forget how beautifully Mother answered him, though the dear, hopeful soul had built much on his success; but with a beaming face she kissed him, saying, ' I call that doing *very well*. Since you are safely home, dear, we don't ask anything more.'

" Anna and I choked down our tears, and took a little lesson in real love which we never forgot, nor the look that the

[1] Sanborn, 309.

tired man and the tender woman gave one another. It was half tragic and comic, for Father was very dirty and sleepy, and Mother in a big nightcap and funny old jacket."[1]

This is a typical picture of the struggle, which, we must believe, the Alcotts carried on against poverty, until eventually Louisa Alcott, gaining literary renown and at the same time fulfilling her youthful ambition to bring relief to her parents, freed them from financial embarrassment. Even Alcott's own increased material success in his later conversations must be attributed in good measure to his daughter's popularity. Over these later years of Alcott's life we need not linger—years that brought the Concord School of Philosophy and with it (to use Miss Alcott's words) "plenty of talk to swim in" and the realization of his long-cherished dream to see himself the American Plato surrounded by a group of admiring disciples.

The simple fact of the case then is—Alcott could not support his family. Others, indeed, supported him; and we cannot help wondering what would have become of him without his staunch friend Emerson, or, still more, without his devoted and talented daughter and his heroic wife. At the very time when Alcott was entering in his Journal, "All day discussing the endless infinite themes,"[2] Mrs. Alcott was doing the endless finite chores. Long afterward when the venerable Dr. McCosh asked Louisa Alcott her definition of a philosopher, it was from her own experience that she spoke when she made the prompt reply: "My definition is of a man up in a balloon, with his family and friends holding the ropes which confine him to earth and trying to haul him down."[3]

Such was Alcott. It is plain that, unconscious as he may have been of it, he was selfish. Nor is it hard to see how it came about. He was—we may almost say—a man of one idea. He saw the unity, not the diversity, of the world; and

[1] Cheney, 69.
[2] Sanborn, 455.
[3] Cheney, 315.

his one idea both blinded[1] him to much of the life around him and exaggerated the sense of his own importance. He saw in it a universal cure for the sins and failures of mankind, and longing to give his whole time to this great theme, how could he do otherwise than chafe under the petty labor after bread?

The diary of Miss Alcott, kept during the Fruitlands experiment (she was then ten years old), which reveals incidentally the pathetic self-consciousness that her father had engendered in her innocent mind, contains a phrase which one is tempted, perhaps maliciously, to turn against Alcott. Here is the entry: "Had good dreams, and woke now and then to think, and watch the moon. I had a pleasant time with my mind."[2] Is not this a description of what her father had too? Such a statement unqualified, to be sure, would be but a half truth, but it is nevertheless a fact that Alcott was too easily tempted to do just this—have a pleasant time with his mind. Thoreau recognized it when he wrote to Emerson (1847): "Mr. Alcott seems to have sat down for the winter. He has got Plato and other books to read. . . . If he would only stand upright and toe the line!—though he were to put off several degrees of largeness, and put on a considerable degree of littleness. After all, I think we must call him particularly *your* man."[3] And Emerson, whose praise of Alcott is unending,[4] was not unaware of the same thing. He writes in 1842: "It must be conceded that it is speculation which he loves, and not action. Therefore he dissatisfies everybody, and disgusts many. When the conversation is ended, all is over. He lives

---

[1] An anecdote, related by Emerson, shows how oblivious he was not merely to the common, but to the beautiful things about him: "One thing I used to tell him—that he had no senses. . . . We had a good proof of it this morning. He wanted to know why the boys waded into the water after pond lilies. 'Why, because they will sell for a cent apiece, and every man and child likes to carry one to church for a Cologne bottle.' 'What?' said he; 'have they a perfume? I did not know it.'" Sanborn, 425.

[2] Cheney, 40.

[3] Thoreau, *Familiar Letters,* 175.

[4] For some of the remarkable tributes of Emerson to the genius of his friend, see Sanborn, 236, 238, 345, 425, 537; *Carlyle-Emerson Correspondence,* I, 122.

to-morrow as he lived to-day, for further discourse,—not to begin, as he seemed pledged to do, a new celestial life."[1]

But now, while we recognize that Alcott's one idea distorted his vision of the world and unfitted him for the practical duties of life, on the other hand let us admit that he had the heroism to sacrifice everything, including his own comfort, to that idea, to stand unflinchingly for principle. Said Henry Hedge, " On the whole Alcott stands in my recollection for the best representative I have known of the spiritual hero."[2] And Emerson wrote to Margaret Fuller (1837), " He has more of the Godlike than any man I have ever seen, and his presence rebukes and threatens and raises. He *is* a teacher. . . . I can never doubt him."[3] Much as we may censure it in our calmer moments, we cannot but admit a certain sublimity in the temperament which, for an ideal, indulges in a splendid disdain of facts. When Sheriff Staples arrested Alcott for not paying his taxes and Miss Helen Thoreau asked him what Alcott's idea was, he replied: " I vum, I believe it was nothing but principle, for I never heard a man talk honester."[4] Reference has been made, too, to the part played by Alcott in the Burns affair. This, and his refusal to dismiss the colored child from his school when he must have known that his action meant its ultimate closing, are typical of his attitude toward any question involving the practical application of his philosophy. In judging Alcott, we must remember this heroic adherence to principle, this determination to live his beliefs at any cost; we must remember, too, his lack of the sense of humor and with it the depth and sincerity of his conviction of a prophetic mission to the world. On the other hand, what we have seen of his life has been ample to show that in his case at least the popular application of the term *transcendental* was far from unfounded. When Emerson called Alcott a " tedious archangel " he put a great deal of truth into two words.

[1] Sanborn, 250.
[2] *Ibid.*, 540.
[3] *Ibid.*, 566.
[4] *New England Magazine*, May 22, 1873.

III

To devote extended space to a consideration of Theodore Parker's relation to the world of practical activity is hardly necessary. Indeed, as one turns from his biography one feels in a mood to ask—such was the literally prodigious amount of labor of the most exhausting, varied, unselfish, and productive kind that he crowded into his prematurely ended life— whether a more active man ever lived. Though in his case, then, our question is answered at the outset, it will nevertheless be proper to collect some of the facts, not alone for the sake of uniformity with the other parts of the discussion, but in order to emphasize certain aspects of his character.

If on the one hand Theodore Parker attained a life of more tangible and doubtless greater activity than Channing, it should be recognized on the other that he did not have the same natively contemplative disposition to struggle against. He was by birth active. How fundamental, both in his public and his private relations, the element of practical common-sense in his nature was, is attested by dozens of anecdotes and by passages from his letters and journals—a single example of which is the fact that his judgment on money matters was considered so good that his friends sought his advice concerning investments involving thousands of dollars. Even Parker's immense reading was done actively rather than meditatively. He misconceived his own nature when he said, "I was meant for a philosopher, and the times call for a *stump orator*."[1] His mind was not primarily metaphysical in cast. He was not an original philosophic thinker. And yet his love of metaphysics was hardly surpassed by that of any other member of the transcendental group. His own account of his spiritual experiences, of which a short review has already been given, serves to show how deep was his interest in and how fundamental his reliance on thought of this kind, and his lecture on *Transcendentalism* is, if anything, an even better revelation of how much his intellectual convictions meant to his religion. "Love of philosophy," he writes in another place, "may be 'the last infirmity of noble minds' [*sic*], but I will

[1] Chadwick, 278.

12

cling to it still. You ask me what effect my speculations have on my practice. You will acquit me of boasting when I say, the most delightful—better than I could hope. My preaching is weak enough, you know, but it is made ten times the more spiritual and strong by my views of nature, God, Christ, man and the Sacred Scriptures."[1] Such was the fascination for him of metaphysical thinking that Parker feared it might carry him too high and so impair his usefulness to his fellow men. "I begin to fear my sermons are too speculative. Is it so? I wish to stand on the earth, though I would look beyond the stars. I would live *with men,* but think with philosophers."[2] As mere symbols of the way in which his life embodied this double purpose it is instructive to place side by side two of his typical "plans of work" while in West Roxbury:

"Things to be done this week.
" 1. Finish two sermons.
" 2. De Wette.
" 3. Jacobi.
" 4. Fichte (Ethik).
" 5. Duty *vs.* Inclination.
" 6. Commence the account of Moses.
" 7. Begin the translation of Ammon's 'Fortbildung Christenthums.'"

"Work to be done this week.
" 1. Plant the other side of the brook.
" 2. Sow the garden vegetables.
" 3. Plough the new land.
" 4. Plant the old alleys.
" 5. Visit Mr. Keith and Chapin in evening.
" 6. See about the Sunday school.
" 7. Get the benches for the vestry.
" 8. Ask Mr. Ellis to be superintendent."[3]

The discussion of Parker's reading has served to show his passion for facts. The degree in which he combined this with

[1] Weiss, i, 110.
[2] *Ibid.,* 115.
[3] Frothingham, 93.

a love of speculation is one of his remarkable characteristics. The outline of his voluminous projected work on the *Development of Religion*[1] is a good illustration of this union of interest. His heart was in the book, but when the imperative call of the anti-slavery cause came, his moral and practical nature ruled, and he relinquished his cherished plan.

It was with this turning of his interest to the slavery question and especially with the arousing of all of the fires of his nature at the passage of the Fugitive Slave Law that the tremendous will-power and activity of Theodore Parker came into greatest prominence. The chapters on this subject in the biographies affirm the indomitable energy and personal heroism of the man. During the years of this controversy, an endless mass of correspondence, lectures, sermons, and addresses was interspersed with deeds of daring moral and physical courage.[2]

Parker was chairman of the Executive Committee of the Vigilance Committee, sheltered fugitive slaves in his own house and aided their escape in all ways possible, took a prominent part in the fugitive slave affairs in Boston, in Faneuil Hall called for open resistance on behalf of Anthony Burns, and was indicted in connection with this case together with Phillips and Higginson, but never brought to trial. Later he came into intimate relations with John Brown, was one of five members of a committee pledged to the support of his enterprises, and contributed money of his own and raised funds from others for that purpose. The entries in his Journal show how much of his time was spent. For example (1859?):

"Feb. 21.—These are sad times to live in, but I should be sorry not to have lived in them. It will seem a little strange one or two hundred years hence, that a plain, humble scholar of Boston was continually interrupted in his studies, and could not write his book for stopping to look after fugitive slaves—his own parishioners!

[1] Weiss, ii, 50.
[2] The period referred to was, of course, after the crest of transcendentalism, but the qualities then conspicuously revealed in Parker were his throughout his life.

" Feb. 22.—Washington's birthday! Very busy with fugitive slave matters.

" Feb. 24.—Not well. Writing report on fugitive slave
petitions, etc.

" Feb. 25.—At home—about anti-slavery business. P. M.
at the State-house with Anti-Slavery Committee. Phillips,
Sewall, and Ellis spoke. Vigilance committee sat at night.

" Feb. 26.—Much time in fugitive slave matters."[1]

A week or two before Buchanan's election, speaking of buying books he wrote, " Last year I bought $1,500 worth. This
year I shall not order $200 worth. I may want the money
for cannons [sic]."[2]

Not the least remarkable feature of his activity was that
through all this period he continued to discharge his minis-
terial duties, preaching the same transcendental theology. At
the end of his life he made an enumeration under eight heads
of some of the most important fields covered by his preaching.
They emphasize the practical nature of the man. These are
the subjects: intemperance; the abnormal desire of accumu-
lating property; public education; the condition of woman;
current political questions of all sorts; the evils of war; slavery;
the errors of ecclesiastic theology.

Some of Parker's remarks on literature and art throw much
light on his common-sense character and show how his moral
dominated and prejudiced his æsthetic nature. We feel constantly that his hatred of selfish things in men like Byron[3] and
Goethe led him to underrate them as poets. As he read
Goethe's life his sympathy was aroused for Frederika Brion;
and so it is more than a coincidence that twice, just after mentioning her, he proceeds to rate Voltaire above Goethe as a
poet. No abstract affinity between his own and Goethe's
transcendentalism can make Parker love him. He says, " He
was a great Pagan. His aim was to educate Herr Goethe.
He leads one to labor, but not for the highest, not by any
means for others. His theory was selfish, and the Christian

---

[1] Weiss, ii, 105.
[2] Chadwick, 331.
[3] Frothingham, 37.

was not in him."[1]   But still more illuminating is the following
from a letter to George Ripley, dated Rome, October 29, 1859:
" I can't attend much to the fine arts, painting and sculpture,
which require a man to be indoors.   And, by the way, the fine
arts do not interest me so much as the coarse arts which feed,
clothe, house, and comfort a people.   I should rather be such
a great man as Franklin than a Michael Angelo; nay, if I had
a son, I should rather see him a great mechanic, who organized
use, like the late George Stephenson in England, than a great
painter like Rubens, who only copied beauty.   In short, I take
more interest in a cattle-show than in a picture-show, and feel
more sympathy with the Pope's bull than his *bullum*.   Men
talk to me about the ' absence of art ' in America (you remember the stuff which Margaret Fuller used to twaddle forth on
that theme, and what transcendental nonsense got delivered
from gawky girls and long-haired young men) ; I tell them we
have cattle-shows, and mechanics' fairs, and ploughs and har-
rows, and saw-mills; sowing machines, and reaping machines;
thrashing machines, planing machines, etc."[2]   Parker evidently appreciated the popular use of " transcendental."

His love of the simple and the concrete is another manifestation of the qualities we are emphasizing.   He writes: " I
have always preferred to use, when fit, the every-day words[3]
in which men think and talk, scold, make love, and pray, so
that generous-hearted philosophy, clad in a common dress,
might more easily become familiar to plain-clad men . . . for
this I must not only plead the necessity of my nature, delight-
ing in common things, trees, grass, oxen, and stars, moonlight
on the water, the falling rain, the ducks and hens at this moment noisy under my window, the gambols and prattle of children, and the common work of blacksmiths, wheelwrights,
painters, hucksters, and traders of all sorts; but I have also
on my side the example of all the great masters of speech—
save only the French . . . —of poets like Homer, Dante,

[1] Weiss, ii, 21.

[2] *Ibid.,* 377.

[3] 91 out of 100 of his words were Saxon. John White Chadwick, *Library
of the World's Best Literature,* xix, 11,077.

Shakspere, Goethe, of Hebrew David, and of Roman Horace: of philosophers like Socrates and Locke; of preachers like Luther, Latimer, Barrow, Butler, and South."[1]

And in this same connection, a sentence or two from Emerson's tribute to Parker must not be omitted: " Theodore Parker was our Savonarola, an excellent scholar, in frank and affectionate communication with the best minds of his day, yet the tribune of the people, and the stout Reformer to urge and defend every cause of humanity with and for the humblest of mankind. . . . What he said was mere fact, almost offended you, so bald and detached; little cared he. He stood altogether for practical truth; and so to the last. He used every day and hour of his short life, and his character appeared in the last moments with the same firm control as in the midday of strength."[2]

Anything but a utilitarian in the technically ethical sense, Parker was to the core a utilitarian in the practical sense. These are the two cardinal facts about him. Frothingham emphasizes one when he declares, " The thing of most moment to say of Parker is, that he was pre-eminently a man of uses,"[3] or when he closes his biography by calling him " the best working-plan of an American yet produced;" C. A. Bartol emphasizes the other when he ventures the assertion that Parker had " a conscience since Luther unsurpassed."[4]

IV

Emerson's three lectures, *The Times, The Conservative, The Transcendentalist,* delivered in Boston at the end of 1841 and the beginning of 1842, are most illuminating documents, for the more often they are read the clearer it becomes that he has both stated and defined his position on exactly the question we are now considering. Especially is this true of *The Transcendentalist.* Through this paper runs a sharp line of distinction pointing out nearly if not exactly that same

[1] Weiss, ii, 505.
[2] Emerson's *Works*, x, 324.
[3] Frothingham, 578.
[4] *Ibid.*, 345.

double meaning of the word *transcendental* which has already been emphasized: that on the one hand it has reference to a certain philosophical way of looking at the world, while on the other it is descriptive of the character and actions of a class of ultra-radical persons who find themselves out of joint with the society in which they live.

With philosophical transcendentalism Emerson seems to declare himself completely at one. " The first thing we have to say," he begins in *The Transcendentalist,* " respecting what are called *new views* here in New England, at the present time, is, that they are not new, but the very oldest of thoughts cast into the mould of these new times." And then, a few paragraphs further on, follows the definition of *transcendental* which we quoted in full at the beginning of our essay.

Toward transcendentalists in the second sense of the adjective *transcendental,* Emerson seems to assume a double attitude. The fact that he refers to them as " this class," " these persons," " these children," is only part of the evidence that he does not intend to identify himself with them. On the one hand, for their conduct considered in itself he has throughout an implied, if never an expressed, censure. Yet on the other hand he seems, as we should expect from his views on fate and individuality, to have not merely a sympathy but almost a justification for them, seeing in the pendulum swing of events, the historical value and necessity for their very extremes and eccentricities. A number of quotations will best present his position.

" It is a sign of our times, conspicuous to the closest observer, that many intelligent and religious persons withdraw themselves from the common labors and competitions of the market and the caucus, and partake themselves to a certain solitary and critical way of living, from which no solid fruit has yet appeared to justify their separation. They hold themselves aloof: they feel the disproportion between their faculties and the work offered them, . . . their solitary and fastidious manners not only withdraw them from the conversation, but from the labors of the world; they are not good citizens, not good members of society; unwillingly they bear their part of the public and private burdens; they do not willingly share in the public charities, in the public religious rites, in the enterprises of education, of missions foreign or domestic, in the abolition of the slave-trade, or in the temperance society. They do not even like to vote. The philanthropists inquire whether Trascendentalism does not mean sloth: they had as lief hear that their friend is dead, as that he is a Transcendentalist; for then he is paralysed and can never do anything for humanity."

Then Emerson gives an amusing colloquy between these people and the world. The former begin by complaining to the latter:

" ' We are miserable with inaction. We perish of rest and rust: but we do not like your work.'

" ' Then,' says the world, ' show me your own.'

" ' We have none.'

" ' What will you do, then?' cries the world.

" ' We will wait.'

" ' How long?'

" ' Until the Universe beckons and calls us to work.'

" ' But whilst you wait, you grow old and useless.'

" ' Be it so: I can sit in a corner and *perish* (as you call it), but I will not move until I have the highest command. If no call should come for years, for centuries, then I know that the want of the Universe is the attestation of faith by my abstinence.' "

It would be superficial indeed to assert that Emerson was unconscious of the element of absurdity in such a position. "There is, no doubt," he says, "a great deal of well-founded objection to be spoken or felt against the sayings and doings of this class." Or again (to pass for a moment from the essay to his Journal): "Buddhism, Transcendentalism, life delights in reducing *ad absurdum*. The child, the infant, is a transcendentalist, and charms us all; we try to be, and instantly run in debt, lie, steal, commit adultery, go mad, and die."[1] But he is far more disposed to commend than to censure (we return to the essay):

[1] Cabot, 413.

" Now every one must do after his kind, be he asp or angel, and these must. The question, which a wise man and a student of modern history will ask, is, what that kind is? . . .

" These persons are of unequal strength, and do not all prosper. They complain that everything around them must be denied; and if feeble, it takes all their strength to deny, before they can begin to lead their own life. . . .

" These exacting children advertise us of our wants. There is no compliment, no smooth speech with them; they pay you only this one compliment, of insatiable expectation; they aspire, they severely exact, and if they only stand fast in this watch tower, and persist in demanding unto the end, and without end, then are they terrible friends, whereof poet and priest cannot choose but stand in awe; and what if they eat clouds, and drink wind, they have not been without service to the race of man."

Finally, the concluding paragraph of the lecture should be quoted, because here, everyone must feel, Emerson is speaking of himself, defining his relation to the age, and as it were, seeking to justify that element which Carlyle criticized. And this relation, it is significant to notice, is precisely the one which Matthew Arnold seized on in his characterization of Emerson.

" Amidst the downward tendency and proneness of things, when every voice is raised for a new road or another statute, or a subscription of stock, for an improvement in dress, or in dentistry, for a new house or a larger business, for a political party, or the division of an estate,—will you not tolerate one or two solitary voices in the land, speaking for thoughts and principles not marketable or perishable? Soon these improvements and mechanical inventions will be superseded; these modes of living lost out of memory; these cities rotted, ruined by war, by new inventions, by new seats of trade, or the geologic changes:—all gone, like the shells which sprinkle the sea-beach with a white colony to-day, forever renewed to be forever destroyed. But the thoughts which these few hermits strove to proclaim by silence, as well as by speech, not only by what they did, but by what they forbore to do, shall abide in beauty and strength to reorganize themselves in nature, to invest themselves anew in other, perhaps higher endowed and happier mixed clay than ours, in fuller union with the surrounding system."

Thus, though Emerson does not identify himself with "these children," and deprecates their excesses, he feels for their general spirit a deep sympathy and clearly considers his own mission and position to be much like theirs. Already in *Nature* he had written of idealism, "It is a watcher more than a doer, and it is a doer, only that it may the better watch."[1] And again, a little later, "I see action to be good, when the need is, and sitting still to be also good. Epaminondas, if he was the man I take him for, would have sat still with joy and peace, if his lot had been mine."[2]

In these quotations we have been listening, to be sure, merely to Emerson's theoretical views about practical life. But it would have been wrong to omit them, for they certainly throw much light on the more important question to which we now come: How did Emerson himself *live?*

A not unprevalent conception of the man is that he was entirely out of touch with the everyday life of the world, and so a sort of living refutation of the value of his own idealism; while on the other hand a widely adopted view makes him out the embodiment in one person of the Plato and the Yankee, a man uniting the ability to inhabit the high heaven of speculative thought, with the plain, practical common-sense of the typical New Englander.

Emerson, like Channing, was of a natively contemplative disposition. His love of meditation, of solitude, was always strong, and at least at one time (which Mr. Cabot calls his "Transcendental apogee"), it seems that he carried this tendency to inaction and reflection to an extreme. It was then that he made that entry in his Journal which we have already quoted,[3] telling of "gray clouds, short days, moonless nights, a drowsy sense of being dragged easily somewhere by that

[1] *Works*, i, 64.
[2] *Ibid.*, ii, 153.
[3] P. 127.

locomotive Destiny, which, never seen, we yet know must be hitched on to the cars wherein we sit." While this on the one hand appears to have been an exceptional condition, there seems to be no evidence on the other that Emerson ever consciously tried to avert these periods of dreamy contemplation.

Perhaps the most illuminating source-book concerning the every-day life of Emerson is the *Emerson in Concord* of his son, E. W. Emerson. This, by means of many anecdotes, personal remembrances of the author, and extracts from Emerson's Journal gives us a vivid picture of the more intimate and domestic aspects of the man. Here we see, as well as Emerson the poet and philosopher, Emerson in the home and in the garden, Emerson on the stage-coach and the railroad, Emerson in contact with his neighbors, fighting brush-fires with his townsmen, or conversing with fishermen and woodchoppers whom he met on his long walks. The reading of this book will tend to corroborate neither of the extreme views above mentioned.

Whatever his nature might have made him had be been brought up under other circumstances, to say that Emerson actually was a practical Yankee, is, it decidedly seems, stretching either the fact, or the meaning of the word. The often-quoted remark of his little son Waldo on seeing his father at work with a spade in the garden, " Papa, I am afraid you'll dig your leg," would in itself perhaps be sufficient to disprove Emerson's title to the name Yankee, without adding his own proud declaration that he could split a shingle four ways with a single nail. He disclaimed it himself again when he said, " God has given me the seeing eye, but not the working hand."[1] The author of *Emerson in Concord*, too, is at pains to point out the mistake in that view of his father which emphasizes his Yankee shrewdness:

" The whole tale of the shrewdness has been told when it has been said that he was usually right in his instincts of the character of the persons with whom he dealt (though often he imputed more virtue than was rightly there), and that he avoided being harnessed into enterprises not rightly his,

[1] Holmes, 365.

lived simply, served himself and went without things which he could not afford, only however, to give freely for what public or private end seemed desirable or commanding on another or better day. These simple rules were his utmost skill. He had no business faculty or even ordinary skill in figures; could only with the greatest difficulty be made to understand an account, and his dealings with the American publishers on behalf of Mr. Carlyle, adduced in proof of his Yankee ' faculty,' really only shows what love and loyalty he bore his friend, that he would freely undertake for him duties so uncongenial and,—but for outside help and expert counsel,—almost impossible for him."[1]

And this too is of interest: " Mr. Emerson cheerfully assumed such duties as the town put upon him. Almost immediately on his coming to Concord he was chosen a member of the School Committee, and later he served on it for many years. He never felt that he had the smallest executive ability, and on the village committee, as later on the Board of Overseers of the University, he preserved an unduly modest attitude, seldom speaking, but admiring the working and reasoning of others."[2] About the same is said of his conduct in the town meetings.[3]

Emerson was one of the earliest of the transcendentalists actively to express sympathy with the anti-slavery movement. As early as May 29, 1831, he permitted an abolitionist to lecture in his pulpit. Though Emerson was too disposed to look at the question historically and judicially to be fully at one with the most radical opponents of slavery,[4] his opposition to that institution, while never actively aggressive, was always firm and sometimes even heroic. In 1835, when Harriet Martineau was nearly mobbed in Boston, he gave her shelter in his home; and shortly after the murder of Lovejoy in 1837, Emerson in his lecture on Heroism ventured to defend him, saying, " It is but the other day that the brave

[1] *Emerson in Concord*, 198.
[2] *Ibid.*, 142.
[3] *Ibid.*, 72.
[4] See Holmes, 211.

Lovejoy gave his breast to the bullets of a mob for the rights of free speech and opinion, and died when it was better not to live." "A cold shudder ran through the audience at the calm braving of public opinion, says an eye-witness."[1] In 1844 at the seizure of colored citizens of Massachusetts from vessels lying in Southern ports, he made a stirring address demanding their immediate release. In 1851 he publicly rebuked Webster, in the face of hisses and groans, for his 7th of March speech. He entertained John Brown at his own home,[2] contributed to the Kansas cause, and later, when Brown was under sentence of death, declared that if he should suffer he would "make the gallows glorious like a cross." Previous to this he had delivered an address in New York on the Fugitive Slave Law and one in Concord after the assault on Sumner. In January, 1861, at the invitation of Wendell Phillips, he faced a stormy crowd in Music Hall, but was unable to make himself heard.

Though this record (which by no means includes all that he did) is far from betokening apathy toward the slavery question, yet it cannot be called one of marked activity. He did not so consider it himself. The following from his Journal in 1852 shows exactly his position and his reasons for it:

"I waked last night and bemoaned myself because I had not thrown myself into this deplorable question of Slavery, which seems to want nothing so much as a few assured voices. But then in hours of sanity I recover myself, and say, God must govern his own world, and knows his way out of this pit without my desertion of my post, which has none to guard it but me. I have quite other slaves to free than those negroes, to wit, imprisoned spirits, imprisoned thoughts, far back in the brain of man,—far retired in the heaven of invention, and which, important to the republic of man, have no watchman or lover or defender but I [sic]."[3]

He expresses this same attitude at the beginning of his

[1] *Emerson in Concord*, 85.
[2] *Ibid.*, 87.
[3] *Ibid.*, 78.

Fugitive Slave address[1] in New York, saying that he has his own spirits in prison and that he hopes he knows his own place.

Even this brief glance at Emerson's connection with the anti-slavery cause is sufficient to put one fact—a most important one for our discussion—wholly beyond dispute: that he possessed high moral courage and an unbending, Puritanical[2] adherence to principle. Indeed his sermon on the Lord's Supper, and his *Divinity School Address,* in point of opposing public opinion, required no small amount of these same qualities.

As we read Emerson chronologically, there is observable a decrease in the purely speculative and an increase in love of anecdote and fact.[3] His interest in such men of action as Napoleon is significant. He apparently never cared for technical metaphysics at any time. "Who has not looked into a metaphysical book? And what sensible man ever looked twice?"[4] Such a passage as the following (written late in life) may be directed merely at system-makers, but perhaps it would not be fanciful to read into it also a slight confession that he had himself indulged too liberally in speculation:

"I confess to a little distrust of that completeness of system which metaphysicians are apt to affect. . . . I share the belief that the natural direction of the intellectual powers is from within outward, and that just in proportion to the activity of thoughts on the study of outward objects, as architecture, or farming, or natural history, ships, animals, chemistry,—in that proportion the faculties of the mind had a

---

[1] *Works,* xi, 205.

[2] It is worthy of remark that even in some cases where it might hardly have been expected (as in his views on the observance of the Sabbath, card-playing, dancing, the theatre, etc.) Emerson held to the old and strict New England customs. See *Emerson in Concord,* 168 and 171; *Works,* Centenary Edition, iv, 345 and 357; and the conclusion of the essay on Shakespeare.

[3] Volume xi, *Miscellanies,* of his works exhibits him especially in the more practical aspect.

[4] *Works,* Centenary Edition, ii, 438.

healthy growth; but a study in the opposite direction had a damaging effect on the mind.

"Metaphysic is dangerous as a single pursuit. We should feel more confidence in the same results from the mouth of a man of the world. The inward analysis must be corrected by rough experience. Metaphysics must be perpetually reinforced by life."[1]

Emerson had then by nature—do not the facts point strongly toward this conclusion?—a respect and love for the simple, plain, concrete things of life, and his speculative and contemplative studies, his idealism, never tended to breed in him disdain for anything of this sort. On the other hand, his life, mainly one of meditation, reading, writing, and lecturing, did (as he himself fully recognized) isolate him from and make him ignorant of many things of everyday concern. Tried by any such standard of activity as that which Theodore Parker set, Emerson's life was inactive and out of relation to the practical. Active and practical of its own kind, exerting an influence not easily overrated, it surely was neither active nor practical in the sense of touching the world at many points or in a large variety of ways. Emerson has himself well summed up his relation to the so-called concrete affairs of life at the begining of his essay on *Prudence*. These are his words:

"What right have I to write on Prudence, whereof I have little, and that of the negative sort? My prudence consists in avoiding and going without, not in the inventing of means and methods, not in adroit steering, nor in gentle repairing. I have no skill to make money spend well, no genius in my economy, and whoever sees my garden discovers that I must have some other garden. Yet I love facts, and hate lubricity and people without perception. Then I have the same title to write on prudence that I have to write on poetry or holiness. We write from aspiration and antagonism, as well as from experience. We paint these qualities which we do not possess."

[1] *Works,* xii, 11. See also on this subject *Ibid.,* viii, 39; x. 289; xii, 6 and 44.

Or again this whole matter might be put in terms of the well-known "Hitch your wagon to a star." Emerson was an authority on stars, not on wagons. He felt it peculiarly his to put the whole emphasis on the star, but though his knowledge of wagons was deficient he does not appear ever to have said or done anything to show that he questioned their usefulness and necessity. If this be so, we perceive then, do we not, that a just estimate of Emerson's personality must lie between the extremes already mentioned? The opinion that Emerson lived his whole life "beyond the clouds" is clearly inadequate, and takes its rise usually, we must believe, from the critic's dislike of speculative writing. On the other hand, the view that would make him out a union of the Plato and the Yankee is again an obvious overstatement. Yet this estimate is surely nearer to the truth than is the other—for, in spite of its exaggeration, it indicates one of the deepest things about Emerson, a doubleness, we might almost say a contradiction, in his nature. He *was* the saint and seer; but he was not less—just the plain citizen of Concord. And there is a profound sense in which he *did* have the power to be at once "standing on earth" and "rapt above the pole."

V

The treatment of Margaret Fuller's relation to the practical may be considerably abbreviated owing to the fact that Mr. Higginson, in his admirable *Life,* has given especial attention to this aspect of her character with a view to readjusting the estimate of her earlier biographers. It would be superfluous to repeat in detail the evidence which he has accumulated. This evidence is scattered through the whole book, though it is the chapter on Miss Fuller's personal traits in which particular attention is given to this subject. Mr. Higginson has pointed out that the authors of the *Memoirs* saw Margaret Fuller almost exclusively on her intense, aspiring side, and hence inevitably—and so quite pardonably—put undue emphasis on this aspect of her nature; he has given proof for his statement that "there never was a year of Margaret Fuller's life, after her precocious maturity, when the greater part of it was not given to daily, practical, commonsense labor, and this usually for other people."[1]

The treatment of her conversations and more especially of her emotionalism and mysticism has already sufficiently emphasized her ethereal elements. There is no doubt that at times she could soar very high. Yet she always asserted that her philosophy was based in experience and that she preferred action to speculation. "That is the real life which is subordinated to, not merged in, the ideal."[2] There is a surprising analogy between Theodore Parker's statement that he would rather be a Franklin than a Michael Angelo and Margaret Fuller's declaration, "Yet would I rather, were the choice tendered to me, draw the lot of Pericles than that of Anaxagoras."[3] She criticized Alcott and his children's school severely, because he rejected experience and longed for "the safe and natural way of intuition." A few sentences, too, may be quoted from a letter (1838) to show the sort of advice she was capable of giving a young friend:

"I think the course of reading you have fallen upon, of late, will be better for you than such books as you formerly read, addressed rather to the taste and imagination than the judgment. The love of beauty has rather an undue development in your mind. See now what it is, and what it has been. Leave for a time the Ideal, and return to the Real.

"I should think two or three hours a day would be quite enough, at present, for you to give to books. Now learn buying and selling, keeping the house, directing the servants; all that will bring you worlds of wisdom if you keep it subordinate to the one grand aim of perfecting the whole being. And let your self-respect forbid you to do imperfectly anything that you do at all.

"I always feel ashamed when I write with this air of wisdom; but you will see, by my hints, what I mean."[4]

To this may be added the statement that Miss Fuller's book

---

[1] Higginson, 304.
[2] *Memoirs,* ii, 30.
[3] Higginson, 310.
[4] *Woman in the Nineteenth Century,* 346.

13

Woman in the Nineteenth Century (preface dated November, 1844), an expansion of an article published the previous year in the *Dial,* gives the reader no impression of being the work of a visionary or of one unacquainted with life as it is; on the contrary it rings with reality.

But there is more substantial evidence on this point than the mere expression of her desires, her condemnation of the purely theoretical, or even her books, and letters of practical advice. The giving up at the death of her father (1835) of her long planned trip to Europe,[1] her struggle for the education of her brothers and sisters,[2] her exactness and care in money matters,[3] her capacity in domestic affairs—these are but a few of the things that might be mentioned to show that she was no mere dreamer, that she was not ignorant nor neglectful of the practical issues of life. To this element in her nature her brother has borne witness. In his editor's preface to *Woman in the Nineteenth Century,* he writes at some length and with feeling—not of her intellectual brilliancy, but of what his sister *did.* He speaks of himself as " one who knew her from childhood up—at *home,* where best the *heart* and *soul* can be known,—in the unrestrained hours of domestic life,—in various scenes, and not for a few days, nor under any peculiar circumstances," as one therefore " who speaks what ' he doth know, and testifieth what he hath seen.' " And then he goes on to tell of the " life of constant self-sacrifice," the " devotion to the welfare of kindred and the race " of one who carried her " Christianity into all the departments of action, so far as human infirmity allows." An extract from a letter to her mother (1837) is a remarkable revelation of this devotion.[4]

Put such a tribute as this one of her brother side by side with some of those passages quoted in the last chapter concerning Miss Fuller's haughtiness and mysticism. What light they throw on one another! Now may be more fully appre-

[1] *Memoirs,* i, 158.
[2] *Ibid.,* 157.
[3] Higginson, 55.
[4] *Woman in the Nineteenth Century,* 344.

ciated what before was hardly open to doubt: that the story of Margaret Fuller's pride and sentimentalism is at the same time the story of a rebellion against that pride and of a struggle against that sentimentalism. This struggle, as in the case of Channing's conflict with his feelings, was a successful one. She did not alter her temperament; but she did more and more gain control over herself; she did work a transforming change in her own character. Especially in the years beginning with her removal to New York—and afterward of course in Italy—when she seems to have come to the full maturity of her nature, does the practical side of the woman come clearly into evidence. She took an active, personal interest in nearly all philanthropic movements for social reform,[1] coming into immediate and vital contact with the convicts, paupers, outcast women, etc., in whom she was so deeply interested. These were some of the subjects on which she wrote her articles for the *Tribune: The Rich Man, The Poor Man, Woman in Poverty, What Fits a Man to Be a Voter? The Condition of the Blind, Prison Discipline, Appeal for an Asylum for Discharged Female Convicts, Politeness to the Poor, Capital Punishment.*[2] "I doubt," Horace Greeley declares, "that our various benevolent and reformatory associations had ever before, or have ever since received such wise, discriminating commendation to the favor of the rich, as they did from her pen during her connection with the 'Tribune.'"[3] Her personal contributions, Mr. Greeley says, were "large in proportion to her slender means."

Though these years in New York came after the crest of the transcendental movement, they came *immediately* after the period of the Conversations and the *Dial.* With a full recognition of the changes that Miss Fuller's character underwent in the course of her life, it must be said that there is no evidence of any transforming development of her nature within a few months such as might superficially be deemed necessary to account for the sudden alteration in the quality of her

[1] For her attitude on the slavery question, see Higginson, 122.
[2] *Ibid.,* 213.
[3] *Ibid.,* 214.

activity. The difficulty lies too deep for any such easy-going explanation. If there be a paradox here, we shall come nearer its resolution by considering to what an unusual degree she united apparently contradictory elements. That Margaret Fuller should have combined in one nature her intense emotional capacities, her critical and intellectual power, and her practical common-sense, is sufficient to prove the complexity of her temperament, and to warn those to look again who think they have understood her at a glance.

What was the relation of the transcendentalists to practical life? This is the question to which, through two chapters, we have been seeking an answer, and yet now, as we approach the end of our discussion, a general conclusion seems, in many ways, impossible. The differences among these men appear more prominent perhaps than do their likenesses. Whatever fundamental identity of spirit they had, Theodore Parker and Bronson Alcott, in their attitude toward the concrete facts of life, stand strikingly, not seldom diametrically, opposed. Between these extremes the others are arranged, and scarcely any general statement can be framed, however guarded in expression, to which one name at least will not be an exception.

Indeed, as we glance back at the course of our investigation, does it not appear to have involved a hopeless contradiction? Do not its two parts—the previous chapter, we mean, and this—stand out, on the whole, in most conspicuous contrast? Do they not clearly reveal the paradox to which we earlier referred? We think they do. Yet it is in this very seeming paradox that the essence of transcendentalism—unless we are in error—must finally be sought. It is this which, in spite of all their differences, unites these men in a singular kinship and stamps them as the product of one set of forces. Let us make sure that we see what the nature of this contradiction is.

In the earlier half of the discussion we saw a power at work whose tendency seemed to be, on the whole, to carry those it touched "beyond the clouds," away from the world of ordinary fact and common-sense. Variously as this force affected the different transcendentalists, not one of them entirely escaped it. An impatience with detail, a turning of the eyes from the ugliness of the world, a lack of accurate scholarship, a proneness to generalize on insufficient data—even these things were sufficient to reveal its presence; while sometimes it amounted to an actual disdain of facts, to a retreat into the recesses of a purely personal experience, or, at last, to a soaring away on the wings of mystical rapture. The philosophy of these men, too—however vital some of its conceptions—must be pronounced one-sided. It showed an inclination, sometimes a hopeless inclination, to overemphasize the spiritual and subjective, to perceive the unity while passing lightly over the diversity of life, to forget the " wagon " while gazing at the " star." The transcendentalists were idealists—but their idealism had not the great objective basis of reality of that of the Dantes and Goethes of the world. They were individualists—but their individualism, whatever its merits, tended only too often to carry with it a blindness to the significance of social and collective forces, to the part that *institutions* must play in human progress. There was a time, the years just before and just after 1840, when this interest in the purely intuitional and ideal ran highest. Then aspirations, oftentimes, came dangerously near being prized for their own sakes; then the self-consciousness that characterized the whole period was most pronounced. The movement in its prime,[1] even among its leaders, showed marks of exaggeration, extravagance, and excess. A religion tending to sweep its disciples up into the thin atmosphere of rapture and speculation—something of this sort, the facts being permitted to speak for themselves, it was the main trend of Chapter III. to find in transcendentalism.

But all this it has, hardly less, been the main trend of the present chapter to deny. The moment we are confronted with the plain facts of their lives, we realize that these men were far enough from inhabiting a purely isolated and ideal realm,

[1] It may be said that transcendentalism *was* what we speak of as " the movement in its prime," that after the crest of the wave had passed the very thing we are discussing ceased to be. One may so use the word if one chooses, but so to limit the term appears to the writer highly unphilosophical. See the closing paragraph of Chapter I.

that there was something in them to balance—partly at least—
the tendency that drove them upward. They did not show, in
their actual living, indifference to that evil whose reality they
philosophically denied. They did not rest content with their
creed, independent of its influence upon others, or unmindful
of its dangers to themselves. In a score of ways—but pre-
eminently in the slavery agitation—they came into vital contact with the great practical issues of the day. Not that the
later facts of our study add nothing to our perception of the
ethereal elements of transcendentalism. The contrary is true
—especially of Alcott; he alone,[1] of the five we have considered, seems open more than once to the charge of being pal-
pably out of joint with common-sense. But the substance of
the chapter goes to prove that these men were not dead to the
real life around them, that they were not blind to facts, that
transcendentalism touched and affected the great human world,
and that to describe it as merely " flighty " and " ideal " is
hopelessly inadequate.

Here then—put in two paragraphs—we have the contradiction.

In none of the other transcendentalists do these opposing
elements appear in such striking contrast as in Margaret
Fuller. In her—the extreme case—is brought out with especial clearness what was true, in its degree, of all the rest. Her
later biographer, emphasizing the more practical side of the
woman, has readjusted the estimate of the earlier historians
of her life. He is right. Yet their account was not false;
it was merely incomplete; it gave but one side of her double
nature. There were two Margaret Fullers: one, the intense,
the imperious, the rapturous Margaret Fuller; the other, the
Margaret Fuller who recognized the pride and hyper-emotion-
alism of her nature and struggled to subdue them. There
were two Channings: the youthful one of vague and sentimental visions, the later one of wide and varied life; yet the ma-
turer Channing was, after all, only the earlier one transformed.

---

[1] The criticism, therefore, which from his life, or the lives of lesser men,
has generalized concerning the whole transcendental group, has not unnatur-
ally done very large injustice.

There were two Emersons: the one—a halo round his head—delivering in the omniscient style his ultimate oracles; the other a plain, kindly New England gentleman ready to turn humorously aside any suggestion of his own omniscience. There were even two Parkers and two Alcotts—though here the opponent forces were matched less equally. The practical Parker has made his presence amply felt; yet Parker had his transcendental flights. With the mystical Alcott we are well acquainted; yet the man who saw the world as one vast spinal column stood, at another hour, ready to defend with his life his anti-slavery convictions.

Transcendentalism then—is not this the logical conclusion?—was in no small measure the union of two contrasting elements, the product of two opposing forces. The essence of the one was in the main impractical; that of the other chiefly practical. The popular charge stands neither refuted nor confirmed.

With these statements the chapter may best be brought to a close; to attempt to analyze and interpret them belongs to the last division of the essay. But meanwhile one fact, repeatedly brought out in the course of the discussion, must here be emphasized. About it there could have been indeed no initial disagreement; yet, for the purposes of our study, it is of unsurpassed importance. And that fact is this: that on the whole the most conspicuous similarity of these transcendentalists was simply their *Puritan character*. We have just been insisting on the differences between Bronson Alcott and Theodore Parker. Great as these were, the man who, it was declared, had "a conscience since Luther unsurpassed" and the man who stood in the mind of his friend as the best type of a spiritual hero he had ever known, are, after all, examples of the same New England character. They and the other chief transcendentalists had the same moral courage, the same adherence to principle, the same purity, nobility, elevation of spirit that belonged to the best of the old New England. The significance of this must already be apparent.

CHAPTER V

We saw at the beginning of our study how, on the surface of the negative and critical age of reason, there slowly developed a great tidal wave of change, which, invading almost every sphere of action and affecting life in a wide variety of ways, swept over Europe at the end of the eighteenth and the beginning of the nineteenth century. In politics and religion, in philosophy and literature—to mention no other departments of activity—revolts were instituted against prevailing standards.

To produce the conviction that transcendentalism was, if a late, still an organic part of this great revolution, there is needed no minute study of historical influences. But when we realize that the forces which led up to the New England outburst were the same as those whose interplay preceded the earlier and more widespread European commotion, we perceive how far beyond the power of the most elaborate study it must be to distinguish absolutely between the American and the foreign streams of tendency making toward the transcendental movement, to tell just how far the one development produced the other, how far the two were merely parallel. The old New England—and with it the ancestors of the transcendentalists—was interested predominantly in matters of religion. Hence it was natural that new ideas, whether widely accepted or not, should early make themselves felt within this sphere of life. This was the actual case; and, as we saw in the first chapter of our study, the story of the long preparation of the soil which alone made possible the later flourishing of transcendental views becomes, in no small measure, the history of the revolt from Calvinism and the rise of Unitarianism. When, then, with the culmination of Unitarianism in transcendentalism, a spirit emerges resembling the spirit which came with the culmination of the age of reason in the French

184

Revolution, we are at a loss to tell just how far French Revolutionary influences have really been at work, and how far we have a case of similar causes producing similar effects.

But, whatever the relative significance of the foreign and domestic contributions may have been, the fact itself remains the same, the fact, namely, that the spirit of New England transcendentalism and the spirit of the French Revolution are, in many respects, astoundingly alike. From the moment when Emerson—to go no farther back—freeing himself from the shackles of the church and calling on his countrymen to cast aside tradition and live their own lives, wrote the opening sentences of *Nature,* transcendentalism was linked forever with that world-movement which began conspicuously with Rousseau. "Man is born free, but he is everywhere in chains"—those words never cease to echo through the utterances of Emerson and Parker, of Alcott and Thoreau. Away with tradition!—Back to Nature!—Down with creeds and institutions!—The Golden Age is before us!—these were the battle cries which, born long before in France, reawakened now in New England, and the transcendental spirit partook to an extraordinary degree of that distrust of the past, that optimistic faith in the future, that confidence in the efficacy of a formula for solving the problems of mankind, which inspired the most sanguine minds of 1789. To the truth of that other mighty ideal of the revolutionary age—that ideal to which, as embodied in the British Constitution, Burke bowed down, and to which he has given, perhaps, the loftiest expression—the transcendentalists were blind, almost as blind as the French Revolutionists themselves. They, like the latter, did not grasp the significance of historical continuity and evolution—seeming indeed, at times, without the slightest feeling for chronology; they did not reverence the authority of experience, nor perceive the complete dependence with which the present rests upon the past; they failed to comprehend the real functions of the church and state, and, exalting the individual, ignored in large degree the social and institutional factors of life. Indeed, the resemblance between the two movements is frequently so close that we are tempted to end the whole matter with the dictum: Transcendentalism was the French Revolution of American religion! Yet the moment we utter such a formula we are constrained to take three-quarters of it back, so vitally different, after all, the two revolutions really were; and the more we reflect the more we feel that this French Revolutionary spirit is rather the indispensable emotional atmosphere in which transcendentalism was to be engendered than the real essence of the movement itself, or, to put it in a slightly different way, that these partly separate and partly blended streams of American and European tendency, of which we have just been speaking, are not so much an immediate as an *indirect* contribution to that movement.

But there was also a *direct* European contribution of prime importance. What this was, our discussion of the reading and studies of these men has, we trust, made clear. As we have already pointed out, with the passing of the age of reason a widespread desire arose in Europe for some new standard of truth, for some avenue broader than that of the pure intellect through which to approach the deepest problems of the world. As one response to this desire, there emerged both in England and on the continent, but preëminently in Germany, a general theory of the world and attitude toward life, which, in spite of the various modifications or even disguises it is capable of assuming, never completely loses its identity and in the end is always recognizable. The view itself—though there be no single satisfactory name for it—is world old. We may call it Platonism or Neo-Platonism, Idealism or Transcendentalism, or a dozen other names (even *Pantheism,* if we dare be so reckless as to employ that hopelessly indefinite term); and yet, widely or even diametrically as philosophies that we so designate may differ in even important respects, they retain a still more radical and essential kinship. During the years following the French Revolution, this general view of the world, in various forms, gained widespread currency, appearing not merely in philosophers like Fichte and Schelling, but in poets[1] like Goethe, Wordsworth, and Shelley.

---

[1] Platonism, it is perhaps superfluous to note, is a highly imaginative system; Plato the most poetic of philosophers. His philosophy has always

While the reason already assigned for the prevalence, during these years, of this philosophy is, we imagine, fairly fundamental, it must not be thought that it is offered as in itself a
sufficient explanation.[1] The immense growth and influence
of modern science was another potent and closely kindred
cause of its appearance (" closely kindred," we observe, because the scientific movement, with its emphasis on the in-
ductive method, seems, at just this historical moment, to
harmonize marvelously with the general revolt against the
deductive method of pure reason). At the beginning of the
nineteenth century the full daylight of the scientific age was
dawning over Europe. But Europe was not willing to aban-
don her religion. The reconciliation of science and religion,
in other words, was one of the great questions of the time.
Now Platonism offers—whether adequate or not—a solution of this problem. Indeed Plato may be said to have
erected his philosophy to solve it. Brought up in the doctrine of Heraclitus, he sought amid the endless flux of things
($\pi\acute{a}\nu\tau a \ \acute{\rho}\epsilon\hat{\iota}$) on which that doctrine puts such emphasis, something eternal and unchangeable—but something eternal and
unchangeable was just what revolutionary Europe now, centuries after Plato's death, was seeking. And so there came to
life in this later age a philosophy which in many ways resem-
bled that of the Academy.

Now of all the elements of change that were comprehended
in the spirit of the time, it was, along with the prevailing
enthusiasm, just this metaphysical attitude which appealed
most to a little group of men and women in New England—
the transcendentalists to be—and had the strongest influence

appealed most strongly to men of the imaginative cast, and has been revived most successfully at times when men's emotions have run high. (The
period of Elizabeth is only one example.) Such a poetical and imaginative
age the one we are now considering preëminently was.

[1] To the question why this metaphysical view appeared so conspicuously
at this time, the history of philosophy (in tracing the development of
thought since Locke) has ready its own answer. But doubtless the history
of philosophy—if by that we mean the history of metaphysical thought—is
in itself inadequate to offer a full explanation, for such an explanation can
hardly be less complex than the very life of the period itself.

upon them. Not only openly, in technical form, did this philosophy make its way, but much more often under some other name, some theological, perhaps, or literary guise. And precisely because this view of the world was not in its essential nature new, other sources were soon contributing their share, and influences were soon coming over the ocean of time as well as over the Atlantic. Ancient India and Persia, Greece and the Middle Ages, and many other times and countries, sent their portion. The springs of influence were world-wide, and they helped to awaken in their turn in New England a cosmopolitan spirit.[1]

But now, when these influences thus made their way across the water, by whom were they welcomed? On what did the seal of this new thought and spirit make its impress? Was there, like the European, no *direct* American contribution to transcendentalism? Were its indigenous elements merely those indirect and preparatory ones already traced in the story of Unitarianism? Far from it. The fact of paramount importance is that these influences came to a group of men who were embodiments in its noblest form of the old New England character. *They were Puritans to the core. This*—and in making the statement it is not forgotten that England was the home of Puritanism—*was the signally American contribution to transcendentalism.* The latter portion of our study has perhaps made this sufficiently apparent, but the significance of the fact is such that we must again dwell for a moment on what was said at the end of the last chapter.

We have ample evidence of the stuff of which these leading transcendentalists were made. Though they had revolted against their ancestral creed, they had kept in its purity their ancestral character. Channing risking a life-long popularity and endangering many a life-long friendship by his stand on the slavery question; Alcott choosing to abide by his principles, and, at the price of its disbanding, to retain a colored

---

[1] Transcendentalists of course could claim no monopoly of the cosmopolitan spirit, especially in literature. The work that Ticknor and Longfellow did, and later Lowell, must not be forgotten. It is worthy of remark that the cosmopolitan spirit brought forth not an imitative, but an American literature. The same spirit wrought a corresponding result in Germany.

child in the school; Emerson sacrificing his position in the ministry to his convictions on the question of the Lord's Supper—these are but typical instances of this survival from the ancient stock of a stern, unbending, uncompromising virtue. These men had in common the sincerity, the purity, the moral heroism, the noble and unselfish adherence to an ideal, which we always think of as the dominant grandeur of the old Puritanism.

Whatever else, then, and however much more transcendentalism may have been, it was, as embodied in its leaders, the mingling of an old world and a new world element, the blending of an idealistic, Platonistic metaphysics and the Puritan spirit, the fusion—at a high, revolutionary temperature—of a philosophy and a character. The white heat of feeling brought out the noblest outlines of that character and touched into actuality the potential mysticism which that philosophy a hundred times has shown itself to hold.

In spite of not a few points of signal congeniality between Platonism[1] and Puritanism, such a fusion, considered merely theoretically, promises at the outset some remarkable features. Idealistic philosophies are not as a rule lacking in insistence on the importance of the moral element of life; and so also on the other hand are the Puritans in one sense, the moral sense, already idealists. They too in a way look upon earthly existence as a dream and shadow. But the old New Englanders united with their moral idealism no inconsiderable measure of practical common-sense. The Puritan is eminently a doer; he is, in spite of his laying up for himself treasures in heaven, in close contact with concrete things. Metaphysical idealism, on the other hand, carries with it, as many examples—Hamlet among the rest—abundantly prove, a marked tendency toward the purely theoretical, toward contemplation, inaction, isolation from the concrete and practical; while these qualities are only accentuated if it become trans-

---

[1] For the sake of convenience, since we must have some single name for this metaphysical attitude, we shall call it "Platonism," using the term, we would have it understood, very broadly and elastically, and waiving entirely the question whether Plato himself was a mystic or a rationalist.

fused with mysticism. Puritan and Platonist!—whatever resemblances of temper they may have, it is not unfair to say, nevertheless, that they present in considerable measure the antithesis of doer and thinker, of action and contemplation, of the practical and the theoretical, of the Occidental and the Oriental. And the union of the two!—is not such a coming together of "mighty opposites" (regardless of the environment in which it happens) bound in itself to generate intense emotion? What, then, is to be anticipated when that union takes place in an atmosphere of revolution?

But now in these two opposing elements are we not face to face again with precisely the contrast, the paradox, the contradiction concerning which the facts of our study have already forced us to say so much? Here on the one hand we have the celestial vapor with which the transcendental balloon was inflated, on the other the ballast that tended to keep that balloon from voyaging beyond the terrestrial atmosphere.

The moment we take this "fusion" point of view, how naturally explicable become the differences of prevalent opinion as to the relation of the transcendentalists to the concrete, daily world; and how justifiable the conclusion which the facts thrust upon us, that no generalization can be made on this point except one that halts between the extreme views. These men were metaphysical idealists—with mystical proclivities—and as a group, they show some of the extravagances and even absurdities into which that type of thinking —and of feeling—exhibits a tendency at times to pass. The Hamlet paradox emerges more than once. But the fact is that these men were at bottom, all the while, utilitarians, utilitarians not in the technically ethical but in the practical sense. The English foundation of their natures was not lost, even though something highly alien to the Anglo-Saxon genius had come down upon it.

Some of the very instances that seem most to prove their impracticality and that have aroused the satire of the scoffers most, are, if we look closely, examples of this utilitarian, not exclusively theoretical tendency beneath. Alcott attempting to put his doctrine of pre-existence and Wordsworth's Ode into practice in his school; Alcott planting Fruitlands; even Alcott consuming "aspiring" vegetables, are cases of this sort. In all we feel the practical element struggling for expression. Emerson had hold of this fact when he wrote, "My quarrel with poets is that they do not believe their own poetry. But Alcott is a poet, the only one in the country; he believes his images." Nothing could better prove that the spirit of this is true than the way in which Alcott's theoretical optimism had its counterpart in his practical serenity even in adversity of the soul-trying kind.

But it is just as well not to go to extreme examples. The great lasting proof of this "union" of which we are speaking is the persistency with which the transcendentalists carried over their philosophy into the sphere of practical religion. They were not proverbial metaphysicians, content in isolation from real life to spin the theory for the theory's sake; nor mystics, content to inhabit a purely subjective realm of ecstacy, oblivious to the world. They were not even primarily teachers. They were preachers. They must put their philosophy into practice; they must feel it; they must live it; they must spread it abroad by establishing schools, by holding conversations, by lecturing, by writing essays, by preaching. The Puritan blood was still within their veins.[1] Transcendentalism was a gospel.

They were not content to affirm abstractly the divinity of human nature; they must apply this belief in their stand on the slavery question. They were not content to rest in a theoretical individualism; they must preach and live lives of conspicuous self-reliance. And it was the union of the iconoclasm of the Puritan character and a philosophy that taught no adherence to "external" authority, even more, probably, than its French Revolutionary roots, that made New England transcendentalism a grand casting off of tradition. And so we might continue. In this union of a philosophy and a character we find a rational justification of a large number of

---

[1] The attitude of most of the transcendentalists toward Byron and Goethe has been brought out and is an example of surviving Puritanism; "the Puritan in me accepts no apology for bad morals in such as *he*," writes Emerson of Goethe to Carlyle.

the facts we have already observed. Even "transcendental pride" may be included here. Platonism grafted on Puritanism gives in an intensified form a certain intellectual positiveness—not wholly alien to either of those spirits—which, if almost wholly free from the narrow intolerance of the latter, is quite one with it in the moral certainty of the everlasting truth of its own convictions. If "transcendental pride" be on the one hand the inspired self-assurance of the mystic, what is it on the other but the Puritan character in a new guise?

Excellently as all these things are illustrated by the careers and characters of those whom we have considered, not one of them—not even Margaret Fuller herself—affords so nearly perfect an example of our thesis as does a man concerning whom, owing to the limited method of our treatment, we have had but little to remark—Henry David Thoreau. It will hardly be in the nature of a digression, therefore, to pause for a moment to notice in what an eminent degree he united the practical and the mystical, the revolutionary and the common-sense.

Thoreau, it should be said to begin with, in spite of the fact that he cared for the metaphysical even less than Emerson, was a true transcendentalist in his view of life, and after his own kind, too, a philosopher. He was, in the next place, the extreme individualist, probably, of the whole group, applying his principles almost to the point of anarchy. But his anarchy, we should hasten to add, was of a harmless variety. On one occasion, as is well known, he refused to pay his taxes and was sent to jail; but when some friend discharged the indebtedness and set him free, he contented himself with being "as mad as the devil," and went back to picking huckleberries in the pastures where "the State was nowhere to be seen"— a course of action which proves not so much that Thoreau lacked consistency and courage as that he possessed at least a fair endowment of common-sense. This element of common-sense, his practical ingenuity and mechanical skill, his moral intensity and determination to live his theories, exemplify one aspect of the man, the New England qualities of his character; but quite another aspect is illustrated by his love of solitude, of communing with nature, or of dreaming away long hours in rapt contemplation, totally oblivious to the external world. Thoreau it is—not Emerson—who is the true Yankee-mystic. The Walden experiment is symbolical of this, and so too in another way are his writings, full of minute observation and detail, but permeated nevertheless with the transcendental spirit. The realistic strain in his works is pronounced, and in this respect at least he has a far closer kinship with the very greatest writers than Emerson can claim. Whether the belief which a few bold critics have advanced .that Thoreau's writings will ultimately outrank Emerson's is at all tenable, is a question of no importance for the purposes of our present study, but surely the strongest argument for one who might wish to defend such a proposition would be precisely this fact that the balance between the real and the ideal is much better maintained by Thoreau than by Emerson.[1] Indeed, in nearly every respect, the "poet-naturalist" embodies almost equally those contrasted elements whose blending, in one proportion or another, we have noticed in all these transcendentalists.

Emerson himself showed that he was conscious of this composition of old world and new world forces and really recognized the main point on which we are insisting, when he said: "there is an ethical element in the mind of our people that will never let them long rest without finding exercise for the deeper thoughts. It very soon found both Wordsworth and Carlyle insufficient."[2] One of the most convincing proofs of the truth of Emerson's remark is simply the political importance of transcendentalism, its relation to the slavery agitation. One is probably not likely to overrate the influence exerted on the North by the conception—even in its abstract form—of the dignity of human nature. Toward spreading this conception the transcendentalists did much. Nor does all the credit for applying the theory to the facts

---

[1] In connection with all this it is at least interesting to remember that Thoreau had both Scotch and French blood in his veins.

[2] *Works,* Centenary Edition, xii, 472.

14

belong to others. They too perceived the connection and carried their thinking into practice.

Indeed it is utterly impossible to draw any distinct line between the transcendentalists and the abolitionists—as, to be sure, it is equally impossible to distinguish clearly the boundary between transcendentalism and most of the radical movements of the day. The Garrison movement, the literary movement which began with Ticknor and was continued by Longfellow and Lowell, the Brook Farm movement, these and many others —even some of the absurd religious extravagances in the less cultured portion of the community—were all reflections of the larger spirit of the time, all aspects of a single tendency, and all idealistic in the sense of seeking a more nearly perfect condition of society and humanity.

These considerations ought, we think, to render clearer than it could be made at the beginning of our study, the relation between Brook Farm and transcendentalism. We do not wish to minimize the reality of that relation. The sources of the two movements were in many respects identical, as the name of George Ripley itself is sufficient to show;[1] and doubtless too the Brook Farmers got most of their ideal enthusiasm from the transcendentalists. The aims of the two movements, likewise, were in a large sense the same, the moral perfection of man and society. But while the transcendentalists sought that moral perfection almost exclusively through the individual and predominantly by means of a philosophical-mystical religion, the Brook Farmers sought it only partly through the individual and very exceptionally or incidentally through anything philosophical. In one sense then Brook Farm was an organic part of transcendentalism;[2] in another sense it seems

[1] It has been declared that Ripley owed his first idea of Brook Farm to a suggestion from Dr. Channing.

[2] Brook Farm was surely an embodiment of the tendency (of which we have had so much to say) to *apply* the theoretical, though the theoretical is not in this case the philosophical. It conformed, too, with the nature of transcendentalism in its Puritanism, an aspect of the experiment which has often been remarked. It is interesting again to remember the practical way in which many of the Brook Farmers—Ripley and Dana, for instance—went to work after leaving West Roxbury.

like a side-issue of the movement, deviating from the main line of its development; in still another sense—and we trust this will not be deemed, in the light of the prevalent conception, impertinently paradoxical—it was most truly a part of transcendentalism in that it was a reaction against it, for it embodied the inevitable return of the pendulum which any extreme manifestation of individualism must ultimately produce. Certainly as far as the leading transcendentalists are concerned, the realm of their activity overlaps that of abolitionism[1] much more extensively than it overlaps Brook Farm.

What we have just been saying should make it sufficiently clear that our description of transcendentalism as a mingling —in the heat of a revolutionary age—of an idealistic philosophy and the Puritan character is not offered as a complete formula for its composition. In proof—if any proof be needed —that the blending of these elements is not in itself enough to account for the results, it is necessary only to point to Jonathan Edwards. In him too we have a union of Puritan character and an idealistic philosophy; and, though he lived in the age of prose and reason, it may be said that, on a necessarily limited scale, he created an environment of enthusiasm. Edwards and his philosophy present many striking analogies—and how beautifully ironical it all is!—to the transcendentalists and their philosophy. Yet he was hardly a transcendentalist himself; and so he both confirms our analysis, and at the same time guards us against its too narrow application. Not every New England Puritan who read Coleridge and Carlyle became a transcendentalist. It was only in especially prepared minds[2] that the new philosophy found congenial soil, in minds possessing among other things, perhaps, an inborn mystical capacity. So if transcendentalism was the union of a character and a philosophy, it was such a union

---

[1] See Higginson, *Margaret Fuller Ossoli*, 129.

[2] As to how far Celtic elements in the natures of its disciples may have contributed to the dreamy, inactive qualities of transcendentalism, it may be interesting to speculate; but it can hardly be more. To adopt a suggested explanation of the movement, and call it a sporadic outcropping of Celticism, would be wildly contrary to the evidence.

taking place at a definite time, in specially fertilized soil, under particular conditions.

In this connection, as we have already hinted, we must not minimize the importance of the connection of transcendentalism with literary romanticism[1]—indeed with the literary spirit in the widest sense—nor forget that its literary ingredients, though obviously less significant than its moral and philosophical, must by no means be neglected. Transcendentalism was in part a literary renaissance. These men awoke suddenly from the narrow culture of New England and beheld, spread out before them in bewildering richness, a whole world of literature. Are we in a position to realize the feelings that sight must have aroused? It must have come as the first glimpse of Homer came to Keats—only with them it was not one new planet, but a whole constellation, a whole firmament, that burst upon their view; it was not one Pacific, but a hundred, whose mysteries allured them. (And critics carp at these men because their scholarship was not minutely accurate!) But, great as it was, we must not overemphasize the relative importance of this element in transcendentalism. The movement obtained its fullest objective expression, to be sure, in a literary enterprise, the *Dial,* a journal whose sub-title, " A Magazine for Literature, Philosophy, and Religion," explains its scope. Yet even in the *Dial* the philosophical and religious elements constantly tended to overbalance the literary (spoiling much of the poetry, it might be incidentally remarked). If these things be true, Emerson's relation to his age, then, may be taken as typically transcendental: he was a poet and literary man appealing to the sense of beauty; he was still more a teacher appealing to the love of truth; but doubtless even more than poet or philosopher, he was the prophet and preacher appealing to the will, to the moral and religious nature of man. So, too, transcendentalism: it was a literary movement, a philosophy, and a religion, all in one. There is a Platonic fitness in the triple relation.

[1] Such facts as the Elizabethan revival and the intensified love of nature are simply two typical examples of the similarities between the two movements.

It is clear, also, that had the facilities for the study of the other arts been as great as those for the study of literature, they would have assumed a much more conspicuous place than they did in the New England renaissance. Even as it is, the new interest aroused in music, and the influence, especially, of Beethoven are far from negligible.

Of the many things that have been written about transcendentalism, Matthew Arnold's essay on Emerson contains, assuredly, some of the most keenly critical and at the same time some of the most sympathetically appreciative—for not a little of what Arnold writes especially of Emerson applies without important qualification to these other transcendentalists. Says Arnold, " by his conviction that in the life of the spirit is happiness, and by his hope that this life of the spirit will come more and more to be sanely understood, and to prevail, and to work for happiness,—by this conviction and hope Emerson was great, and he will surely prove in the end to have been right in them." Emerson, to be sure, was a genius in a sense in which none of the rest of this group[1] were, and if all of them were not full sharers of the " hopeful, serene, beautiful temper " of that genius, yet there was not one but had a portion of it, and each too was in his degree " the friend and aider of those who would live in the spirit "—a phrase which sums up, with the rarest insight, the positive and lasting achievement of transcendentalism.

And Arnold suggests a reason why many have failed to judge this movement soundly: " Emerson's points are in themselves true, if understood in a certain high sense; they are true and fruitful. And the right work to be done at the hour when he appeared was to affirm them generally and absolutely. . . . The time might come for doing other work later, but the work which Emerson did was the right work to be done then." This is in reality simply an appeal—not frequent in Arnold— for an historical judgment. To the attempt to judge transcendentalism absolutely, without taking into account the pecu-

[1] We refer, of course, to those we have been discussing, not including Thoreau therefore.

liar conditions of the time when it appeared, may be attributed, we imagine, a majority of the one-sided and misleading estimates of its nature. To be to unawakened earth the trumpet of a prophecy[1]—this was the wish of the transcendentalists. To be judged as philosophers who offered one more solution of the riddle of existence—this has too often been their destiny. As philosophers, inevitably, they failed—transcendentalism, which averts its ken from half of human fate, is no unravelling of the master-knot. But as inspirers of their generation, they succeeded. He, therefore, who has a wish to understand this movement aright must endeavor to put himself back in the Massachusetts of 1835. Hard enough, even then, will it be for him to appreciate the glow at the hearts of those who watched this renaissance of feeling dawn over New England, at the hearts of the men and women who awoke to perceive that " the sun shines today also."

Youthful—that is exactly what this movement was. It had the hope and the imagination and the passion of youth; it had, too, youth's extravagance, its impatience with detail, its overconfidence in its own powers. Characteristics like these, it is true, even among those still immature, may justly bring a smile to the lips of experience and age, but that experience would little deserve its name which should blame the young for possessing those very qualities that constitute the youthful spirit. Ours, in judging transcendentalism, is the experience which the passage of time has brought, and as we look back on the men of a generation so strangely different from our own, nothing is easier than to fall into a satirical mood: to ridicule their amateurish seeking after culture, to point out how their vaunted wisdom only exposed their ignorance, how their boasted cosmopolitanism only revealed their provincial limitations, to call them sciolists and dabblers and to moralize on the disastrous results of their inaccurate and disorderly habits of thinking or their wild notions of the function of books, habits and notions which have been described—and not

" I do not propose to write an ode to dejection, but to brag as lustily as chanticleer in the morning, standing on his roost, if only to wake my neighbors up."—Thoreau, *Walden*.

with entire injustice—by the phrase " literary Epicureanism."
Smile, we must. But if we smile cynically rather than kindly,
if we fail to perceive that many of these qualities were what
constituted the very essence of the age and were themselves
instrumental in imparting to it, and to the age that followed,
high purposes and hopes—how much wiser shall we prove
ourselves than the man to whom experience and the passing
years have brought only intolerance for the extravagance of
early life? For—let it be carefully noted—it is extravagance
and excess, essential qualities of youth, not moral obliquity,
its frequent but inessential attendant, whose counterpart we
find among the leading transcendentalists. Idealism run mad,
individualism run mad, though there were suggestions of even
these extremes in the youthful spirit of these men, it was,
after all, a spirit tempered with moral sanity and productive
not merely of aspirations but of deeds. Whence these contrasted elements were derived, we have already seen, but in
the light of our present analogy, it is worth while again to call
to mind their sources. The grandsire of transcendentalism
was the French Revolution; its mother was a mystical philosophy; its father was the Puritan spirit—rapture and revolution
were in its veins, but because moral integrity was in those
veins as well, it was preserved, in the main, from those romantic and anarchical excesses to which, in the case of not a few
related European movements, rapture and revolution, morally
unrestrained, had led. Because these transcendentalists
breathed their ancestral New England air, their footsteps were
kept steady, nor did they wander into that abyss of decadence
and moral death along whose brink the narrow and dangerous path of mysticism has been proved, a thousand times, to
lie. It is this moral element which redeems transcendentalism
and puts in a different light its bewildering exaggerations.
Had its apostles uttered their extreme statements simply as
philosophers, had it been as mere theorists that they put their
disproportionate emphasis on the ideal side of life, we should
feel less disposed to judge them mildly; but because they
uttered those statements and put that emphasis as prophets

and preachers, and exemplified their doctrines in pure and noble lives, we can almost applaud their very exaggerations.[1]

That there were men and women in New England at this time who were affected by these same ideal and revolutionary influences, but who lacked the moral balance of the Puritan character, it would be venturing little to assume. That such actually did exist the records of the period amply prove. And does not this suggest—here at the end of our inquiry—that the seemingly arbitrary limitation which we placed upon ourselves at the beginning corresponds, roughly at least, to a real distinction? While it may be impossible to draw a sharply distinguishing line between the two, surely it is not fanciful to perceive a real difference in kind between transcendentalists of the type of Emerson or Parker and men who, having many or all of the other elements of transcendentalism, lack the Puritan character.

To which of these two groups the term "transcendentalists" may be more properly applied is, perhaps, an open question. Possibly it would be more in accord with popular usage to reserve it for the latter, falling in with a prevalent tendency to attach the epithet *transcendental* to a man in proportion as his nature loses all balance and he himself evaporates in a cloud of ideal vapor. We have not chosen to do so. The way, however, in which the word is to be used is after all a minor matter, provided the distinction itself be clearly grasped and the confusion between two profoundly different types be thus prevented, provided, that is, we do not lump promiscuously together every mad "come-outer" and "apostle of the newness" on the one hand and on the other men whose visionary and anti-social tendencies were corrected by the healthiness of their moral natures. And some of these same considerations, in a very different way, must be kept in mind in any attempt to estimate men who trace their spiritual lineage to Emerson and his circle. Walt Whitman, for instance, is a

[1] " I desire to speak somewhere *without* bounds; like a man in a waking moment, to men in their waking moments; for I am convinced that I cannot exaggerate enough even to lay the foundation of a true expression."— Thoreau, *Walden*.

mystic and a revolutionist, and the immediate source, too, of his main conceptions is apparent; but his is not the Puritan spirit, and to him must be denied—in our sense—the name of transcendentalist. Much more must it be denied to lesser men who, imbibing somewhat of the individualism and idealism of their masters, have not been equally careful to imitate their character. Were Emerson alive today he would doubtless fail to recognize many who claim to be his legitimate offspring.

What harmful effects transcendental doctrines may have had in natures of this sort[1]—natures that lacked the proper moral balance—it is not our part, if indeed it were within our power, to trace. But to the benefits which have flowed from the teaching and example of the transcendentalists we fortunately have ample witness. The influence of Emerson on such men as Arnold and Tyndall, men so unlike Emerson in many ways and in many ways so unlike each other, is typical of the inspiration which this movement spread abroad. Many a tribute has attested this; and there is no more fitting way than with one of these to conclude what we have had to say of New England transcendentalism:

" . . . in a copy of Mrs. Jameson's Italian Painters, against a passage describing Correggio as a true servant of God in his art, above sordid ambition, devoted to truth, 'one of those superior beings of whom there are so few;' Margaret [Fuller] wrote on the margin, 'And yet all might be such.' The book lay long on the table of the owner, in Florence, and chanced to be read there by a young artist of much talent. 'These words,' said he, months afterwards, 'struck out a new strength in me. They revived resolutions, long fallen away, and made me set my face like flint.' "

[1] See T. W. Higginson, *The Sunny Side of the Transcendental Period,* Atlantic Monthly, xciii, 11. Reprinted in *Part of a Man's Life,* 1905.

APPENDIX

GERMAN LITERATURE IN NEW ENGLAND IN THE EARLY PART OF THE NINETEENTH CENTURY

A passage from the *Life, Letters, and Journals of George Ticknor* (vol. i, p. 11) shows clearly the lack of interest in things German, in the New England of the middle of the second decade of the nineteenth century. Ticknor, on deciding to go to Göttingen to study, made an attempt before leaving home to learn something of the German language. The following, telling of the difficulties he encountered, has reference to the summer and autumn of 1814 (he sailed in May, 1815):

" At Jamaica Plains there was a Dr. Brosius, a native of Strasburg, who gave instruction in mathematics. He was willing to do what he could for me in German, but he warned me that his pronunciation was very bad, as was that of all Alsace, which had become a part of France. Nor was it possible to get books. I borrowed a Meidinger's Grammar, French and German, from my friend, Mr. Everett, and sent to New Hampshire, where I knew there was a German Dictionary, and procured it. I also obtained a copy of Goethe's ' Werther ' in German (through Mr. William S. Shaw's connivance) from amongst Mr. J. Q. Adams' books, deposited by him, on going to Europe, in the Athenæum, under Mr. Shaw's care, but without giving him permission to use them. I got so far as to write a translation of ' Werther,' but no farther."

The inevitable inference from this passage, that German books were exceedingly scarce in New England about 1815, is confirmed by the booksellers' auction catalogs of the time, which contain only very infrequently any German works. An unusual number of German entries is found in the catalog of a sale occurring in Boston, December 20, 1815: " Goethe's Works, German, 4 vols.; Sorrows of Werther. Jacobi, Works, German, 3 vols. Mendelssohn, Philosophical Works. Lessing, Dramatic Works, 2 vols. Schiller, History of the Thirty Years' War, German; Conspiracy of Fiesco." At a sale of the library of Rev. Samuel Cooper Thacher, Boston, June 18, 1818, we find: " Goethe, 1 vol., including ' Die Wahlverwandtschaften.' " At another auction two months later: " Elements of the Critical Philosophy, London, 1798." In connection with Ticknor's remark about the German dictionary in New Hampshire, it is interesting to note that in 1824 the Library of the Philological Society of Middlebury College, Vermont, contained Schiller's works, complete in eighteen volumes, and twenty volumes of Goethe.

It was especially, as was stated in Chapter I., the return, about 1819, of several young American students from Göttingen that stimulated New England interest in German literature and German educational methods. " From 1815 to 1817 Everett, Ticknor and Cogswell were studying in Germany and meeting many German scholars and literary men, whose interest in Harvard College they aroused, so that in the next two years following books were received by the College Library from Eichhorn, Blumenbach, Schaeffer, Wolf, Hermann, Jacobs, and Kästner; also from Spohn, Spitzner, Bouterwek, van der Kemp, Glasenwald, the Grimm brothers, and Goethe."[1] (An exhaustive account, by Mr. L. L. Mackall, of Goethe's gift to Harvard and the circumstances attending it was published in the *Goethe Jahrbuch* for 1904.) " When Everett went abroad, he was given $500 by the Harvard Corporation to spend in Germany, and a few months later $500 more for the same purpose."[2] The coming of Charles Follen to Harvard as instructor in German about 1825 also did much to increase enthusiasm for things German, and what had been accomplished in this direction in a decade or a little more is indicated by a glance at the *Catalogue of Books in the Boston Athenæum, Boston, 1827*, and *A Catalogue of the Library of Harvard University in Cambridge, Massachusetts, Cambridge, 1830*. To the former the following " Advertisement " was prefixed:

[1] From a letter to the writer from Mr. William C. Lane, Librarian of Harvard University.

[2] From the same letter referred to in note 1.

" Several thousand volumes of Books were ordered for the Athenæum during the last summer. As none of them are rare, or difficult to be procured, they will no doubt soon be received; and it has, therefore, been thought best to insert their titles in this Catalogue. They can easily be distinguished, because no number of a shelf is attached to them, and no note of the time or place where they were printed."

A large number of these books were German and included: Goethe—Sämmtliche Werke; Herder—Sämmtliche theologische, historiche, und literärische Schriften; Jacobi—Werke; Lessing—Sämmtliche Werke; Novalis—Schriften; Richter—Domstücke, Vorschule der Aesthetik, Titan, Levana; Schiller—Sämmtliche Werke; Schlegel, A. W.—Dramatische Kunst, Lectures on Dramatic Literature (translated), Gedichte; Schlegel, Fried.—Geschichte der Literatur der Griechen; Tieck—Sämmtliche Werke; Uhland—Schriften; Wieland—Sämmtliche Werke. German works and translations from the German actually in the Athenæum at the time when the catalog of 1827 was published included: Goethe—The Sorrows of Werther, tr. from the G., Chiswick, 1822; Herder—On Man, tr. from the G., London, 1803; Schiller—History of the Thirty Years' War, tr. from the G., vol. I, Dublin, 1800,—Don Carlos, a Tragedy, London, 1798; Schlegel, Fried.—Lectures on the History of Literature, from the G., 2 vols., Phil., 1818; Wieland—Oberon, a Poem, tr. from the G., London, 1805,— the same, Boston, 1810.

The Harvard Library in 1830 was (actually) much richer in German works than the Athenæum was in 1827. Among others we find:

Goethe. Werke, 20 Bände, Stuttgard und Tübingen, 1815–1819. Nine other entries.

Herder. Ten entries, originals and translations.

Kant. Critik der reinen Vernunst, Riga, 1790. Critik der practischen Vernunst, Riga, 1792. Critik der Urteilscraft, Berlin, 1793. Elements of the Critical Philosophy, London, 1798. Four other entries.

Lessing. Fragmente und Antifragmente, Nürnberg, 1788.

Lessing und J. J. Eschenburg. Zur Geschichte und Litteratur, 3 Bände, Berlin und Braunschweig, 1781–1793.

Schiller. Werke, 18 Bände, Carlsruhe, 1817. Wallenstein, translated by Coleridge, London, 1800.

Schlegel, A. W. Ueber Dramatische Kunst und Litteratur, 3 Bände, Heidelberg, 1809–11. Course of Lectures on Dramatic Art and Literature, tr. from the G., London, 1815.

Schlegel, Fried. Geschichte der alten und neuen Litteratur, Wien, 1815. Lectures on the History of Literature, from the G., Phil., 1818.

Schleiermacher. Six entries, including five volumes of his translation of Plato.

The accession books of the Harvard Library contain these two entries:

"June 18, 1830. Three boxes of Books, German mostly."

"September 21, 1831. One box of German Books."

No detailed entry is given under the former head, but accession dates in the books of the Library show that these "three boxes" of 1830 must have contained among other things: Lessing—Sämmtliche Werke, Berlin, 1825; Kant—Vermischte Schriften; Jacobi—Werke; Wieland—Sämmtliche Werke, Leipzig, 1818. Under the second head detailed entries are made. The list includes a few volumes of Kant, Fichte, and Schelling, but the two largest sets are the complete works of Müller (27 vols.) and of Herder (45 vols. in 41).

Auctioneers' catalogs of the latter part of the fourth decade of the century show, by comparison with those referred to above, how widely interest in things German had developed in twenty years. For example, in a catalog of books, the stock of S. Bardett, a bookseller, sold at auction in Boston, November 11, 1837, the entries are numbered according to languages as follows:

English, Greek, and Latin, 1–77.

Spanish, 78–231.

German, 232–480.

Italian, 481–651.

French, 652–1032.

The German entries include Richter, Herder (63 vols. in 22), and especially a large number of editions of Goethe and

Schiller, both broken and complete. The German entries in a sale at Boston, June 21, 1838, extended from 2262 to 2429, and include Goethe, Schiller, Herder, and Lessing.

Among the early private libraries in New England containing many German books were those of F. H. Hedge, Convers Francis, and George Ripley. A list of some of the most important works in the collection of Ripley will be found in Frothingham's biography of Ripley, page 46.

BIBLIOGRAPHY

The following bibliography makes no attempt to include the numerous essays and magazine articles, mainly of a critical nature, which have been consulted, nor the large number of works, biographies, etc., of men indirectly connected with New England transcendentalism, such as, for instance, Kant, Coleridge, and Carlyle. It omits also histories of literature (except American literature) and philosophy, as well as works of the type of Leslie Stephen's *English Thought in the Eighteenth Century.*

For the sake of convenience, magazines are included in a list by themselves.

Aikin, Lucy. Memoirs, Miscellanies, and Letters of the late Lucy Aikin. London, 1864.

—— **and Channing, William Ellery.** Correspondence from 1826–1842. Ed. by A. L. LeBreton. London, 1874.

Alcott, Amos Bronson. Concord Days. Boston, 1872.

Conversations with Children on the Gospels. 2 vols. Boston, 1836–37.

Ralph Waldo Emerson; an Estimate of his Character and Genius. Boston, 1888.

Table-talk. Boston, 1877.

Tablets. Boston, 1879.

Alcott, Louisa May. Life, Letters, and Journals. Ed. by Mrs. E. D. Cheney. Boston, 1889.

Silver Pitchers, and Other Stories. (Containing " Transcendental Wild Oats.") Boston, 1902.

Allen, A. V. G. Jonathan Edwards. Boston, 1889.

Bartol, C. A. Amos Bronson Alcott; his Character; a Sermon. Boston, 1888.

Brooks, C. T. William Ellery Channing, a Centennial Biography. Boston, 1880.

Brownson, H. F. Orestes A. Brownson's Life. 3 vols. Detroit, 1898–1900.

Brownson, Orestes Augustus. Works: Collected and Arranged by H. F. Brownson. 20 vols. Detroit, 1882–1887. (See especially vi, 1–134.)

Charles Elwood; or, The Infidel Converted. Boston, 1840. (Reprinted in Works, iv, 173.)

Cabot, J. E. Memoir of Ralph Waldo Emerson. 2 vols. Boston, 1887.

Cary, Elizabeth Luther. Emerson, Poet and Thinker. New York, 1904.

Chadwick, J. W. Theodore Parker, Preacher and Reformer. Boston, 1900.

William Ellery Channing, Minister of Religion. Boston, 1903.

Channing, William Ellery. Works, Fourteenth Complete Edition, with an Introduction. Six vols. in three. Boston, 1855.

Channing, William Henry. The Life of William Ellery Channing, D.D. The Centenary Memorial Edition, by His Nephew. Boston, 1899.

Cheney, Mrs. E. D. Reminiscences. Boston, 1902.

Clarke, James Freeman. Autobiography, Diary, and Correspondence. Ed. by E. E. Hale. Boston, 1891.

Memorial and Biographical Sketches. Boston, 1878.

Cobbe, Frances Power. Life; by herself. Boston, 1894.

Conway, M. D. Emerson, at Home and Abroad. Boston, 1882.

Cooke, George Willis. Ralph Waldo Emerson; his Life, Writings, and Philosophy. Boston, 1881.

The Poets of Transcendentalism; an Anthology; with introductory essay and biographical notes. Boston, 1903.

Unitarianism in America; a History of its Origin and Development. Boston, 1902.

Dall, Caroline Healey. Margaret and Her Friends, or Ten Conversations with Margaret Fuller. Boston, 1895.

Edwards, Jonathan. The Works of President Edwards. 4 vols. New York, 1857.

Ellis, George E. A Half-Century of the Unitarian Controversy. Boston, 1857.

Emerson, Edward Waldo. Emerson in Concord; a Memoir. Boston, 1889.

Emerson, Ralph Waldo. Works, Riverside Edition. 12 vols. Boston, 1883–1894.

Complete Works of Emerson, Centenary Edition. 12 vols. Boston, 1903–1904.

A Correspondence between John Stirling and Ralph Waldo Emerson. Ed. by Edward Waldo Emerson. Boston, 1897.

Carlyle, Thomas, and Emerson, Ralph Waldo. Correspondence, 1834–1872. Ed. by Charles Eliot Norton. 2 vols. Boston, 1886.

Emerson, R. W., and Grimm, H. F. Correspondence. Ed. by T. W. Holls. Boston, 1903.

Letters to a Friend, 1838–1853. Ed. by C. E. Norton. Boston, 1899.

Memoirs of Margaret Fuller Ossoli, by R. W. Emerson, W. H. Channing, and J. F. Clarke. 2 vols. Boston, 1874.

Parnassus. Boston, 1875.

Fuller, Margaret. See Ossoli.

Frothingham, Octavius Brooks. Boston Unitarianism, 1820–1850; the Life and Work of Nathaniel Langdon Frothingham. New York, 1890.

George Ripley (American Men of Letters). Boston, 1882.

Memoir of William Henry Channing. Boston, 1886.

Theodore Parker; a Biography. Boston, 1874.

Transcendentalism in New England, a History. New York, 1876.

Garnett, Richard. Life of Ralph Waldo Emerson. London, 1888.

Hale, Edward Everett. Ralph Waldo Emerson; with two early essays of Emerson. Boston, 1902.

Hawthorne, Nathaniel. Blithedale Romance. Boston, 1895.

15

Higginson, Thomas Wentworth. Cheerful Yesterdays. Boston, 1898.

Contemporaries. Boston, 1899.

Margaret Fuller Ossoli (Amercan Men of Letters). Boston, 1884.

Old Cambridge. New York, 1899.

Holmes, Oliver Wendell. Ralph Waldo Emerson (American Men of Letters). Boston, 1885.

Howe, Julia Ward. Margaret Fuller (Marchesa Ossoli). Boston, 1883.

Ireland, Alexander. Recollections of Emerson. Boston, 1903.

Judd, Sylvester. Margaret, a Tale of the Real and the Ideal. Boston, 1846.

Lee, Eliza Buckminster. Memoirs of Rev. Joseph Buckminster, D.D., and of his son, Rev. Joseph Stevens Buckminster. Boston, 1849.

Mead, E. D. The Influence of Emerson. Boston, 1903.

Nichol, John. American Literature. Edinburg, 1882.

Norton, Andrews. A Discourse on the Latest Form of Infidelity. Cambridge, 1839.

Ossoli, Sarah Margaret (Fuller), Marchesa d'. At Home and Abroad. Boston, 1874.

Life Without and Life Within. Boston, 1890.

Love-Letters, 1845–1846; with an introduction by J. W. Howe. New York, 1903.

Papers on Literature and Art. London, 1846.

Summer on the Lakes, in 1843. Boston, 1844.

Woman in the Nineteenth Century, and Kindred Papers, etc. Boston, 1855.

Parker, Theodore. The Critical and Miscellaneous Writings of Theodore Parker. Boston, 1843.

Speeches, Addresses and Occasional Sermons by Theodore Parker. 2 vols. Boston, 1852.

An Humble Tribute to the Memory of W. E. Channing; a Sermon preached Oct. 9, 1842. Boston, 1842.

Transcendentalism; a Lecture. Boston, 1876.

Peabody, Elizabeth Palmer. Record of Mr. Alcott's School. Boston, 1874.

Reminiscences of William Ellery Channing. Boston, 1880.

Quincy, Josiah. History of the Boston Athenæum. Cambridge, 1851.

Renan, Ernest. Études D'Histoire Religieuse. Paris, 1864.

Richardson, C. F. American Literature, 1607–1885. 2 vols. New York, 1887–1889.

Ripley, George. "The Latest Form of Infidelity" Examined; a letter to Andrews Norton. Boston, 1839.

Specimens of Foreign Standard Literature; edited by George Ripley. 14 vols. Boston, 1838.

Salt, H. S. Life of Henry David Thoreau. London, 1890.

Sanborn, Frank B., and Harris, W. T. A. Bronson Alcott: His Life and Philosophy. 2 vols. Boston, 1893. (The life of Alcott is by Mr. Sanborn; the essay on Alcott's philosophy, by Mr. Harris.)

Sanborn, Frank B. Henry D. Thoreau (American Men of Letters). Boston, 1882.

Ralph Waldo Emerson. Boston, 1901.

The Genius and Character of Emerson; Lectures at the Concord School of Philosophy (1884). Ed. by F. B. Sanborn. Boston, 1885.

The Personality of Emerson. Boston, 1903.

The Personality of Thoreau. Boston, 1901.

Swift, Lindsay. Brook Farm; its Members, Scholars, and Visitors. New York, 1900.

Thoreau, Henry David. Writings, Riverside Edition, 11 vols. Boston, 1895–1898.

Ticknor, George. Life, Letters, and Journals of George Ticknor. 2 vols. Boston, 1877.

Trent, William P. A History of American Literature, 1607–1865. New York, 1903.

Walker, Williston. A History of the Congregational Churches in the United States. New York, 1894.

Wendell, Barrett. A Literary History of America. New York, 1900.

Weiss, John. Life and Correspondence of Theodore Parker. 2 vols. New York, 1864.

Winsor, Justin. The Memorial History of Boston. Ed. by
Justin Winsor. Vol. iii. Boston, 1881.
Woodbury, C. J. Talks with Ralph Waldo Emerson. New
York, 1890.

MAGAZINES

Biblical Repertory; Biblical Repertory and Theological Re-
view; Biblical Repertory and Princeton Review; Pres-
byterian Quarterly and Princeton Review, Various
Places, 1825–71.
Biblical Repository, Quarterly. Andover and New York,
1831–1850.
Boston Quarterly Review. Ed. by O. A. Brownson. Boston,
1838–1842. (Merged in the *Democratic Review.*)
Brownson's Quarterly Review. Boston and New York, 1844–
1875.
Christian Disciple (1813–1818), and Christian Disciple and
Theological Review (1819–1823). Boston, 1813–1823.
(Continued as *Christian Examiner.*)
Christian Examiner. Boston, 1824–1869.
The Dial; a Magazine for Literature, Philosophy, and Reli-
gion.[1] Boston and London, 1841–1844.
The Harbinger, devoted to Social and Political Progress.
Published by the Brook Farm Phalanx. New York
and Boston, 1845–1849.
The Massachusetts Quarterly Review. Boston, 1848–1850.
Monthly Anthology and Boston Review. Boston, 1804–1810.
North American Review. Boston, 1815–

Bibliographies will be found in Garnett's life of Emerson,
in Sanborn's life of Emerson, in Chadwick's life of Parker,
in Higginson's life of Margaret Fuller, and in Lindsay Swift's
Brook Farm.

[1] *The Dial* has been reprinted by The Rowfant Club of Cleveland. Cleveland, 1900–1903. See also George Willis Cooke, *An Historical and Biographical Introduction to accompany the Dial as reprinted in Numbers for
The Rowfant Club,* 2 Vols. Cleveland, 1902.

INDEX.

(This index does not include the material in the appendix.)

213

217